# HAPPINESS

ALSO BY THE AUTHOR

*The Antisocial Personalities*
*A Tremor in the Blood: Uses and Abuses of the Lie Detector*

# HAPPINESS

## WHAT STUDIES ON TWINS SHOW US ABOUT NATURE, NURTURE, AND THE HAPPINESS SET-POINT

# Dr. David Lykken

Contemporary Psychology (APA Review of Books)
Robert J. Sternberg, Editor
Department of Psychology, Box 208205
Yale University
New Haven, CT 06520-8205

Golden Books
New York

*Golden Books*®

888 Seventh Avenue
New York, NY 10106

Copyright © 1999 by David Lykken
All rights reserved, including the right of reproduction
in whole or in part in any form.
*Golden Books*® and colophon
are trademarks of Golden Books Publishing Co., Inc.

Designed by Stanley S. Drate/Folio Graphics Co., Inc.

Manufactured in the United States of America

10  9  8  7  6  5  4  3  2  1

This book contains references to actual cases the author has worked on over the years. However, names and other identifying characteristics have been changed to protect the privacy of those involved.

**Library of Congress Cataloging-in-Publication Data**

Lykken, David Thoreson.
    Happiness : what studies on twins show us about nature, nurture,
  and the happiness set-point / David Lykken.
        p.   cm.
    Includes index.
    ISBN 1-58238-004-X (hardcover : alk. paper)
    1. Happiness.   I. Title.
  BF575.H27L85   1999
  158—dc21                                                            98-27790
                                                                        CIP

To my grandchildren:
Laura, Erik, Sara, Zeke, Adin, Karl, Jake, Roxanna, Oliver, and Ezra, who share a surname, *Lykken*, that in Norwegian means *The Happiness*.

# CONTENTS

# INTRODUCTION

I came to write this book in a curious, serendipitous fashion. An article in *Psychological Science*, the journal of the American Psychological Society, reported that subjective well-being or happiness is largely unrelated to income level or educational attainment, to social status, or to whether one is married or single.[1] The authors, David Myers, of Hope College in Michigan, and Ed Diener, of the University of Illinois, are highly respected researchers and their findings, however surprising they might seem, had to be taken seriously. It occurred to me that I already had in the computer data on thousands of middle-aged people, who constituted a highly representative sample of the population of Minnesota, data that included scores on the Well Being scale of a personality inventory developed by my colleague, Auke Tellegen. Because we also knew the basic demographic facts about these people—how far they had gone in school, their approximate annual income, their occupations, and so on—we could replicate Myers's and Diener's findings to see if they held up on this different sample, employing somewhat different measures of the relevant variables.

Moreover, our subjects were twins whom we had identified through birth records and subsequently tracked down and recruited. Therefore, we could also determine whether genetically identical twins, grown up and living their own separate lives, were more similar in their reported happiness than same-sex fraternal twins, who share only half their genes, on average. If so, that would suggest that one's average level of subjective well-being is to some extent influenced by the outcome of the great genetic lottery that occurs at conception. Tellegen and I therefore got busy analyzing our data and what we found, reported in the same journal in 1996,[2] caused an almost unprecedented stir in the popular press. Articles appeared in the *New York Times* and

1

the *Los Angeles Times*, in the *Washington Post* and the *Wall Street Journal*, in the *London Times, Daily Telegraph* and *Daily Mail*, in Rome's *La Repubblica* and Toronto's *Sun*, in Germany's *Stern* magazine, in Spain's *El Tiempo*, in Canada's *Maclean's*, in *Newsweek, Fortune,* and *Forbes* magazines, as well as in journals such as *Science, Science News*, and *Nature Genetics,* catering to the scientist reader. Tellegen and I received endless requests for radio interviews (Tellegen's mellifluous Dutch accent is especially appealing). Not surprisingly, in retrospect, people are interested in happiness.

All of this media attention began to make me increasingly uncomfortable about one sentence toward the end of our *Psychological Science* article. Having found that happiness has strong genetic roots, that an identical twin's well-being now can be predicted from his cotwin's score years earlier, just as it can from the first twin's own score at that earlier time, we had written, "It may be that trying to be happier is as futile as trying to be taller and therefore is counterproductive." For reasons that will become evident later, that pessimistic conclusion is not impelled by the data and, in fact, I believe it is wrong. When John Brockman, a distinguished literary agent, suggested that I might write a book explaining what I think we really know about the sources of human happiness, and about some of the sources of unhappiness, the *happiness thieves*, I decided it would be a worthwhile and interesting project and also a chance to set the record straight.

I am indebted (in so many ways) to my wife, Harriet, and to my sons, Jesse, Joseph, and Matthew, who have read many chapters in draft and made useful suggestions. My former mentor and longtime friend, Paul Meehl, and his wife, Leslie Yonce, have also generously read and commented helpfully on portions of the text. The interested reader is encouraged to look at David Myers's excellent *The Pursuit of Happiness*,[3] which covers some of the same material and much else as well.

# PART ONE

# THE HERITABILITY OF HAPPINESS

Happiness and misery depend as much on temperament
as on fortune.

—La Rochefoucauld

Life is like a sewer; what you get out of it depends on what
you put into it.

—Tom Lehrer

M y purpose in this book is to recant the claim I made earlier that, because happiness has strong genetic roots,
"trying to be happier is like trying to be taller." Then I
shall illustrate some of the ways in which one can raise one's
happiness "set point" (or that of one's children) above the level
that one's genetic steersman would be likely to achieve if left in
complete control.

Most professional psychologists, even those trained as I was
in the bygone days of radical environmentalism, are aware of the
modern evidence that all members of our species share in some
degree inborn proclivities that were adaptive in far ancestral
times. Moreover, it has been shown that nearly every psychological trait or tendency that we can measure reliably owes part of its
variation from person to person to genetic differences between
people. Some people, however—for ideological reasons or
through misunderstanding of what the recent research with

3

twins really implies about human freedom and modifiability—resolutely turn their faces from these fascinating findings.

Most lay persons, in contrast, have always found it natural to suppose that people differ in their inborn behavioral and emotional tendencies. The idea that human baby brains, like brand-new Macintosh computers, are all identical with no "ROMs" or preprogramming, is a sophisticated sort of error, normally available only to persons holding Ph.D. degrees. On the other hand, many people tend not to think of happiness as a trait at all. Traits, they say, are tendencies like aggressiveness, impulsiveness, or cleverness. Happiness is a goal, a reward, a kind of Holy Grail; how can individual differences in happiness have anything to do with one's genetic blueprint?

For all of these reasons, the two chapters that comprise part I of this book are devoted to laying the necessary foundations so that we can all, so to speak, start on the same page. Chapter 1 introduces the reader to the new (or reborn) discipline of evolutionary psychology, a field that I believe provides a useful and productive vantage point from which to study many problems in psychology. Evolutionary psychology is more like history than it is like science, because its assumptions and many of its deductions cannot be subjected to experimental tests. On the other hand, some unexpected predictions by evolutionary psychologists have been tested and confirmed empirically. In particular, one such prediction—that most modern *Homo sapiens* exist on the happy side of hedonic neutrality most of the time—has been repeatedly confirmed, to the surprise of many.

Chapter 2 explains how it is possible to estimate the extent to which individual differences in traits, such as IQ or irritability or happiness, are associated with genetic differences between people. It then addresses the difficult question (which some people consider unanswerable) of how it can be that our genes, whose function is to synthesize the production of enzymes and other proteins, can possibly influence, much less determine, complex psychological tendencies or traits.

# 1

# THIS HAPPY BREED

Human nature is, moreover, a hodgepodge of special
genetic adaptations to an environment largely vanished,
the world of the Ice-Age hunter-gatherer.
—E. O. WILSON

The genes sing a prehistoric song, that must sometimes be
resisted, but which cannot be ignored.
—BOUCHARD ET AL.

The aristocratic philosopher Bertrand Russell, author of
*Principia Mathematica* and other light classics, published
in 1930 a really heavy tome called *The Conquest of Happiness*. Although short and written in English rather than symbolic
logic, *Conquest* sits like lead on one's lap because its author was
a lifelong depressive who said he eschewed suicide as a youth
only because he wanted to learn more mathematics. This English
lord, who made many of his intimates unhappy, began his manual for happiness attainment by explaining: "My purpose is to
suggest a cure for the ordinary day-to-day unhappiness from
which most people in civilized countries suffer, and which is all
the more unbearable because, having no obvious external cause,
it appears inescapable."

With what Russell calls the "art of reading faces" in the street,
at work, even at parties, he sees, like Blake,[1] "A mark on every
face I meet, marks of weakness, marks of woe."

From Ecclesiastes to Roger Bacon, from Byron to a curious
American named Joseph Wood Krutch who wrote a despairing

5

book called *The Modern Temper*, Russell amasses examples to show that intellectuals, at least, are naturally unhappy because there is after all so much to be unhappy about. Why he fails to quote Strindberg is a puzzle: "He who views the world without scales before his eyes would have to be a swine to enjoy it!" Perhaps the two men were too much alike with their series of failed love affairs to be compatible. But it is a grim beginning, rather like watching ten Ingmar Bergman films in a row.

The premise upon which this book is based is very different. I believe it possible to show that happiness is the natural condition of humankind, that indeed most people are happy most of the time, and that we are equipped with a remarkable capacity to tolerate the slings and arrows of outrageous fortune or to quickly recover from their effects. Some people are happier than others, of course. Some have more of the inborn happiness talent, others have bad habits that prevent them from exploiting their happiness potential. Finally, I believe that most people, even people like gloomy old Lord Russell, can learn to bounce along above their innate happiness set points most of the time.

During the late 1980s, my colleagues and I administered a questionnaire to more than four thousand twins who were born in Minnesota from 1936 through 1955. They were identified through birth records and then tracked down to their current whereabouts. Apart from being twins, these people are a remarkably representative sample of Minnesotans. They live in cities, small towns, farms; some are highly educated, most are not. Part of our questionnaire looked like this:

In this next set of questions you are asked to compare yourself with other people on the specified trait or ability—where do you think you would rank compared to other people of your age and sex? This will be difficult for some of these traits, but please make the best estimate that you can. For each of the items in this section, please using the following rating scale:

| 1 | 2 | 3 | 4 | 5 |
|---|---|---|---|---|
| Lowest 5% | Lower 30% | Middle 30% | Higher 30% | Highest 5% |

1. **Abstract Intelligence:** The ability to solve intellectual problems, to understand complicated issues, to figure things out: "school intelligence."

2. **Capacity for Happiness:** The ability to really enjoy the good things in life, if and when they come your way; to experience pleasure, enthusiasm, satisfaction. Not whether you *are* happy now but whether you can be truly happy, joyful, "high," when things go right for you.
3. **Capacity for Misery:** The tendency to suffer when things go wrong, to feel despair, regret, disappointment, anguish. Not whether you *are* miserable now but whether you are likely to really suffer when things go wrong for you.
4. **Contentment:** Taking the good with the bad, how happy and contented are you on the average now, compared with other people?
5. **Recent Memory:** The ability to quickly learn new names, facts, numbers, and to recall them easily on demand.

You might want to rate yourself on these five items now, before I tell you how our middle-aged Minnesotans rated themselves.

I can tell you first that our subjects followed our instructions very well on many of the items. On 5, Recent Memory, for example, just 4 percent gave themselves a 1 and another 5 percent rated themselves 5. On 1, Abstract Intelligence, the proportions in the categories 1 through 5 were 2, 15, 43, 34, and 6 percent, in that order. Garrison Keillor says that in his hometown of Lake Wobegon, Minnesota, "all the children are above average," but this no longer is entirely true once they reach middle age. On most of these items, men and women rated themselves similarly, but on both 2, Capacity for Happiness, and on 3, Capacity for Misery, the women rated themselves higher than the men. On the tendency to feel really bad when things go wrong, 25 percent of the women, compared with just 16 percent of the men, thought they were in the upper 35 percent of people in general. But on Capacity for Happiness, the ability to really enjoy the good things in life, 65 percent of the men and 80 percent of the women thought they were in the upper 35 percent! When asked how happy or contented they were right then, *most* of our subjects thought they must be happier than are two-thirds of people in general!

Can we put any trust in what people say about themselves on such questionnaires? Psychologists have invested a great deal of effort in researching this topic and their basic conclusion is yes, you can place real faith in self-report, providing you ask the right questions, and providing also that the con-

## CONTENTMENT BY GENDER

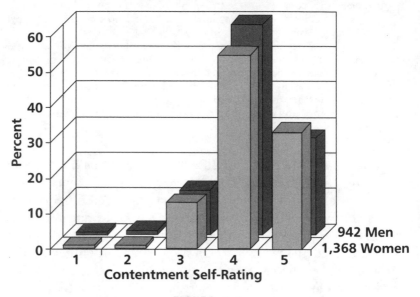

FIGURE 1.1

Self-ratings on "contentment" by middle-aged Minnesotans who were asked to rate themselves 1 if in the lower 5 percent of people in general, 2 if in the next 30 percent, 3 if in the middle 30 percent, 4 if in the higher 30 percent, and 5 if they thought they ranked with the upper 5 percent in contentment.

text is one in which people are not motivated to misrepresent themselves. But perhaps we asked an unreasonable question: How can people be expected to know how they compare in their Capacity for Happiness with people in general? And clearly it is not mathematically possible for the vast majority of people to be "happier than two-thirds of people in general." One interpretation of this result is that our subjects assumed that the average person is neither happy nor unhappy and that all those who thought themselves generally happy rated themselves as above average.

This accords with what other investigators have found, asking the questions somewhat differently. For example, one team asked,

How satisfied are you with your life as a whole these days?[2]

| Completely Dissatisfied | | | Neutral | | | Completely Satisfied |
|---|---|---|---|---|---|---|
| 1 | 2 | 3 | 4 | 5 | 6 | 7 |
| 0.9 percent | 2.1 percent | 3.7 percent | 11.3 percent | 20.7 percent | 39.6 percent | 21.7 percent |

Here the middle choice was clearly specified as neither "satisfied" nor "unsatisfied" and 82 percent of this sample placed themselves on the satisfied (or, presumably, happy) end of the continuum.

Another group, believing apparently that a picture is worth at least more than a few words, asked the question this way: Here are some faces expressing various feelings. Which face comes closest to expressing how you feel about your life as a whole?[3]

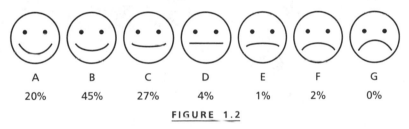

| A | B | C | D | E | F | G |
|---|---|---|---|---|---|---|
| 20% | 45% | 27% | 4% | 1% | 2% | 0% |

FIGURE 1.2

This time, 92 percent said that they were on the happy side of neutral. Thus, asked of different samples and in different ways, it appears that the vast majority of typical English-speaking adults feel that, by and large, they are *happy*.

This (happily) turns out to be a common finding, not just in Minnesota but in most of at least the more-developed countries of the world. The figure below, taken from the World Values Surveys organized by Ronald Inglehart at the University of Michigan, shows the average responses of citizens of twenty-four countries to the question "How satisfied are you with life as a whole?"[4] Responses could range from 0, or extremely dissatisfied, to 10, a state presumably of complete beatitude. The form of this question is not quite right for our purposes because "satis-

fied with life as a whole" rather invites an appraisal of external
circumstances, the economy, the crime problem, who won the
last election, and so on.

I think it is for this reason that the figure shows a strong
correlation (r = .67) between satisfaction and the per capita
wealth of the nation (e.g., the Swedes and the Swiss, who are
prosperous and satisfied, are in the upper-right of the figure
while the Portuguese and the Greeks, less rich and less satisfied,
are in the lower-left). But what is striking also about this figure
is that the average citizens of *all* of the twenty-four countries,
from South Africa to Sweden, expressed a satisfaction level above
5.5 on the scale from 0 to 10. Had the question asked instead:

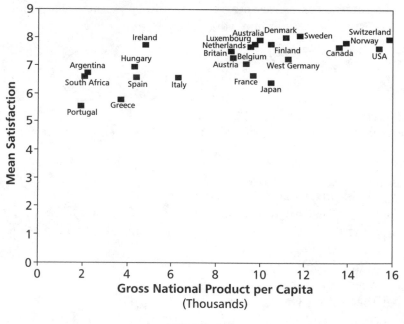

FIGURE 1.3

Average ratings of "satisfaction with life as a whole" for groups sampled from
twenty-four countries. The rating scale ran from 0 (extremely dissatisfied) to 11
(supremely satisfied), so that a score of 5.5 would indicate neutrality. Source:
Ronald Inglehart © 1990. *Culture Shift in Advanced Industrial Society.* Princeton
University Press. Used with permission.

"How happy and contented do you usually feel?," then I believe that the twenty-four national averages would have been even more similar, say, between 7.0 and 8.0 on this graph.

We shall be talking about correlation coefficients quite a bit in this book and, if you are not yet acquainted with this statistic, you are in for a treat, because it is a very useful concept. Because we shall use correlations mainly to quantify the similarity of twins, let us suppose we have one hundred pairs of identical twins, all adult males, and we want to know how similar they are in height. Applying the correct formula,[5] we will get a twin correlation (usually represented by R) for stature of about R = .90. If identical cotwins all were exactly the same height, R would be 1.00, indicating perfect similarity. It is hard to find a score on which identical twins are completely unrelated, so we have to do something artificial to illustrate an R of 0. Suppose, instead of heights, we give each man a score equal to the value of the coins each happens to have in his pocket, and then correlate these scores within pairs. That should give us an R of about 0. The twins will correlate in weight about R = .78, less than for height, because these men's weight is influenced by their eating habits and also, perhaps, by their wives. The correlations for fraternal twins in height and weight will be about half the values for identical twins, because fraternal twins share only about half their genes, on average.[6] But both types of twins will correlate about R = .70 for birth weight because weight at birth largely depends on gestational age and both members of any twin pair tend to be born at about the same time.

Most people feel reasonably happy most of the time. And that is a good thing—an *adaptive* thing—because happy people get sick less often and they get well faster when they do get sick or injured. Norman Cousins, the former editor of the *Saturday Review,* was stricken with a devastating disease of his connective tissues for which there seemed to be neither cure nor hope. With the help of an unusually open-minded physician, Cousins had himself transferred to a hotel (which cost, complete with full room service, about one-fourth of what his hospital was charging) where he proceeded to heal himself with laughter—funny films and funny stories—and he later wrote a book about it.[7] In addition to being healthier, happy people are usually more attractive to other people, more enjoyable to live with and work with, more likely to be welcomed when they come a-courting, and, later on, likely to be better parents. During the time when our species was evolving, back in the Pleistocene, it seems probable that the grouches and the doleful were less likely to survive long enough to become ancestors and, if they did survive, that they did not do as well in the mating game. Thus, there seems every reason to believe that those genes that combine to produce a happy person—perhaps by making brains that are somehow tuned for happy feelings or perhaps by creating combinations of attributes that tend to elicit happy experiences—were favored by natural selection so that we are, on average, a happy breed.

## Evolutionary Psychology

"Hold out your hands and close your eyes and I'll give you something to make you wise." Suppose we play this child's game and, when you open your eyes, you find in your left hand a large, dead spider and, in your right hand, a small Derringer pistol. The chances are that you will drop the spider the moment you recognize what it is, but you will not drop the pistol. Yet guns are more dangerous than dead spiders. Why do we have this instinctive fear and revulsion for spiders and snakes but not for guns, knives, electric sockets, and similar artifacts that pose a greater threat in the lives of most of us?

A million years or so ago, when our earliest ancestors were evolving into the species to which we all belong, there were no guns or knives or electric sockets, but there were snakes and spiders and some of them were poisonous. Some of those early hominids were more likely than others to pick up and examine creepy-crawly things, and those rash individuals were therefore more likely to get bitten before they had offspring. Those early humans whose genetic makeup made them inclined to shy away from snakes and spiders were therefore more likely to survive long enough to pass their genes along and to become our ancestors. This is Darwin's process of natural selection, the same mechanism that gave us our large brains, our ability to walk on our hind legs, and our opposable thumbs. Natural selection works slowly, over hundreds or thousands of generations; guns and electric sockets have not been around nearly long enough for us to have evolved an instinctive fear of them.

About 200,000 years ago, perhaps in Africa, there lived a woman known as Mitochondrial Eve. Every cell in her body, including the eggs from which her babies grew, was powered by a multitude of bacteria-like fragments of life called mitochondria. Like all the other mothers in the band of hunter-gatherers to which Eve belonged, she passed along her mitochondria to her children to energize their cells. Males do not pass on their mitochondria; a sperm has room for only enough to power its swimming movements. The mitochondria drop off with the sperm's tail when sperm meets egg. Therefore, mitochondria are handed down only in the female line. Yours came from your maternal grandmother, who got them from *her* maternal grandmother, and so forth on back. All of the other mothers in Eve's time passed their mitochondria along just as she did, but some of them did not have girl babies, so their line of mitochondria stopped with them. Others did not have female grandchildren, so their legacy ended in the second generation. Only Eve's line was unbroken, from mother to daughter all the way down to my mother and yours; in that sense, Eve was the mother of us all.[8]

Eve and her relations, near and distant, already looked more like us than they resembled *their* ancestors, the great apes. Like us, they were social creatures, living together in extended-family groups. There were many benefits of membership in those early hominid communities. The elders could teach one how to make tools and clothes and fires, how to find or make a shelter from the elements, how to hunt game, what plants were edible or medicinal or poisonous—all the accumulated wisdom of their ancestors. If Ogg made the best hunting bows, he might make one for Igg in exchange for a haunch of meat or a tiger's tooth Igg found somewhere. If a member became sick or injured, his colleagues would feed him and nurse him back to health. With the coordinated effort of many men, one could hunt really big game and lay in stores of protein. One's children would be more likely to survive with the extended family to help look after them. As they slowly migrated away from the tropical savannas into colder climates, survival became increasingly complex for our ancestors and the practical wisdom and mutual assistance of the group became increasingly important. The stories told by the returning hunters and warriors provided information about the larger world outside, and the myths told by the old ones would have made that world seem more orderly and perhaps less frightening.

Therefore, it was adaptive to belong to such a group and to be able to partake in these advantages. Some of Eve's relatives tried to go it alone and did not survive. Others could not learn to obey the group's rules or refused to cooperate in the group effort for survival; they were likely to be excluded for such reasons and therefore failed to become ancestors. At some point, whether before or after Eve's time we do not know, certain of our ancestors became able to vocalize in more varied and complex ways than other primates could and, more importantly, to associate specific meanings with those vocalizations. If Eve could do this, she would have been more likely to mate with a male who could do it too, and their children would have had the great advantage, over the offspring of some other couples, of being able to talk with one another. Over the millennia, any small genetic differences that increased the chances of survival, especially those differences that improved one's chances of maintaining and profiting from group membership, gradually separated our ancestors from the also-rans.

One of these adaptive differences, surprisingly, was an innate tendency to look on the bright side and to be happy. All mammals are equipped with neural circuitry that causes them to do things, and to learn to do things, that make them feel good. These ancient tendencies evolved because most things animals do to feel good are good for them and help them to survive and to reproduce their kind (since the advent of fermented beverages and psychoactive drugs, this rule is no longer strictly true for our species). What is surprising is that most humans apparently manage to behave in ways that keep them feeling good, and reasonably happy, most of the time.

If you think that appealing to the early days of human evolution is mere speculation, pointless and unnecessary today, consider this familiar story. When the Minnesota Twins baseball team won the World Series in 1987, and again in 1991, 4 million otherwise rational Minnesotans acted as if something wonderful and important had happened. People who had never attended a Twins game, who could not previously have named a single player on the team (except, of course, for Kirby Puckett), were glued to their televisions. Walking my dog one chilly evening during the 1991 Series, I could hear the sound of people cheering inside their closed-up houses in my quiet neighborhood. We groaned when the other team got a hit, cheered when one of our boys made a good play, and we generally acted as if we believed that those twenty-five highly paid athletes, born in other states or even other countries, none of whom we'd ever met, were all members of our family and that the National League players were enemy invaders. In all of the press talk about the fans' reaction to those games, no one ever asked the most obvious and puzzling question: *Why did we care?* Those men were not "our boys" at all; the team belonged to a rich banker named Carl Pohlad, not to us. Why did we agonize, cheer, exult with pride? What actual difference could the result of those games possibly make in our individual lives? The fact that most of us reacted the same way makes the question sound silly at first: of course we cared. But when we take a second look there is really no denying that— unless we had bet the farm on the team's success—our reaction to the event was irrational. And yet it was also somehow deeply inevitable and natural.

The only way I think we can make sense of such phenomena is to remember that the innate predilections we now carry around with us evolved when our ancestors lived in small bands of hunter-gatherers and the fate of the band frequently depended upon the success of the band's young men in combat with the young men of other bands. Those extended family groups in which the women and children encouraged and honored their warriors, inspiring the boys to want to grow up to be fighters themselves, would have been, on average, more successful in repelling invaders, more likely to survive to breed again.

## Evolutionary Change and Genetic Diversity

A basic principle of evolutionary theory is that the organism is the gene's way of reproducing itself.[9] Just as humans do today, the ancestral hominids differed from one another genetically, due both to the occurrence of random mutations and to the new genetic configurations that are created at every conception when a random half of the mother's genes combines with a random half contributed by the father. We know today that virtually every psychological trait that can be reliably measured owes an appreciable part of its variation in the population to genetic variation (see chapter 2). Therefore, we can safely assume that our earliest ancestors, because of their genetic variability, also varied one from another in their behavioral tendencies.[10] Those genetically influenced behavior tendencies that increased the likelihood of viable children and grandchildren (or nieces and nephews) were for that reason likely to be more frequent among succeeding generations.

Genetic variations that confer important adaptive advantages will become fixed characteristics of the species, given sufficient environmental stability and enough time for all the less-adaptive variants to disappear from the gene pool. Why is there, then, so much genetic variation left in so many of the psychological traits of modern humans? First, there has not been enough time. Our species has been in place for only 100,000 years or so, which is not long as time is reckoned by evolutionists. Second, the environment has been far from constant. The psychologically relevant environment embraces all of human culture and technology (and is much broader than the aspects of environment that influence physiological development) and it has been changing at an ever-increasing pace. Many human talents and propensities that are important now were irrelevant in far ancestral times so that evolutionary pressures could not act upon them. If a child with Shakespeare's or Newton's genetic blueprint (genome) had been born in some band of Paleolithic hunter-gatherers, it is not at all clear that he or she would have been considered to be special or, if special, wonderful.

Moreover, many psychological traits may turn out to be genetically complex, involving configurations of genes that are pleiotropic—that is, genes that have other functions apart from their contribution to the trait in question. Such traits are hard to get to "breed true," whether natural selection is doing the job or a human breeder of domestic animals. The record-setting Thoroughbred racehorse Secretariat provides one example that we shall discuss in the next chapter. Many human traits presumably have become less variable over the millennia, such as the traits of socialization and other happy-making characteristics that are considered here. Other psychological traits may have an even greater range of genetic variation now than in ancient times (e.g., there may be more very smart humans now than there once were, due to assortative mating for intelligence).

## Success Does Not Yield Happiness

People who go to work in their overalls and on the bus are just as happy, on the average, as those in suits who drive to work in their own Mercedes. Although men still retain a perilous grip on most of the reins of power in our society, they are not any happier than are women. In spite of racism and relative poverty, African Americans enjoy on average the same feelings of subjective well-being as do white Americans. Psychologists David Myers and Ed Diener reported in 1995 that there is no appreciable correlation between happiness, on the one hand, and social status, income, gender, or skin color on the other.[11] These at first surprising findings have been replicated by others using different techniques. When I first read the Myers and Diener paper, I realized that we could test most of their findings with data we had already collected from our large sample of middle-aged twins. Our sample ranged in age from thirty to fifty-five. Some had only

a fourth-grade education, while others had M.D.'s or Ph.D.'s;
some were currently unemployed or on welfare, while others
were doing very well as professionals or businesspeople or farm-
ers. About 90 percent of them had been married at least once
and some 20 percent had been divorced. Among other questionnaires they had completed for us was the Multidimensional Personality Questionnaire (MPQ), an inventory constructed by my
colleague, Auke Tellegen, which measures eleven basic traits of
personality or temperament.

One of the MPQ scales measures Well Being, and its items
ask whether the respondent is interested in his daily activities,
enthusiastic about the way things are going, optimistic at least
about her own current and future prospects—that is, whether he
or she is *happy*. Because it gets at this question of happiness with
many items rather than just one, the MPQ-WB scale is a more
reliable measure than our single "Contentment" item discussed
earlier. Other happiness researchers have not used Tellegen's
scale; I personally believe that his is best. But the important point
is that it is *different,* so that when we compare our twins' scores
on Well Being to their social status, income, marital status, education, and the like, we can be sure that our getting the same
results as Myers and Diener is not due simply to our use of the
same (and possibly invalid) instrument. And we did indeed get
the same results: Well Being accounts for about 2 percent, a trivial amount, of the variation across our subjects in status, income,
and education. The married twins were slightly happier than the
single ones, but the difference was not enough to sneeze at. The
mean difference between men and women was even smaller,
with the women slightly higher.

Myers and Diener (and others) had suggested that religious
commitment might be both a bulwark against despair and an
open door to feelings of subjective well-being. Another of the
MPQ scales measures a characteristic called Traditionalism; people high on Traditionalism are generally conservative, they en-
dorse family values and conventional morality, and are likely to
earnestly subscribe to some form of established religion. But the
correlation we found between Traditionalism and Well Being was

only .05 ($\pm$ .016) or very nearly 0. More recently we have administered the MPQ to some 3,300 parents of eleven- or seventeen-year-old twins, and we also have a more specific and detailed measure of the current religious commitment of these men and women. We know how regularly they attend religious services, how often they seek guidance or forgiveness through prayer, how important they consider their religious faith to be in their daily lives. The correlation between this specific measure of religious commitment and the MPQ-WB score was just .07; it is "statistically significant," as the professionals would say, but it is trivial. Religious people are not noticeably happier than the freethinkers. Perhaps this is the purpose of revival meetings, to revive one's faith and also the sense of well-being that comes from a renewed religious commitment.

## Adaptation

> There was a danger that Abram might become too well
> pleased with his own good fortune. Therefore God seasons
> the sweetness of wealth with vinegar.
> —John Calvin

How can we explain the fact that success—winning the gold, getting that promotion, making more than old Dad ever did, getting that degree, being made a partner—does not actually bring us to the promised land as we always had assumed it would? Darwinian theory, once again, suggests the answer. The ancients did not have bank accounts or corporation CEOs, but they did have tribal chiefs. What if each newly christened chief had felt so proud, so continuously happy and content with his new status, that he ceased striving, having new ideas, networking, solving problems, doing the kinds of things that led to his election in the first place? What if each success that anyone achieved had permanently diminished that individual's initiative? What if a child who learns at last to add is so permanently elated that he never bothers to learn to subtract, much less to multiply or do long division? What if a bad experience, a failure, a loss, bereavement, an injury, should continue to hurt, month after month, as intensely as it did when it first happened? Would people made like that be likely to survive and to leave their genes behind in the next generation?

One important trait that scientists think all mammals share is the ability to adapt to rather wide-ranging changes in environmental conditions. We gradually get used to the new circumstances and our nervous systems become habituated to the changes in stimulus input. Psychologists have studied ordinary habituation for years and know something about it. My favorite real-life example has to do with my big grandfather's clock, which commits an assault upon the eardrums every quarter hour. The few times that I actually hear the clanging of this clock are now and then when I'm awake in bed, separated from the clock by a floor, a closed door, and a considerable distance. When my wife and I are reading in the living room, neither of us is inclined to hear the clock because we are habituated to its racket. When guests are in the room, however, conversation ceases and they may even jump when Grandfather goes into his chiming routine. If the identical sounds were recorded on tape and played back unexpectedly from the backseat of my car while I'm driving to work, there would probably be an accident. By some poorly understood mechanism, when I am in my living room, my brain tunes out when the clock strikes, and I don't even hear it. The repeated presentations of a stimulus that we need not react to produces habituation so that some unconscious mechanism identifies the stimulus as a familiar and, at least for now, meaningless stimulus and then attenuates its impact so that we either do not notice it at all or, if we do, its intensity is much reduced.

Bill Iacono and I have studied habituation in the laboratory by presenting repeated noise blasts (or even harmless but painful electric shocks) to subjects who are initially startled by them and react with strong physiological disturbance.[12] After many repetitions, however, habituation supervenes and the reactions diminish and, for most people, cease altogether. We have shown, in fact, that some people habituate much more readily than others do and that individual differences in habituation have strong genetic roots; if one identical twin is able to rapidly habituate, it is very likely that the cotwin will do so as well.[13]

There is no standard way of measuring the speed with which different individuals get over the effects of a success or a failure, of bereavement or of a triumph. My guess is that the same people who habituate rapidly to loud noises in the laboratory may be the ones who more readily get back to their former equilibrium after some good or bad event has temporarily displaced their normal hedonic or happiness levels up or down. But I cannot be sure of this.

Happily, however, researchers at the University of Illinois have made an important advance in our understanding of this phenomenon.[14] They began by measuring their subjects' current levels of subjective well-being, using the methods developed at Illinois by Ed and Carol Diener. Then they asked each subject to report on every significant event, positive or negative, that had increased or decreased their happiness levels during the preceding year. People who had suffered some misfortune within recent weeks turned out to have lower scores on subjective well-being. Those who had experienced cheering, happy-making events recently were happier than average. But if the good or bad experiences were as far removed as three months back, their effects on present mood were nearly impossible to distinguish and, if as long as six months earlier, no residual effects were visible.

Like most other mammals, ours is a remarkably adaptable or accommodating or habituating species (there seems to be no ideal name for this trait). People who have been desolated by the loss of a loved one often feel a guilty surprise to find, six months later, that they can smile and enjoy life again. People who have suffered crippling and permanent injuries typically recover psychologically quicker than we luckier ones would have believed possible. I have a colleague who was a gymnast in his youth and broke his upper back in a fall at age nineteen. Yet he went on, a near quadriplegic, to earn a Ph.D. in biostatistics, to marry and raise a family, and to become a favorite (and funny) teacher and academic colleague. The film star Christopher Reeve suffered a similar accident at the height of his career yet, within a year, he found that he "had discovered joy again." Helen Keller, born blind, deaf, and mute, became a productive and happy adult. In 1995, Jean-Dominique Bauby, editor of the French periodical *Elle*, became a prisoner within a body totally paralyzed by a massive stroke. He could communicate only by blinking in a letter code. Yet by 1997 he had composed in this laborious way a book, *The Diving Bell and the Butterfly*, with sentences that "soar, unburdened by self-pity or despair," according to *The New Yorker*.[15]

We "get over" or adapt to success and good fortune just as readily. Lottery winners have been interviewed a year later and, alas, the great high of their winning had largely evanesced by that time. Carl Imhof, of Pine Island, Minnesota, won $9.4 million in 1996 but still gets up before dawn five days a week to get to his job driving a forklift in a warehouse. He says he "can't just sit at home, life would get boring." There seem to be no permanent ups or permanent downs; natural selection has made us this way because, by accommodating to both adversity and to good fortune in this fashion, we remain more productive, more adaptable to changing circumstances, and more likely to have viable offspring.

## Happy-Making Traits

In October 1996, Astronaut Shannon Lucid returned after spending a record 188 days circling the earth in the *Mir* space station. She was plainly very happy to be back, but was she happy— could *anyone* be happy?—during her six months of solitary confinement in that isolation chamber? Apparently Dr. Lucid was in good spirits most of that long period, but not just because she is an innately happy person. She was able to tolerate what might have been a mind-numbing ordeal because she had things to do, important things that she knew how to do well, and she had things to look forward to. She had significant scientific experiments to monitor, she could communicate with her family by e-mail and with her NASA controllers by radio, she had two hours daily of vigorous exercise to keep fit, and she had books to read. A chimpanzee in her situation would not have been able to dream about her eventual triumphant homecoming or look forward to the next e-mail from home, the visit of the resupply ship in August, or a new stock of M&Ms. Happy people may have more responsive "happy centers" in their brains, but those centers need some happy-making input to respond to; happy people do not just sit around in perpetual bliss but, rather, they are inclined to *do* things that stimulate interest, enthusiasm, contentment, and joy. Some of the things that happy humans do to maintain that desirable state, some of the traits we have evolved that operate to keep our average levels of contentment above the zero mark, are reviewed below.

## Effectance Motivation

Slick Willie, my bull terrier, knows three different games to play with tennis balls. Yard ball is much like ordinary "fetch," but because bull terriers find it very difficult to release a ball once it is clamped in their mouths, Willie needs to play with two. When he gives up one to be thrown again, he still has the other under control. Stair ball is more complicated, and corner ball, played in the kitchen, is more complex still. Willie's eagerness to play these games is laughable; knowing these games plainly has enriched his life. Bull terriers do not often invent games on their own, not being very smart, but Border collies instinctively love to herd things; they will herd chickens or children or houseguests if nothing else is available. A Border collie trained to herd sheep on command will work happily at this task day after day.

But it is our species, far more than any other, that has evolved the capacity to create games and other goal-oriented tasks, to develop truly extraordinary skills at such endeavors, and to thoroughly enjoy the process. A psychologist would say that we humans have a strong effectance motivation, a desire to impact our environment, to make things happen in predictable ways, to control events. It was obviously adaptive for our ancestors to invent weapons and other tools, to construct shelters, and eventually to cultivate gardens, but it appears that they evolved not only the ability to do these things but also an inherent enjoyment in the doing, in productive labor for its own sake. We know this because some of the things that they worked at were not merely means to some material end. They made cave paintings, for example, and they decorated their weapons and their eating bowls. We also know this because we, their descendants, enjoy developing and exercising skills, playing games, making things, growing things, learning things. Often we work just because we have to or in response to some cultural imperative, like the Protestant ethic. Yet it remains true that productive activity is one of the most dependable sources of human happiness. Prison inmates who are unable to work, to develop or exercise a skill, are not happy people. I can imagine no stronger inducement to escape attempts, the construction of "shivs" or other weapons, the formation of hierarchical inmate gangs and the incitement of inter-gang warfare, than a prison in which inmates have nothing constructive to do, nothing licit that they can take pride in. On the other hand, some inmates of more enlightened prisons learn there for the first time the satisfaction of doing something useful or of doing something well.

## Nurturance

Young animals are vulnerable and relatively helpless so we, like other mammals, evolved a tendency for parents to behave in a nurturant and protective way toward their offspring. The greater probability that nurtured and protected offspring would survive to breed themselves was the cause of this evolved proclivity. But the actual mechanism that evolved to yield this useful tendency is relatively nonspecific. Like many other mammals, we seem to have an innate disposition to be protective of the helpless and vulnerable. A mother dog can sometimes be induced to accept a nursing kitten and, once used to the idea, becomes maternally protective of the foundling. It is a fact that most human adults feel an innate tenderness toward an infant, even an infant not related to themselves and, having once accepted responsibility for its care, may come to love it as their own. My guess is that nurturing helps to generate love, as well as the other way around.

Doing things for an infant, a younger sibling, a pet animal, seems to enhance its value to us as well as our feelings of empathy.

This nonspecific feeling of tenderness toward the helpless and vulnerable, this innate pleasure that we take in their nurturance and care, constitutes the proximate cause of parenting behavior. It did not evolve because it was nonspecific but, rather, it evolved as a nonspecific tendency because that was sufficient to accomplish the evolutionarily important result of inducing parental nurturance. But because it is nonspecific, this tendency may have unanticipated consequences. It may explain, for example, the curious fact that many humans can feel the full range of parental emotions and nurturing impulses toward pet animals, a tendency that seems unlikely to have evolved on its own.

The important principle that this example illustrates is this: Adaptations, including behavioral dispositions, that were selected because they increased inclusive fitness in ancestral times, may have effects wholly extraneous to those effects that were responsible for their original selection in the "environment of evolutionary adaptation,"[16] effects that, under the greatly altered conditions of modern life, may even detract from reproductive fitness. One grim example is our trait of xenophobia—fearing, and therefore hating, persons different from ourselves—which was adaptive once when strangers were likely to be bent upon raiding our village and stealing our women. But xenophobia has accounted for endless carnage and misery since we became "civilized."

But it is also important to see that nurturance, feeding, fondling, making nice for those we love (including, for many of us, critters of various types), is inherently enjoyable and therefore is a happy-making trait. Nurturance is clearly higher in women than in men. When our more than four thousand middle-aged twins rated themselves on nurturance, among many other traits, 78 percent of the women scored above the mean self-rating of the men. According to my expense records, my wife, who is very critter-oriented, spends as much each year feeding Willie, the three cats, numerous birds, six squirrels, and a spider, as she spends feeding me (the spider's meals, dead insects, don't cost anything, actually, and her flock of crows eat mainly table scraps). It is one of the important satisfactions in her life.

## Self-Awareness

Although the great apes, whose genetic blueprints differ from our own by only a few pages, seem to have a rudimentary sense of self—like human children, they can learn to recognize themselves in mirrors, for example—only members of our species develop a detailed mental picture of ourselves and of our attributes, a *self-concept*. Because we are irresistibly inclined to evaluate other people, admiring this one, disdaining, even despising that one, we tend to evaluate our pictures of ourselves using similar criteria. This means that having a self-concept can be a curse as well as an advantage. If I see myself doing things or having characteristics that I look down upon in others, then I will not be a happy person, at least not until I change my ways enough to merit self-esteem. Fortunately, we are constructed in such a way as to be motivated to do just that. We try to become like the people we admire and, once achieved, a positive self-concept is a treasure that we try to live up to. As Samuel Johnson said, "That kind of life is most happy which affords us most opportunities of gaining our own esteem." This important point is developed further in the later chapter on parenting.

Unfortunately, some bad people, who have pictures of themselves that would make you or me feel awful, maintain high self-esteem because they have different values and they esteem people whom we fear and despise, hence the admiring expression "He's a real bad-ass." Self-esteem and happiness, sadly, are not reserved only for the kind and good. Unfortunately, also, there are good people whose self-concepts are bad because they are inaccurate. These people used to be called neurotic before modern psychiatry changed the rules. What they need is psychotherapy, preferably something like rational emotive therapy (RET), which is designed to help the patient to develop a more accurate, realistic picture of himself and his world.[17]

## Future Perspective

Our species also is the only one able to contemplate the distant future. Other mammals clearly can make short-term plans. When my dog Willie's clock tells him it is 4:00 P.M. (his clock seems accurate to ± five minutes or so), he comes to tell me that it is time for our daily game of yard ball. Our cats announce their mealtimes (their clocks always run early), and Polly Peachum, our previous bull terrier, plainly decided before each evening's walk which route she wanted to take that night. She would put her head down as we exited the driveway and head determinedly left, right, or across the street before I could possibly make a different choice. Animals, however, cannot plan for next week, cannot work today for a reward tomorrow, cannot happily antici- pate some distant future joy; neither can they anticipate with dread some future grief or loss. Like self-awareness, our human future perspective is no guarantee of happiness. Yet I am certain that the sum of the enjoyment I have experienced in my long life would have been greatly diminished had I not been able to anticipate future reunions, accomplishments, rewards, and other satisfactions, some highly probable and others less so.

## Vicarious Experience

Our ability to share vicariously in the experience of others is another trait peculiar to our species that can influence our sub- jective well-being in important ways, both positive and negative. Because we can (learn to) empathize with others, we can there- fore learn without getting burned ourselves that the fire is hot or, without getting sick, whether these berries are good to eat. Although nature did not plan it that way, we can also enjoy at secondhand the experiences of some soap opera character, feel a safe thrill at a horror movie, or participate in "our team's" victory as we watch the ball game on TV. As every confirmed couch potato knows, these vicarious enjoyments pale after a while and become more sedative than pleasurable. Some vicarious plea- sures do more than entertain. The ones that teach us true things about the world we live in, and the people in it, not only give us the satisfaction of accomplishment but also make us better equipped to understand and deal with new experience, to avoid pain and derive pleasures later on. Good books and honest drama pay bigger dividends in the long run, but even the lightest entertainment, so often based on vicarious experience, has its place in anybody's life.

## Aesthetic Pleasures

One truly mysterious characteristic of our species is our ability to take delight in certain sensory experiences that have no Darwinian relevance that is obvious, at least to me. I am not talking about gustatory or sexual or nurturant pleasures, because they serve the obvious Darwinian purpose of keeping us alive and making babies and making sure that they survive. I am talking about the curious fact that, on my evening walks with Willie during the long Minnesota winters, I can get real sensuous pleasure from looking at the trees, their leafless branches making beautiful and complex patterns against the evening sky. Some old oaks, limbs awry, look for all the world like gruff old men or mountain trolls, and some young maples and ash trees, isolated against the blue-gray background, look like demure and comely maidens. There is a small and rather spindly elm tree that we pass that is plainly an arboreal representation of Blanche Dubois in Tennessee Williams's *A Streetcar Named Desire*. Scientists interested in aesthetics are just beginning to think about these things from an evolutionary perspective.[18]

Why do we get such joy from listening to music? I have a poor ear and no musical knowledge, yet I listen to music, great music wonderfully played, for at least an hour or two every day, a delight once available only to kings. E. O. Wilson, a founding father of evolutionary psychology, lists "music" in the index of his (splendid) book *On Human Nature*, but he does not hazard any answer to the question "Why?" If I were a young evolutionary psychologist, I would think very hard about why it was that we evolved our musical appreciation. Since I am not, I am content to enjoy the fact that we did evolve it.

I know even less about visual art, and looking at paintings has not been a high priority for me. Yet I have enjoyed the galleries I've visited, and I have at least a suspicion about what it is that painters do for the rest of us. It seems very probable that human infants and young children have a more intense emotional response to visual sensation than do older children or adults. The infant has so much perceptual learning to do that nature makes most visual stimulation inherently rewarding so as to maintain the child's attention. One summer day, forty years or so ago, I was walking along a residential street when an rich, earthy scent wafted my way and triggered, as smells are wont to do, a vivid recollection. Like Dorothy stepping out of her front door into the Technicolor Land of Oz, I remembered another summer's day when I was four years old, playing in a bank of warm, black dirt in the backyard of my home. I had a little red toy car for which I'd made a road slanting up the face of the dirt bank and, in my recollection, I was "driving" the car up this mountain road while making motor noises. That's all there was, no real action, yet the memory, in the few seconds before it faded away, was redolent with the smell and feel of the warm dirt, the bright color of the toy, the hot sun—with simple but intensely pleasurable sensory experience. When I read Aldous Huxley's account of his mescaline experience, of his feeling that the colors, shapes, and textures of his books on the shelves across the room were as intense an experience as he could bear and that he dared not look outside at the flowers in the garden, I thought of my brief revisitation of my childhood.

Presumably, this intensity of sensory experience does fade when its work of facilitating perceptual learning is accomplished, because it would be maladaptive in adults. Those ancients who sat around all day entranced by colors, smells, and textures would have never gotten the venison cooked or the berries picked; they would have been easy meat for prowling tigers and unlikely to become ancestors. But, since all our species-specific traits and predilections occur in varying degrees in different people, perhaps some modern humans, people like Paul Gauguin or Vincent van Gogh, retain much of that childish way of seeing vividly and then help us, through their reproductions of their own experience, to see it as they saw it. Why is the recounting of an event, a scene, or an idea more moving when it is done in poetry rather than in mere expository prose? Perhaps the words and rhythms of the poet, like the shapes and colors of the painter, somehow, in Huxley's phrase, "open the doors of our perceptions."

Much more certain than any of these speculations is the fact that our species, for reasons that are as yet inscrutable, derives joy from music, from the beauties of nature or of human art, and from the gifted use of words in poetry or prose. Because it is mysterious, perhaps we should regard this trait as divinely inspired and be sure to make the most of it. Those of us incapable of creating beauty of this sort must cherish and facilitate the ones who do, for they brighten all our lives.

## Curiosity

We share our trait of curiosity with other mammals to some extent, but no other species has our drive for understanding ourselves and our environment nor our delight in discovery. The Darwinian sources of this trait are not at all mysterious. To understand is to predict, and to predict correctly is to maximize one's chances to survive in the end. Because we have these big brains, we spend more time and effort trying to figure things out than other species do and, perhaps for the same reason, we get a bigger kick out of finding the right answers. I get great satisfaction out of learning of other people's discoveries and how they did it. Eratosthenes, a Greek who lived in Alexandria in Egypt about 250 B.C., learned of a village some distance to the south where there was a deep well in the marketplace in which the full face of the sun could be seen reflected in the bottom at noon of the summer solstice. Knowing (somehow) the approximate distance from Alexandria to this village, Eratosthenes measured the angle of the sun's rays at noon on the solstice in Alexandria and, from these facts, he estimated the circumference of the earth within a few percent!

Karl Friedrich Gauss (1777–1855), who later became one of the princes of mathematics, while a ten-year-old pupil in a village school, was told by the school master, thinking to keep his class busy for an hour, to add up all the integers from 1 to 100. The class had no more settled down to work when the master was startled to see young Gauss at his desk with the answer, 5,050, written on his slate. The little prince (whose father was a stonemason and whose mother was illiterate) had seen at once that if one were to write the numbers 1 to 50 left to right in one row and the numbers 51 to 100 right to left beneath them, then each vertical pair of numbers would add to 101; so, there being fifty such pairs, the total sum must be $50 \times 101 = 5{,}050$! "There 'tis," as little Karl said.

Psychologists like me get even more pleasure from contemplating the people who figure these things out than we derive from the answers themselves. I believe that human genius, like Secretariat's astonishing racing ability, is often the result of a unique configuration of genes never seen before or since in that individual's lineage.[19] But all of us can get satisfaction from knowing things, even just the names of things—birds, songs, trees, politicians, constellations, movie stars—while knowing how to figure things out, to solve problems, to find answers, is a still-greater gratification.

## To Sum Up

Most people, given basic food, shelter, and reasonable security, feel reasonably happy most of the time. When outrageous fortune drives their hedonic levels down into despair, most people soon recover. We know that "this too shall pass away," that current grief or disappointment will usually have faded in some three to six months' time. The joys that good fortune brings also fade in time, so we must "live in an ascending scale when we live happily, one thing leading to another in an endless series."[20] As the English novelist C. L. Morgan advised, "The art of living does not consist in preserving and clinging to a particular mode of happiness, but in allowing happiness to change its form without being disappointed in the change; happiness, like a child, must be allowed to grow up." Natural selection gave us the ability to experience happiness, not to be kind, but to serve as a carrot with which to lead us donkeys to behave constructively, to adapt to our environment so as to survive, and then to have and nurture babies. Remember that we human "donkeys" are just our genes' way of reproducing themselves.

Unless we currently are trapped in some desperate, life-threatening situation, especially one that continues on until our reserves of resiliency are totally depleted, it is unlikely that any single event, accomplishment, or stroke of good fortune will produce an enduring increase in our level of subjective well-being. Just as most slings and arrows produce only temporary downturns in our current contentment, so, too, the victories and good fortunes we experience yield only upticks that also fade with time. The search for happiness is a never-ending quest—nature planned it that way for her own ends.

# 2

# THE HAPPINESS SET POINT: How and Why People Differ in Their Average Feelings of Well-Being

> My life has no purpose, no direction, no aim, no meaning, and yet I'm happy. I can't figure it out. What am I doing right?
>
> —*Charlie Brown* (Charles M. Schulz)

O ur ancestors must have differed genetically, one from another, in their talent for happiness in order for their "happy genes" to have been passed along selectively to us. People today still differ in their average feelings of well-being— what psychologists call their hedonic levels—although the average for the group is well above 0. Nearly all psychological traits and tendencies—irritability, extroversion, aggressiveness, enthusiasm, fearfulness, even IQ—vary over time in response to circumstances. I am smarter and quicker, in the morning than in the afternoon, for example, and not smart at all when I'm really tired or sick. On rare occasions in my youth, I felt aggressive enough to actually hit someone and even now, most of my fires out, I feel kind of irritable from time to time (but with no urge to hit). Happiness is notoriously variable in this way. Can there be any normal adult who cannot remember ever feeling really joyful?

I talked about happy memories recently with a notoriously successful drug dealer. It happened in a seminar on criminology at Oak Park Heights, the maximum security prison in Stillwater, Minnesota. This inmate participant was explaining ruefully why he had been transferred that week out of the education unit back to the general population. "It was in my critical thinking class," he said. "We were supposed to tell about the time in our lives when we had been the happiest. I said it was the time I escaped from Lompoc [a prison in California.] That was a tricky and rather dangerous proposition, and when I realized that I was really out, that I'd made it and was free again, I think I felt better than I've ever felt before or since." The scandalized instructor, a stuffy martinet, had put him on report for his "uncooperative attitude" and had him transferred out. This inmate's wry conclusion was: "I guess I should have told her that the happiest time in my life was when Dad took the training wheels off my bike." The odd thing about this man, and most of his fellow inmates in this well-run prison, is that—once they have had a few months to adjust to their confinement—they appear to be about as happy as the members of the prison staff, who can go home to their families every day.

And who has not said to himself at other times, "How weary, stale, flat, and unprofitable seem to me all the uses of this world!" (at least those of us who quote Shakespeare to ourselves)? If our genetic makeup has anything at all to do with our happiness, then surely it must be our *average* hedonic level that we owe to our genetic blueprint (to our genome), rather than these sporadic highs and lows that are due instead to fortune's favors. My colleague Auke Tellegen and I have shown, in fact, that most of the variation among people in the level of their happiness set points is associated with genetic differences between them. How much of one's average feeling of well-being is genetic, how we know this, and how and whether we can do something to reset our set points (or to rise above them) are the subject of this chapter.

## What Is Your Own Happiness Level Right Now?

The Contentment scale you may have scored yourself on in chapter 1 is good enough for a rough approximation, but you can get a much more precise and reliable estimate of your current level of subjective well-being by answering (honestly) the eighteen items listed below. These are the items of the Well-Being scale that is part of Tellegen's Multidimensional Personality Questionnaire, or MPQ,[1] the same inventory we have administered to thousands of twins and also to twins reared apart. The instructions printed at the top of the MPQ read like this:

These items are statements that you might use to describe your opinion, interests, or feelings. To the right of each item there is a scale like this: **T t f F**. The meaning of the four possible answers is given below:

> T = Definitely True
> t = Probably True
> f = Probably False
> F = Definitely False

So, if the statement or item is definitely true for you, then you should circle the T like this: Ⓣ **t f F**. If the statement or item is probably true for you (or more true than false), then you should circle the t like this: **T** ⓣ **f F**.

| | | | | |
|---|---|---|---|---|
| 1. I am just naturally cheerful. | T | t | f | F |
| 2. My future looks very bright to me. | T | t | f | F |
| 3. It is easy for me to become enthusiastic about the things I am doing. | T | t | f | F |
| 4. I often feel happy and satisfied for no particular reason. | T | t | f | F |
| 5. I live a very interesting life. | T | t | f | F |
| 6. Every day I do some things that are fun. | T | t | f | F |
| 7. Basically I am a happy person. | T | t | f | F |
| 8. I usually find ways to liven up my day. | T | t | f | F |
| 9. I have several pastimes or hobbies that are great fun. | T | t | f | F |
| 10. I seldom feel really happy. | T | t | f | F |
| 11. Most mornings the day ahead looks bright to me. | T | t | f | F |
| 12. Most days I have moments of real fun or joy. | T | t | f | F |
| 13. I often feel sort of lucky for no special reason. | T | t | f | F |
| 14. Every day interesting and exciting things happen to me. | T | t | f | F |
| 15. In my spare time I usually find something interesting to do. | T | t | f | F |
| 16. I am usually light-hearted. | T | t | f | F |
| 17. For me life is a great adventure. | T | t | f | F |
| 18. Without being conceited, I feel pretty good about myself. | T | t | f | F |

(MPQ items © University of Minnesota Press, used with permission.)

To find your total well-being score, give yourself a 3 for every item answered T, a 2 for every t, a 1 for each f, and 0 for each F. For item 10, you must reverse the scoring so that T equals 0 and

F equals 3. The maximum possible score is 18 x 3 = 54. To compare your score with the middle-aged people in our large samples, look at table 2.1. If your score on the well-being scale was 47 or higher, then your current happiness level is higher than 90 percent of men and higher than 88 percent of women. A score of 37 puts you right in the middle; half of both sexes score 37 or less. If your score is less than 26, then you need to read this book carefully.

| Well Being Score | Men: Percentile | Women: Percentile |
|---|---|---|
| 47 | 90 | 88 |
| 43 | 80 | 77 |
| 41 | 73 | 68 |
| 39 | 63 | 61 |
| 37 | 50 | 50 |
| 35 | 39 | 39 |
| 33 | 30 | 30 |
| 31 | 21 | 22 |
| 26 | 10 | 10 |

**TABLE 2.1**

Percentile scores for some two thousand middle-aged men and women (the parents of eleven- or seventeen-year-old twins in the Minnesota Twin/Family Study). If your score on the MPQ Well Being scale was 41, for example, as shown in the left-hand column, then 73 percent of men and 68 percent of the women scored lower than you did.

If your score was 37 or higher, then—today, at least—you are probably feeling better currently about your life than half or more of your neighbors and friends.[2] But, of course, things may be going especially well for you now or perhaps you are still enjoying the glow from some recent happy event. To get an estimate of your average happiness level, we should have to repeat the test—say, monthly—for some time and then average your scores. Such an average, especially if taken over a number of years of your life, would be an estimate of your happiness set point, the level to which your feelings of well-being tend to return after being displaced, up or down, by the turn of events.

## Assessing the Heritability of Happiness

How is it possible to estimate the extent to which a trait is determined genetically? Even more puzzling, how is it possible that any complex psychological trait, traits like IQ or aggressiveness or the talent for happiness, *could* be "determined by" genetic factors? It makes sense to take these questions in the order given, since there is no point in worrying about how something happens unless we can show first that it does, in fact, happen.

Stature is a good trait to begin with because no one doubts that how tall one is must be in part determined by one's genes. To assess the heritability of stature we are going to make use of a convenient experiment of nature, human twins. Identical or monozygotic (MZ) twins start their existence as a single fertilized ovum that began the usual process of cell division—into two cells, four cells, eight cells, and so on—on the road to becoming a single human individual. However, for reasons yet unknown, about three times in every one thousand such beginnings, the developing embryo splits, some time during the first ten days or so after conception, into two equal and viable halves, and then each half continues to develop into, first, a fetus, then a baby. That original fertilized ovum contained in its nuclear DNA the genetic blueprint—like all such blueprints, at least slightly different from any others seen before upon this earth—and that same packet of DNA is contained in every daughter cell of both half embryos that develop into MZ twins. Dizygotic (DZ) or fraternal twins occur when, again for unclear reasons, the mother produces two (or more) ripe ova in the same ovulation period. Each egg is then fertilized by a different sperm so that DZ twins are genetically like ordinary siblings who happen to be the same age. Each DZ twin or sibling will get a random half of Dad's and Mom's polymorphic genes (that fraction of the total set of genes that varies from person to person and causes individual differences). Therefore, DZ twins share on average about half of their polymorphic genes.

Suppose we take a random sample of one thousand adult male MZ twins and measure their heights. Some of these men will be shorter (or taller) than their cotwins because of little glitches in their development in the womb. No two battleships or buildings built according to the same set of plans ever turn out to be truly identical. In constructing in just nine months' time the most complicated mechanism in the known universe, starting with a single fertilized egg, it is astonishing that Nature usually manages to produce a baby that is as close to the blueprint specifications as, in fact, she does. But there will always be small differences (e.g., the fingerprints of MZ twins, while similar, are not identical). Some twin pairs will differ in height due to an accident or illness that affected one but not the other. A few of these pairs might even have been adopted-away at birth and raised by different parents who provided different qualities or quantities of nourishment while the twins were growing up.

Environmental differences of these kinds can have an effect on stature beginning from conception onward. We know that the within-pair height differences in this sample of MZ twins must be due to environmental factors (and we shall, in fact, find some pairs that differ by as much as several inches). Therefore, the within-pair similarity in our sample must be due to their genetic identity. We measure similarity by means of the twin correlation[3] which ranges from 0, when the twins are no more alike than random pairs of men, to 1.0, if both members of each pair have identical scores. When we do this experiment, we find that the MZ twin correlation for stature is about .90, and we conclude that the heritability of stature in adult males is 90 percent. The same experiment with adult female MZ twins gives similar results.

Now there is a hitch in the logic of what I've just asserted and, if you have discerned what it is, you go to the head of the class. The argument above was based on the assumption that (all of) the similarity within pairs of MZ twins must be due to their genetic identity. But what if the parents of some twins fed them well while others did not? What if both members of some pairs were exposed to the same polio virus and their stature was similarly reduced as a result? Twins who are reared together are likely to be exposed to similar experiences and they may become more similar in consequence. It may seem possible, perhaps even likely, that the similarity of MZ twins reared together (MZT twins) will overestimate the heritability of the trait in question. What we really need, therefore, is a sample of MZ twins who were separated in infancy and reared apart in different adoptive families; they are called MZA twins (A for apart). But twins who were separated from infancy until adulthood are rarer than diamonds (and they are *like* diamonds to the student of behavior genetics). Fortunately for us and for science there exists at the University of Minnesota the headquarters and data bank of the largest and most intensive study of these rarities ever conducted, the Minnesota Study of Twins Reared Apart, owned and operated by my colleague, T. J. Bouchard, Jr.

## The Minnesota Study of Twins Reared Apart (MISTRA)

This project began in 1979, when Tom Bouchard, a professor of psychology at Minnesota, noticed an item in the paper reporting on a pair of identical twins, thirty-nine-year-old men, who had been separated a few weeks after they were born and adopted by families living in two different towns in Ohio. Seeking to learn about his birth family, one of them had discovered to his astonishment that he had a twin brother out there somewhere and he proceeded eagerly to track him down.

I had already been studying twins for some years, on the principle that any research one might think of doing with human subjects will be more interesting if one uses twins as subjects. Since roughly two people out of every one hundred are twins, they are as plentiful as the college sophomores psychologists usually employ as subjects, and twins are in most ways more representative of people in general than are sophomores. Twins are also wonderfully cooperative with researchers as a rule because they know they are of special interest, and they share that interest.

Bouchard came to me and suggested that we get a small research grant, bring this reared-apart pair to Minneapolis, and do a case study. I thought it seemed like a lot of work for just a case study, but Bouchard went ahead, raised the money, and recruited the twins and their wives to spend a week at the university being tested and interviewed and studied in every way he could think of.

It turned out that, by coincidence, both sets of adoptive parents had named their baby boy James, so we came to call this pair the "Jim twins." Blood testing confirmed that they were indeed MZ twins. It also turned out that their both being named Jim was just the first of a truly astonishing set of similarities between these twins, some surely also coincidental and others perhaps not coincidence at all. Both men had divorced women named Linda and then married women named Betty (surely coincidence?). Both had produced a son, named James Alan in one case and James Allan in the other (nothing strange about the same first names, but the second?). Both had dogs as youngsters and each had named his dog Toy (names again). A reporter for the *Smithsonian* magazine visited both Jims at home in their separate towns and took pictures of each man smoking a Salem cigarette in his basement woodworking shop. The reporter noted that each man had constructed a white lawn seat around the trunk of a tree in his backyard.[4] The wives of both twins discovered that each husband had the endearing habit of leaving little love notes around the house. Both men drove Chevrolets, were chain-smokers, chewed their fingernails, drank Miller Light beer, had worked as deputy sheriffs in their respective counties, and enjoyed stock car racing but disliked baseball. As they became better acquainted, the two families learned that, well before their emotional meeting as adults, both had taken spring holidays on the Gulf Coast of Florida, driving down in their Chevrolets to the same quarter mile stretch of beach!

Because of these and other rather spooky similarities, and because the Jim twins were so good-natured about everything, there was much media attention, including appearances, with Professor Bouchard, on national television programs such as the Johnny Carson show. As a result of this publicity, Bouchard began receiving news of other reared-apart twins who had found

*Separated at birth, the Mallifert twins meet accidentally.*

**FIGURE 2.1**

Drawing by Charles Addams © 1981, *The New Yorker* Magazine, Inc.

each other. A retired social worker in England who had been helping adoptees locate their birth families began to notify Bouchard of cases involving twins. What began as a case history of a single pair gradually developed into the most extensive and intensive study of these rare experiments of (human) nature ever attempted. As of this writing, 120 pairs of reared-apart twins plus four sets of reared-apart triplets have come to Minnesota for a week of intensive study, and many of them have been brought back, ten years after their first visit, to repeat much of the testing. One of Bouchard's graduate students has estimated that each MISTRA subject responds to some fifteen thousand questions, on paper or in interviews, during their visit.

An early summary of some of the data was published in *Science* in 1990.[5] One at-first surprising finding was that, for most of the psychological traits measured on the MZA twins, they proved to be as similar as are garden variety MZ twins reared together. What this means—and this conclusion has been supported many times over by other kinds of evidence—is that being reared together in the same broadly middle-class homes does not tend to make siblings more alike, not even if they are MZ twins. Unrelated adoptive siblings reared together, for example, resemble one another modestly as children, but once they have grown up and left their joint adoptive home, they are no more alike than other unrelated persons reared separately. This rule holds at least for average homes with average parents who provide adequate nutrition, shelter, socialization, and educational opportunities. Children reared together by really bad, incompetent, or neglectful parents are likely to remain unsocialized and are similar at least in that respect.[6]

Most twin samples studied by researchers are recruited from the broad middle class and had the generally adequate nutrition, health care, educational opportunity, and so on that characterize such families. Therefore, thanks to Bouchard's and the other studies of MZA twins,[7] we are reasonably safe in assuming that heritabilities estimated from typical MZT samples are reasonably accurate for most traits, including physical traits like stature, psychophysiological traits like habituation, mentioned earlier, plus a host of psychological traits from IQ to happiness.

## Some Examples of Heritable Psychological Traits

Nearly all psychological traits or tendencies that can be reliably measured turn out to have heritabilities ranging from about 25 to 80 percent.[8] That is, among persons of European ancestry—for IQ, extroversion, neurotic tendency, musical talent, creativity, scientific and other interests, even for religiousness, authoritarianism, and for happiness itself—from one-fourth to four-fifths of the variation from person to person is associated with genetic differences between those persons. (As recently as

1980, fewer than 2 percent of births in Minnesota were to African, Asian, or Native Americans combined, so our findings may not generalize to those groups.)

## Interests

Like the Jim twins, many of Bouchard's twins had remarkably similar interests. There were two "dog people" in Bouchard's sample: one showed her dogs in competitions while the other taught canine obedience classes—they were an MZA pair. There were two professional firefighters in the group, and two amateur gunsmiths, both pairs of MZA twins. (There were also two habitual criminals and drug addicts in the group, but they were a DZA pair.) We have measured the recreational and occupational interests of twins reared both together and apart.[9] Table 2.2 shows the MZT, DZT, and MZA twin correlations for a few of these interests.

The table shows, first, that about 60 percent of the variation between people is related to their genetic differences. Secondly, interest in things like hunting and fishing or in church work tends to begin in the childhood home, so that DZ twins are more than half as similar in these interests as are MZ twins. Interests

| Interest | MZT Twins | DZT Twins | MZA Twins |
|---|---|---|---|
| Hunting and fishing | .60 | .49 | .72 |
| Church work | .62 | .40 | .74 |
| Husbandry* | .67 | .33 | .75 |
| Passive entertainment | .68 | .24 | .60 |
| Intellectual | .64 | .22 | .55 |
| Performing artist | .64 | .15 | .74 |
| Professional writer | .61 | .14 | .67 |

TABLE 2.2

Twin correlations for some representative recreational and occupational interests.

*"Husbandry" is our name for an interest in repairing or making things, cleaning, and fixing up one's belongings or living space.

in being a performing artist or a writer, however, show the same strong MZ correlations, while the DZ twins are very little more alike than unrelated pairs would be. Traits like these are especially interesting because, while rather strongly genetic, they run only weakly in families. As we shall see, the happiness trait behaves the same way, so it will be useful here to explain how this can happen.

## Genetic Traits That Do Not Run in Families

Stature, which we discussed earlier, does, of course, run in families. Stature is a polygenic trait, which means that your genetic height as specified in your DNA is influenced by many genes, each of which contributes small amounts to the total. That is, the gene effects combine additively, so that your height depends on how many "tall" genes were present in the random halves of your father's and your mother's genomes that you received at your conception. The organs we all share as humans—the eyes, the heart, the kidneys—are also polygenic, but the many genes involved do not combine additively. Instead, they are like workers on an assembly line, each making a different contribution to the final result. Therefore, if one or a few of your eye genes are missing or defective, you do not get just a smaller eye but rather a qualitatively different and probably defective eye. We can express this difference in the genetic process by saying that the polygenes for these emergent genetic traits (I call them emergenic traits[10]) combine configurally rather than additively.

My favorite example of a clearly emergenic trait is the still-unequaled prowess of the great Thoroughbred racehorse Secretariat. Old-fashioned hereditarians used to make much of the notion of breeding, a concept that has been pushed to the extreme by exponents of the sport of horse racing. Through careful breeding in the early part of the nineteenth century, the Thoroughbred racehorse got steadily stronger and faster and the record times recorded at old English racecourses steadily fell. Along about 1900, however, this curve leveled off as the initial additive variance was bred out of the line. The modest improvements in performance over the next seventy years or so are largely attributed to better training, nutrition, and veterinary techniques.

And then along came Secretariat, the great red American stallion who lay down and took a nap on the day of his Kentucky Derby in 1973 and then got up and broke the course record,[11] not by just a whisker but by seconds. He did the same thing at Pimlico and then won the Belmont—and the Triple Crown—by more than thirty lengths. Put out at once to stud, where only the most promising mares could afford his fees, Secretariat sired more than four hundred foals—most of them disappointments, none of them remotely in their sire's class. Secretariat had a distinguished lineage, of course, although none of his forebears could have run with him, but whatever he received at the great lottery of his conception could not be passed on easily in random halves. It seems a reasonable conjecture that Secretariat's qualities were configural, emergenic.

At last, in 1988, one of Secretariat's sons, Risen Star, finished third in the Kentucky Derby, won the Preakness, and then won the Belmont by some fourteen lengths, albeit a full two seconds behind his sire's record pace. After more than four hundred attempts, Secretariat managed to produce a winner; although emergenic traits do not "run in families," they are more likely to reappear in a carrier family than in a random lineage. No doubt Risen Star's dam contributed key elements of the emergenic configuration.

## Intelligence

The publication in 1995 of Richard J. Herrnstein and Charles Murray's *The Bell Curve* created a firestorm of controversy (in which many of the most ardent participants seem never to have actually read the book) because it presented lots of data showing that people with money, status, and position tend to have higher IQs on the average than the people who work for or wait on them *and* that IQ is strongly heritable. I can't help wondering if the angst and alarm engendered by these findings would not have been mitigated if the debaters had read chapter 1 of this book. After all, the problem with accepting *The Bell Curve*'s conclusions is that it seems so *unfair* that the bosses and the other rich got where they are in part because they were better endowed with hereditary smarts. Yet what we learned in chapter 1 was that, although the bosses and their pals may be richer than the rest of us, *they aren't any happier*. Because we had MPQ Well Being scores and IQ scores on the MISTRA twins, we were able to compute the correlation of happiness with IQ. The result, R = .06, is close enough to 0 not to be worth mentioning. Therefore, gentle reader, knowing that your subjective well-being is not limited by your IQ score, you will not be disturbed to learn that IQ truly is determined in large part by the great genetic lottery. And the intelligence story is so interesting and informative that I cannot resist going into it here.

Psychologists define general intelligence as the capacity measured by the intelligence quotient, or IQ. The average IQ is 100, and IQ scores of 140 and above, attained by perhaps four in every thousand youngsters, used to be classified as in the "genius range." Stanford University's Lewis Terman, who was responsible for revising and standardizing the first individually administered IQ test, the Stanford-Binet, identified some fifteen hundred gifted children with IQs in this range, and Terman's gifted group has now been followed through middle age. Most of them have led relatively successful lives, but none of them, so far as I am aware, would be classified as geniuses today.

At the other end of the IQ scale, a rare few of retarded or autistic persons, known as savants, can quickly specify the day of the week on which any date in history fell, or, although unable to read music, can play any composition on the piano after just a single hearing. These highly specialized abilities seem all the more remarkable in people whose general intelligence may be so low that they are dependent on others for their care and sustenance. Autistic savants are not geniuses either, of course, but these remarkable people seem to me to illustrate an important fact about the structure of the mind.

## Autism and the Modular Brain

Autism was first described in 1944 and is extremely variable in its manifestations. Some autists seem to be profoundly retarded and never develop language. Others, often labeled as having Asperger's syndrome, have normal or superior IQs. One common theme in autism is an extraordinary lack of social motivation and social intelligence. Most autistic children are unresponsive to people, even to their mothers, and dislike being held or fondled. Unlike normal children, they do not seem to see other members of their species as especially interesting, to be studied and imitated. This may explain why even high-level autists tend to be slow in language development and why, in spite of sometimes high general intelligence, they remain insensitive to social cues. Asperger children seem to be unable to identify with other persons and therefore unable to anticipate how others will react to what they do. Another rare congenital abnormality, Williams' syndrome, presents the antithesis of autism. Children with Williams' syndrome are verbally and socially precocious, they "often appear exceptionally self-possessed, articulate, and witty, and only gradually is their mental deficit borne in on one."[12]

We have seen that human toddlers back in the Pleistocene who instinctively avoided snakes and spiders were somewhat more likely in consequence to live to maturity and to become our ancestors. Since natural selection works slowly, such a reaction to electric sockets has not yet evolved. In a similar way, it was adaptive for ancestral infants to be fascinated by their mother's faces, to recognize an affinity with other creatures like themselves, to study and imitate them. This special-purpose "mental module" facilitated learning language and the other skills required for social living. It would appear that this social intelligence module is well developed in Williams' syndrome, in spite of low general intelligence, but poorly developed in Asperger's syndrome, even when general intelligence is normal.

Retarded or autistic savants seem to betoken the existence of other special-purpose modules that are capable of efficient functioning even in the presence of a low IQ. Neurologist Oliver Sacks describes some of these prodigies, such as Jedediah Buxton, a simpleminded laborer, who was a prodigious calculator. "When asked what would be the cost of shoeing a horse with 140 nails if the price was one farthing for the first nail, then doubled for each remaining nail, he arrived at the figure of 725,958,096,074,907,868,531,656,993,638,851,106 pounds, 2 shillings and 8 pence."[13] When asked to square this number, he produced the seventy-eight-digit answer after ten weeks' time during which he did his work, held conversations, lived his life (and apparently quite happily), while his astonishing calculating engine continued to grind away at the problem. A savant studied by Sacks personally could recite the entire nine volumes of Grove's 1954 *Dictionary of Music and Musicians*, which had been read to him once by his father.

"Blind Tom," a retarded slave child, was born in the 1850s nearly blind, and he was unable to speak until age five or six. Yet from the age of four, "seated at the piano, he would play beautiful tunes, his little hands having already taken possession of the keys, and his wonderful ears of any combination of notes they had once heard."[14] Tested at age eleven by musicologists, who played for him two entirely new compositions, thirteen and twenty pages in length, Tom "reproduced them perfectly and with the least apparent effort." Like Mozart, Tom could perform on the piano with his back to the keyboard and his hands inverted. It is important to understand that the gifts of these autistic prodigies seem to go far beyond extraordinary rote memory. Leslie Lemke, a modern "Blind Tom," who also is congenitally blind and retarded, "is as renowned for his improvisational powers as for his incredible musical memory. Lemke catches the style of any composer, from Bach to Bartok, after a single hearing, and can thereafter play any piece or improvise, effortlessly, in that style."[15] The autistic man who could recite Grove's entire *Dictionary* was also a musical prodigy. Martin, although retarded, "had a musical intelligence fully up to appreciating all the structural rules and complexities of Bach, all the intricacies of contrapuntal and fugal writing; he had the musical intelligence of a professional musician."[16]

Sacks also describes artistic prodigies such as Nadia, who "suddenly started drawing at the age of three and a half, rendering horses, and later a variety of subjects, in a way that psychologists considered 'not possible.' Her drawings, they felt, were qualitatively different from those of other children; she had a sense of space, an ability to depict appearances and shadows, a sense of perspective such as the most gifted normal child might only develop at three times her age."[17] Stephen, a profoundly autistic child, was consigned at age four to a London school for the developmentally disabled. When he was five, Stephen began drawing, primarily cars and sometimes "wickedly clever" caricatures of his teachers. At age seven, he began to specialize in drawing buildings, such as St. Paul's Cathedral "and other London landmarks, in tremendous detail, when other children his age were just drawing stick figures. It was the sophistication of his drawings, their mastery of line and perspective, that amazed me—and these were all there when he was seven."[18] Stephen could draw from memory a complex scene (e.g., a construction site) viewed only for a few seconds, but he also had an intuitive grasp for artistic and architectural style. Repeated drawings from memory of Sacks's house over the period of a year varied considerably in detail but not at all in style. Similar repeated renderings of Matisse paintings varied also, proving that he was not "merely" faithfully copying a vivid visual memory but, rather, that he was improvising à la Matisse.

We shall consider later the importance, to human happiness, of effectance motivation, the desire to accomplish something or make something. It seems relevant to note in this connection that many autistic savants, who seem cut off from the human sharing and caring that is so important to most of us, can nonetheless experience obvious joy and satisfaction in the exercise of their extraordinary talent. Sacks says of Stephen: "When he was little, nothing was amusing to Stephen. He now finds all manner of things funny and his laughter is incredibly infectious. He has gone back to caricaturing people around him, and he takes great pleasure watching his victims' reactions."[19]

Examples like these have led psychologists to postulate the existence of numerous special intelligences, which are seen in these savant cases in especially stark relief against a background of general intellectual poverty. It is of great importance to realize that such savantlike talents can also coexist with high intelligence and in the absence of autism. The literary genius, Vladimir Nabokov, possessed "a prodigious calculating gift, but this disappeared suddenly and completely, he wrote, following a high fever, with delirium, at the age of seven."[20] The intellectually normal Chinese artist, Yani, displayed her artistic powers as early as did Nadia or Stephen. Sacks describes another gifted young man, now doing fundamental research in chemistry, who could read fluently and with comprehension at age two, or repeat and even harmonize with any melody at the same age, and who did remarkable drawings with perspective at age three. Blind Tom and Leslie Lemke shared some of Mozart's prodigious talents, but they were retarded and he was not. Thus, it does not seem to be the case that savantlike gifts result from the conscription of all intellectual resources in the service of a single function.

This idea of a modular intelligence contrasts with the view of the brain as merely a general-purpose computer, the power of which can be assessed just by a single number, the IQ. The role of general intelligence may be like that of the conductor of an orchestra in which the brass, percussion, strings, and woodwinds are the special-purpose modules. Like the best orchestral conductors, the computer intelligence knows all of the parts but cannot play the flute as well as the flutist can; the conductor's function is to evaluate and to coordinate. Temple Grandin, a highly intelligent autistic woman and a college professor, learned to use her general intelligence to compensate for her deficient social sensitivity.[21] For example, when she first started teaching, she would often talk facing the blackboard instead of her class. That part of the brain that leads you and me instinctively to look at the people we're addressing is the part that is deficient in Dr. Grandin's brain. After being informed that teachers are supposed to face their class while speaking, she made a point of doing so thereafter.

## The Heritability of IQ

Thus, mental ability is not *just* IQ, although IQ is very important. Every acknowledged human genius, for example, seems to have had at least a good general intelligence *together with* an assortment of other gifts or attributes that, in mutually facilitating cohabitation, led to the extraordinary achievements that are the ultimate basis for classification into this special category. One of the ingredients in the recipe for genius, and which I believe may be as essential as general intelligence, is an exceptional degree of mental energy, permitting protracted periods of intensely focused concentration on the project in hand.[22] Genius aside, a relatively high IQ seems to be required for success in a number of fields of human endeavor. People with IQs lower than about 115, for example (and that includes about eight people out of every ten), are unlikely to get through medical or law school.

Over the past sixty years or so, countless studies have shown that the correlation for IQ between pairs of related individuals is proportional to their genetic correlation. MZ twins, whose genetic correlation is 1.0, are twice as similar within pairs in IQ as are DZ twins, whose genetic correlation is .50 and the IQ correlation for DZ twins, in turn, is about four times that of first cousins, whose genetic correlation is .125. Moreover, pairs of unrelated adoptive siblings reared together, once they are grown and out of the adoptive home, correlate in IQ about 0.[23] Perhaps the best evidence we have of the heritability of IQ among adults of European ancestry comes from five studies of MZA twins, done in Britain, Denmark, Sweden, and in the United States and totaling 163 of these rare twin pairs. The MZA IQ correlations in these studies (each one a direct estimate of heritability) ranged from .64 to .78 and the grand average correlation was .75.[24] This means that our best estimate of the heritability of IQ is about 75 percent; about three-quarters of the variation across people in IQ is associated with individual differences at the level of the genes.

It is important to understand that the heritability of most psychological traits tells us as much about the given culture as it does about human nature. It is likely (although we cannot be sure of this) that the amount of genetic variability among people within each human culture or breeding group is about the same. But environmental opportunities vary widely both within and between cultures. We would not expect to find a mathematical genius in a preliterate tribe in Papua New Guinea. In the Middle Ages, peasant children had poorer nutrition and much less opportunity to develop their intellectual capacities than the children of princes, and the heritability of IQ would have been decreased by this large amount of environmental variation. On the other hand, the fact that the heritability of IQ among the citizens of modern Western democracies is on the order of 75 percent suggests that these cultures have succeeded in providing environmental opportunity that is tolerably equal for all their children. This is true at least for white children; we are less sure about the heritability of IQ among African or Hispanic Americans, for whom the relevant environmental variation (e.g., the proportion of their children reared in poverty by overburdened single parents) is much greater.

## How Do Genetic Differences Produce Psychological Differences?

We cannot yet begin to trace the many steps that intervene between the protein-making activities in which the genes are directly engaged and their ultimate influence upon individual differences in complex psychological traits. We assume that behavioral differences are associated with nervous system differences. Some of the latter undoubtedly are "hard-wired" biological differences. We can imagine, for example, that some brains work faster or more consistently than others or that the inhibitory mechanisms that enable focused concentration are biologically stronger or more reliable in some brains than in others. It is probable that the brain mechanisms responsible for the feelings of happiness and satisfaction are more easily activated in some people than in others, and that the same thing is true of those mechanisms involved in the negative emotions that inhibit well-being. But surely many of the brain differences that account for differences in personality, interests, and attitudes (differences in the "software") are the result of learning and experience. Yet, if nurture or experience is the proximal cause of individual differences in these traits, how can one explain the strong association between these differences and genetic variation (i.e., nature)?

A major insight of behavior genetics is that one important way in which the genome exerts its influence upon the brain is indirect; the genes help to determine the effective environment of the developing child through the correlation or the interaction of genes with environment.[25] Passive gene-environment correlation is exemplified by John Stuart Mill, whose philosopher-father had him reading Greek and Latin classics, in the original languages, by age six. Bright parents tend to give their children both "bright genes" and intellectual stimulation. (This may be why the correlation of IQ for adult MZT twins, reared by the same parents who provided their genes, is five to ten points higher than that for MZA twins.)[26] Children reared by biological parents who are athletic are likely to receive strong bodies as well as athletic encouragement and example.

Partly for genetic reasons, some infants are fussy and irritable, whereas others are happy and responsive; these differences elicit different responses from their adult caretakers. This process, which of course continues throughout life as our (primarily social) environment reacts differentially to our innate temperament, talents, and physical appearance, is called *reactive* or *evoked* gene-environment correlation. And there is no question that both children and adults who exhibit positive emotions are likely to elicit reactions in others that are more positive and happy-making than those engendered by people who are doleful or grouchy.

Partly for genetic reasons, different children attend to different aspects of their environment, and seek out or create environments attuned in some way to their genetic makeup. An active toddler, for example, who climbs on things, exploring, taking occasional tumbles or stimulating a maternal rebuke, can have many experiences unknown to his more passive or less venturesome sibling. These are examples of *active* gene-environment correlation. The first day in school or a first roller-coaster ride will be a pleasurable excitement for some children, stimulating growth and self-confidence, but a terrifying and destructive experience for other children; that is, the same fire that melts the butter hardens the egg—this is gene-environment interaction.

As stated earlier, a mother's face is an instinctive source of fascination to the nonautistic infant, her smiles are gratifying, and her vocalizations stimulate an innate urge to imitate. These genetic proclivities set the occasion for the learning of language and other essential social skills. The great mathematician Karl Gauss taught himself to calculate; when only three, he was able to correct his father's sums and, at age ten, to amaze his teacher. These manifestations of his genetic gifts led the adults in little Karl's environment to provide him educational opportunities but, even more important, we must assume that the exercise of these gifts was inherently so gratifying that it became habitual, a preferred activity. Bright children read more and think more about what they read. They ask more and better questions and adults tend to treat their inquiries with more respect and to answer them carefully. In a similar way, a happy temperament tends to elicit friendly and happy-making responses from others.

## A Truly "Self-Made" Man[27]

A distinguished amateur ornithologist was relieved to learn, at age eleven, that he was adopted; this discovery explained for him why he was so different from his parents and their relatives. His adoptive parents did not read or own books, but the boy always had a library card and used it regularly. The parents had neither talent for nor interest in sports but the youngster, in summer, carried his baseball mitt with him in case of the chance for a game and won recognition for his prowess at basketball and tennis. This man's biography is a chronicle of active gene-environment correlation, and his quest for experiences compatible with his innate proclivities contrasts with his failure to respond to influences that were readily available but with which he did not resonate. One interest that the other members of his adoptive family shared was religion, but our acquaintance never joined with them in this.

In his late middle age, this man undertook to discover his biological parentage. He found that his parents had married after he had been given up for adoption and they had produced several other children, his full siblings, whom he discovered to be well-educated, active, and successful people like himself. One uncle had been dean of my university's graduate school. This man's adoptive parents, like most parents, were "permissive" in the sense that they did not determinedly or effectively shape his behavior or influence him by their provocative or charismatic example. They might have prevented him from engaging in sports, but they merely did not encourage these activities. Had they been readers themselves, with quick minds and lively intellectual interests, they might have given different or additional directions to his reading and thought. Had their religious practices been either emotionally or intellectually stimulating, he might well have been more interested in them.

Had this man, in adulthood, found that he had an MZA twin reared by a different set of similarly "permissive" adoptive parents in some other American town, I believe they would have discovered that they shared not only similar aptitudes and interests, but similar developmental histories as well. Had the cotwin been adopted by the father of John Kennedy or of John Stuart Mill, however, or by Dickens' Fagin, or a Mafia godfather, then, having traveled markedly different environmental paths, the cotwins' differences might have been as interesting as their residual similarities.

## The Heritability of Happiness

In the same large twin study referred to in chapter 1, my colleague, Auke Tellegen, and I found the twin correlation of MPQ Well-Being scores for 663 pairs of MZT twins and 69 pairs of

MZA twins reared apart, with the results shown in table 2.3. These MZ correlations indicate that 40 percent to 50 percent of the variation across people in current happiness levels is associated with genetic differences between people, at least for people in the broad middle class. This is the same as saying that the *heritability* of single measurements of subjective well-being is more than 40 percent.

But remember that happiness level obviously varies from day to day, certainly from month to month, depending on recent events. Twin A, the first-born member of an MZ pair, may be feeling a bit down on the day she takes our Well Being questionnaire because she recently got laid off or one of her children is sick. Twin B, on the other hand, might be feeling especially good because her husband got promoted or her daughter just graduated with honors. Their similarity on this one occasion of testing therefore will underestimate their true genetic similarity, the similarity of their average happiness scores or the set points to which their levels of well-being return as they get over the effects of these temporary highs or lows. When we retested 410 twin individuals about nine years later, their Well Being scores on the first occasion correlated only about .55 with their own scores the second time around. That very modest stability confirms our expectation that some of those who were the happiest on the first occasion would be less so later on and vice versa.

As can be seen in table 2.4, however, the MZ twins' scores, on the first test, correlated .54 with their cotwins' scores nine

| | Number Of Pairs | Twin Correlation |
|---|---|---|
| Twins reared apart: | | |
| Monozygotic | 69 | .53 ($\pm$.06) |
| Dizygotic | 50 | .13 ($\pm$.09) |
| Twins reared together: | | |
| Monozygotic | 663 | .44 ($\pm$.03) |
| Dizygotic | 715 | .08 ($\pm$.04) |

**TABLE 2.3**

Within-pair correlations on the MPQ Well Being scale.

*"I could cry when I think of the years I wasted accumulating money, only to learn that my cheerful disposition is genetic."*

**FIGURE 2.2**

Drawing by Handelsman © 1996, *The New Yorker* Magazine, Inc.

|  | Number Of Pairs | Twin Correlation |
|---|---|---|
| Cross-time or retest correlation: | 410 | .55 (±.02) |
| Cross-time cross-twin correlations |  |  |
|     MZ twins | 131 | .54 (±.03) |
|     DZ Twins | 74 | .05 (±.07) |

**TABLE 2.4**

Nine-year retest correlations of the MPQ Well Being scale.

years later. The 131 pairs of MZ cotwins correlated with each other over this long interval about as strongly as they correlated with themselves over that period! Think what this result means. If we correlated all the twins' scores at Time 2 with their bank account totals at that same time, the result would be trivial, about R = .12. We could predict each twin's happiness level much more accurately from his cotwin's score obtained nine years earlier than we could from that twin's own current income, socioeconomic status, or his marital status. Moreover, we can estimate that the heritability of the stable component of well-being, of the happiness set point, is about .54/.55 or close to 100 percent. Nearly 100 percent of the variation across people in the happiness set point seems to be due to individual differences in genetic makeup!

## Happiness Is Emergenic

Because the correlation for MZ twins on one-time measurements with the MPQ WB almost certainly lies somewhere between .40 and .54, well-being is assuredly at least partly genetic in origin. For traits like stature, traits that run in families, the DZ correlation will be about half the MZ value. But the correlation for 733 pairs of DZT twins was only .08 (±.04) and that for 50 pairs of DZA twins was .13 (±.09) (notice that the MZA and DZA values have larger errors associated with them because the sample sizes are much smaller). This seems to indicate that siblings and other first-degree relatives (such as parents versus their grown children)[28] resemble one another only slightly if at all; that is, happiness does not seem to run in families.

We do not really understand traits like this as yet but they seem to come about when the contribution of one component to the strength of the trait is dependent upon the value of other components. The quality of a voice, for example, depends upon the size and shape of the "voice box," the characteristics of the nasopharynx, of the larynx, the tongue, and hard palate, and so on. Each of these anatomical features was constructed under the direction of different sets of genes. Enrico Caruso got some of the genes in each set from both parents, neither of whom may have sung well at all. Yet, combined in the unique recipe that created Enrico, those genes fabricated a voice box that made beautiful sounds.

Why is happiness emergenic? We can only guess at this point and my guess goes like this: I think each person's happiness set point is determined, at least in part, by the compatibility or fit among that person's innate tendencies or traits. Having a strong desire for warm intimate relationships (as measured by the MPQ's Social Closeness scale) and also a high score on Aggression, for example, would be a bad fit. Having a strong urge to take charge in social situations (the MPQ's Social Potency scale measures this attribute), combined with a low score on Harm Avoidance, which measures fearfulness and shyness, would constitute a good or happy fit. Being high both on Social Potency and on Aggression is a good match for people in management or in politics, although perhaps not so happy for the people who work under them. These examples are oversimplified, of course, but they give the idea. If your innate strengths and weaknesses are compatible with one another, then doing the things that make you happy will come easier than if your various proclivities pull in different directions. You will share your unique configuration with your MZ twin, since you two share all your genes, but you are unlikely to share it with your siblings or to pass it along intact to your children.

But there are exceptions to all good rules, as exemplified by this letter from an English lady prompted by an article about our happiness research that appeared in the British press:

> How right you are about "happiness." Of my six brothers and sisters, three girls and one boy possessed the gene. The boy, my eldest brother, was killed in the second World War and his obituary in The Times read "He had an uncommon talent for happiness." I was eighty last Monday and am a widow. I have lived alone for thirty years and am as happy now as I ever have been and conscious of it and grateful for it every day. I just can't help being happy.

## Changing Your Happiness Set Point

If the heritability of people's average happiness levels is nearly 100 percent, does this mean that those of us with lower levels of subjective well-being are stuck with them? Are we just puppets dancing (or drooping) on strings pulled by our genes? If the answer were yes, I would not have written this book. Many people drudge along well beneath their real happiness set points because of bad habits that I call happiness thieves, which I shall discuss at length in later chapters. All of us, I believe, can learn to bounce along above our basic set points by learning some new habits, by observing some simple rules that are also discussed later on. Parents do *not* have to assume that their offspring must simply accept whatever sense of well-being they were born with, because skillful parents can guide their children along the true primrose path that leads toward a happy and contented life. The basic point one must remember is that the genes affect the mind largely indirectly, by influencing the kinds of experiences people have and the kinds of environments they seek out. The true formula is not Nature *versus* Nurture but, rather, Nature *via* Nurture. If your happiness set point is below average, that means that your genetic steersman is guiding you into situations that detract from your well-being and is tempting you to behave in ways that are counterproductive. If you let your genetic steersman have his way, then you will end up where he wants to go. But it is *your* life and, within wide limits, you can choose your own destinations instead of having them all chosen for you.

# PART TWO

# HAPPINESS MAKERS

Nature has placed mankind under the government of two
sovereign masters, pain and pleasure . . . they govern us in
all we do, in all we say, in all we think: every effort we can
make to throw off their subjection, will serve but to
demonstrate and confirm it.

—JEREMY BENTHAM

"Nature, Mr. Allnutt, is what we are put in this world to
rise above."

—KATHARINE HEPBURN TO HUMPHREY BOGART,
in *The African Queen*

The fact that we humans have a capacity for happiness
(contentment, feelings of well-being, pleasure, joy) is not
because Nature was just being kind. Both pleasure and
pain are adaptive because they get us moving away from dangerous situations and toward beneficent ones. How would you teach
your children all the dos and don'ts they need to learn if they
were insensitive to pain and pleasure, if they experienced neither
euphoria nor dysphoria?

One curious failure of science fiction, which generally hues
to what is scientifically plausible, is its humanlike robots, or an-
droids, are usually depicted as immune to either pain or pleasure
and without moods. But an android is not just a remarkable computer running predetermined programs. It is an entity that
makes choices—and what would determine those choices with-

out some sort of analogue of pain or pleasure? In his excellent book *Emotional Intelligence*, Daniel Goleman points out that the characteristics of *Star Trek*'s hyperrational character, Mr. Spock, are based on a failure to acknowledge that "rationality is guided by feeling." In the sequel, *Star Trek: The Next Generation*, the android, Data, is portrayed as yearning for human feeling, but yearning itself *is* a human feeling, and Data could not behave as he does if some analogue of pain and pleasure had not been built into his circuitry.

The pain of loss or disappointment motivates us to strive to avoid those consequences, but when they occur anyway, we have a remarkable ability to adapt and recover. If we did not, the accumulated sum of life's inevitable losses would soon put us out of action altogether, and that is not Nature's plan. Similarly, the pleasure we derive from doing Nature's bidding (although no one thinks of it in those terms) motivates that sort of adaptive behavior. But it, too, must fade, else we should eventually be immobilized in beatitude, and that is as much at variance with Nature's plan as terminal dejection. What all this means is that happiness is an active state on the whole. We can stop and smell the flowers, admire the view, reflect on our good fortune for a while, but before long, we have to be up and doing again or that sense of well-being fades.

My theory about happiness goes like this: We each have a certain baseline or set point level of subjective well-being (SWB). Think of it as a lake on which our ship is sailing and the higher the lake level, the better we feel. That level seems to vary from person to person for genetic reasons. It also varies within people from time to time for physiological reasons. Mine is higher if I've had a good night's sleep, lower if I'm feeling stressed out. The individual SWB also varies as a consequence of recent events, going down when something unpleasant happens and up when something good happens, but it doesn't *stay* down or up. I can droop along under my personal SWB if I allow some of those happiness thieves (discussed in part V) to obtrude, if I let myself stay mad or anxious, or if I let a spell of the blues lead me into thinking blue thoughts. But I can bounce along *above* my personal SWB by seeking activities and experiences that I enjoy. The problem is that these positive experiences cannot permanently raise my set point but only produce a temporary wavelike increase that soon recedes to where I started. Therefore, I have to vary the input, ideally to become an "epicure of experience," like a gourmet at a buffet, alternating a little of this with a little of that, all things I like to do, never too much of just one.

Some people, like children at their first buffet, go just for the desserts, the entertainments. Desserts have their place, but the mainstay of any happiness diet is productive effort, developing and exercising skills, doing something that needs doing—that is worth doing—and especially doing it well. All children (and many adults) have dreams of glory, and of what does this glory consist? It is not candy and ice cream and unlimited television watching but, rather, the adulation of the multitudes for some spectacular achievement. What most children (and most adults) fail to realize, however, is that the satisfaction of even the most spectacular achievement fades after a while and new accomplishments are needed to keep that SWB bouncing up into the higher reaches of the plus zone.

We need a metric for happiness and I propose the "hap." A good meal when you are hungry is worth about one hap; if you prepared the meal yourself and others share (and appreciate) it, then it might yield two haps. The Nobel prize would be worth ten haps in my reckoning, especially since they give these awards to economists (who seldom do anything really useful) but not to psychologists. (I'm using a logarithmic scale like the Richter scale for earthquakes, so ten haps is a much bigger wave than two haps.) A phone call saying that I have won the lottery would be worth about eight haps; I know I would quickly start worrying about all the problems that come from sudden wealth. A hole in one would be worth one hap to me, because of the novelty of the experience, but perhaps several haps to a real golfer who would regard it as a proof of skill. If my SWB set point equals about five haps—if my lake is five haps deep—then the two haps I get from finishing a chapter of this book, or the one hap that results when my lemon meringue pie comes out perfectly (as usual), will be like little waves on that lake. Each one would lift me briefly higher than my usual five-hap level.

Big waves, like the Nobel prize, take longer to subside, maybe as long as six months. Big achievements, like big earthquakes, are also followed by aftershocks. I feel sure that Nobel prize winners get little half-hap kicks every time someone alludes to their achievement. I published a book in 1995 that was a source of many happy waves while I was working on it, perhaps a three-hap wave when I found a publisher, another hap or two when the first bound copies came in the mail, and good big waves when the reviews started to appear. But if these book waves had been the only activity on my five-hap lake these past two years, my average SWB would have been lower than in fact it was during that period. Besides the book waves (happily), there were visits with my children and grandchildren, my giving an occasional one- or two-hap lecture, lots of half-hap useful tasks done around the house, quite a few lemon pies and loaves of bread (I make really good sourdough bread), a splendid three-hap production of *She Stoops to Conquer* at the Guthrie Theatre—things like that and lots of other activity on my lake keeping me bouncing along above my genetic set point.

This "lake" metaphor needs some adjustment, lest it become misleading. First of all, this lake is peculiar in that it can produce waves without troughs and also troughs without waves. The positive-going waves produced by happy-making experiences fade back to, but not necessarily below, the normal level, while negative waves (troughs) produced by unhappy experiences are not necessarily followed by anything more than a return to normal. Secondly, it is important to be clearer about the role of genetic differences.

We know that there are "pleasure centers" in the brain, and we can be sure that your feelings of euphoria are produced by activity in specific (but as yet unidentified) neural networks in your brain. There are other brain mechanisms associated with negative emotions such as fear or anger, and activity there tends to inhibit activity in what I shall call the "happy center." We can be sure that the reactivity of each of these mechanisms varies from one brain to another because the existence of individual differences is a kind of basic rule of biology. Because we know that variations in SWB have strong genetic roots, it seems likely that the reactivity of the pleasure centers and the negative emotion or "distress" centers—as well as the basic level of the happiness lake—all vary from person to person for genetic reasons.

Recall the self-ratings we obtained from more than four thousand adult twins on Capacity for Happiness, Capacity for Misery, and Contentment, discussed in chapter 1. It seems reasonable to suppose that the first of these, as the name implies, is at least a rough measure of a person's responsiveness to pleasure and positive input, that Misery Capacity measures the reactivity of the distress centers, and that these two determine, respectively, the size of the increases or decreases that good or bad events produce in one's level of Contentment. What I think all of this means is this: If we could get inside the heads of one thousand randomly selected people when they just wake up in the morning and measure the levels of their happiness lakes, some would be higher and others lower due to differences in their brain chemistry. If we then have room service deliver to each one his or her favorite breakfast on a tray with flowers, this treat would produce two-hap waves in the lakes of those with high Happiness Capacities and half-hap waves in those with lower innate responsiveness of their pleasure centers. Similarly, if we arranged things so that all of these one thousand guests would get up to find their bathrooms devoid of hot water or toothpaste or toilet paper, those with hyperactive distress centers would experience big troughs in their happiness lakes while those whose Capacity for Misery was weak would not be greatly bothered. Thus, already we can see at least three different ways in which genetic differences can influence a person's average level of subjective well-being.

But that lake is almost never still because people keep having experiences, some of which make troughs and others make waves. To a very considerable extent, the kinds of experiences people have result from what they do and what people tend to do is also strongly subject to genetic influences. Some people are genetically inclined to get into confrontational, angry-making situations or to cultivate antagonistic feelings. Some people miss out on happy-making experiences because of fear or shyness. Other people are temperamentally disposed to do the sorts of things that make positive waves on their happiness lake. If I let my genetic steersman have his way, then my DNA will largely determine the number and size of the troughs and waves on my lake, and thus my average level of SWB. But, at least within broad limits, I can steer my own boat; I can avoid doing some of those negative, trough-making things that my genes would get me into if I'd let them, and I can proceed instead to do some positive, wave-making things that I might miss out on if I let my four grandparents collectively do the steering.

In this section, we shall consider some of the ways in which one can make more and bigger positive waves on one's lake of happiness.

# 3

# EFFECTANCE VS. ENTERTAINMENT

If you ask any man in America, or any man in business in
England, what it is that most interferes with his
enjoyment of existence, he will say, "The struggle for life."
—BERTRAND RUSSELL

I don't know how many Americans Lord Russell actually questioned before leaping to this conclusion (or why Americans
all are to be thought comparable only to Englishmen "in business"), but his impression is at variance with mine. I remember
arriving early for a luncheon at a restaurant when, after being
seated to await the other guests, I began to eavesdrop shamelessly on the conversation at the next table (psychologists are
permitted to eavesdrop shamelessly). There were four men at
that table, young enough so that it was easy to picture them at
their high school graduations not so many years earlier. They
were talking with animation and real interest about a subject
that clearly held for them great fascination. Was it sex, the last
Vikings football game, was it politics, religion, or how to catch
the walleyed pike? No, they were talking about *linoleum*. They
were in the business, you see, and they knew quite a lot about its
fine points, prices, new products, profit margins, and installation
problems. My thought at the time was how they would have
scoffed, at the actual time of their high school graduations, if

anyone had told them that a few years hence they would be en-thralled by . . . linoleum! But my point here is that plainly these young men now *were* enthralled, fascinated by what they'd learned about the linoleum business and optimistic about its prospects. They were not at all like Russell's imaginary Ameri-cans, cut off from the enjoyment of their existence by their need to "struggle for life"—they were *enjoying* the struggle and they were plainly happy.

Ours is the only species that can learn to talk, that can de-velop a conscience, and that enjoys making things—cave draw-ings, body ornaments, sonnets, lemon pies, new kitchen floors, or holes in one. But, like our capacities for language and for socialization, our innate ability to enjoy making things has to be elicited, shaped, and reinforced during childhood. Many things are innately reinforcing, of course—food, wine, sexual stimula-tion, certain aesthetic experiences, certain chemicals, and enter-tainment. Sometimes we foolishly imagine that a life replete with such pleasures would be heaven. But if we do not permit the denizens of that heaven ever to do anything constructive, to cre-ate anything, to learn and then exercise some skill, then I think that heaven would be a kind of hell.

I write this paragraph with numbed fingers because I have just returned from playing a game of fetch-the-tennis-ball on a Minnesota winter's afternoon, with the temperature just above zero Fahrenheit. Willie, my foolish bull terrier, insists on his regular 4:00 P.M. game in almost all weathers, and he will desert his food dish with alacrity if I walk by enticingly with a couple of tennis balls in hand. Willie enjoys gemütlich passive enter-tainments—he curls up in a chair (preferably what is normally *my* chair) during the cocktail hour, for example—but most often he would rather actively be *doing* something. People are the same way, only more so.

*What* a person will enjoy actively doing depends both on the person and on what she has been doing lately. For example, al-though I enjoy reading and read quite a lot, I am left in the dust by my friend and colleague Paul Meehl,* who reads several books to my one. William Gladstone, when he was not busy governing Victorian England, is said to have read some twenty thousand books in five languages. One difference between me and Meehl (certainly) and Gladstone (probably) is that they remember(ed) what they read better than I do, so that each page for them is an accomplishment, a step forward, whereas reading for me is more like evanescent entertainment. I enjoy reading most when I am *looking up* something, so that I know that the endeavor will have a useful product.

For both Meehl and Gladstone, however, reading—not detective stories but meaty stuff—is (was) equivalent to making something, growing something, slaying a *Deinotherium* and bringing home haunches of meat, and it is (was) therefore gratifying, inherently rewarding. We can think of each chapter, read and tucked away somewhere in their cerebrums, as equivalent to a beefsteak to a hungry man, producing a wavelike increase in their current sense of well-being, both at the time and perhaps later, when they reflected back on what they learned (or on the savor of that meal). Both of them also enjoy(ed) another kind of mental work, *problem solving*. Many others can join with them in this, even people with poorer memories like me, whether the problems involve chess positions, the linoleum business, scientific puzzles, or how to explain something clearly in readable prose.

## Mental Energy

Most recognized geniuses seem to possess remarkable powers of concentration. Archimedes's awesome mathematical talent was augmented by an ability to devote himself single-mindedly to any problem at hand in extraordinary periods of intense,

---

*Regents Professor Emeritus Paul E. Meehl, Fellow of the National Academy of Sciences, and holder of nearly every gold medal or similar award that is available to eminent psychologists.

focused concentration. At such times, the more mundane concerns of life were simply ignored. We learn from Plutarch that Archimedes would "forget his food and neglect his person, to that degree that when he was occasionally carried by absolute violence to bathe or have his body anointed, he used to trace geometrical figures in the ashes of the fire, and diagrams in the oil on his body, being in a state of entire preoccupation, and, in the truest sense, divine possession with his love and delight in science."[1]

Referring to Isaac Newton, John Maynard Keynes has said,

> His peculiar gift was the power of holding continuously in his mind a purely mental problem until he had seen straight through it. I fancy his preeminence is due to his muscles of intuition being the strongest and most enduring with which a man has ever been gifted. Anyone who has ever attempted pure scientific or philosophical thought knows how one can hold a problem momentarily in one's mind and apply all one's powers of concentration to piercing through it, and how it will dissolve and escape and you find that what you are surveying is a blank. I believe that Newton could hold a problem in his mind for hours and days and weeks until it surrendered to him its secret. Then being a supreme mathematical technician he could dress it up, how you will, for purposes of exposition, but it was his intuition which was pre-eminently extraordinary—"so happy in his conjectures," said de Morgan, "as to seem to know more than he could possibly have any means of proving."[2]

Psychologists are not yet able to measure individual differences in mental energy, independent of motivational factors, but there can be no doubt at all that some people have more of this resource than others do, and I am confident that these are differences in native endowment. People, of course, also differ innately in their resources of physical energy, and our adult twins had no difficulty in making this discrimination in their self-ratings. The questions we asked them, like the ones about happiness in chapter 1, were straightforward:

In this next set of questions you are asked to compare yourself with other people on the specified trait or ability. Where do you think you would rank compared to other people of your age and sex? This will be difficult for some of these traits, but please make the best estimate that you can. For each of the items in this section, please use the following rating scale:

| 1 | 2 | 3 | 4 | 5 |
|---|---|---|---|---|
| Lowest 5% | Lower 30% | Middle 30% | Higher 30% | Highest 5% |

**Physical Energy:** The capacity for sustained physical activity—working, playing, moving about, getting things done—without tiring and having to rest.

**Mental Energy:** The capacity for sustained mental work—thinking, planning, reading difficult material, figuring things out—without tiring and losing your concentration.

**Abstract Intelligence:** The ability to solve intellectual problems, to understand complicated issues, to figure things out: "school intelligence."

**Contentment:** Taking the good with the bad, how happy and contented are you now on the average, compared with other people?

**Capacity for Happiness:** The ability to really enjoy the good things in life, if and when they come your way; to experience pleasure, enthusiasm, satisfaction. Not whether you *are* happy now, but whether you can be truly happy, joyful, "high," when things go right for you.

**Capacity for Misery:** The tendency to suffer when things go wrong, to feel despair, regret, disappointment, anguish. Not whether you *are* miserable now, but whether you are likely to really suffer when things go wrong for you.

**Neatness:** High scorers keep their rooms, houses, workshops, offices, neat and clean and orderly; they keep the snow off their sidewalks, the weeds out of their gardens, the dust out of the corners; their belongings are put neatly away after each use.

We also obtained these self-ratings twice, about three years apart, from 102 pairs of MZ twins and 96 pairs of DZs. From these data we could estimate the within-pair similarity in the true or stable values of these seven variables with the retest variability canceled out. These correlations are shown in the next table.

Look first at the similarity in Abstract Intelligence, based on two widely spaced self-ratings (the MZ correlation estimates the *heritability* of intelligence). The correlations of .85 and .41 for MZ and DZ twins, respectively, are almost exactly what we would expect if we had used individually administered IQ tests rather than self-ratings as our estimate of IQ. This permits some reasonable confidence in the methods we are using. Next, note

|                        | 102 Pairs of MZ Twins | 96 Pairs of DZ Twins |
|------------------------|:---------------------:|:--------------------:|
| Physical energy        | .48                   | .16                  |
| Mental energy          | .61                   | .22                  |
| Contentment            | .73                   | .35                  |
| Capacity for happiness | .45                   | .12                  |
| Capacity for misery    | .60                   | .36                  |
| Neatness               | .58                   | .25                  |
| Abstract intelligence  | .85                   | .41                  |

TABLE 3.1

Cross-twin, cross-time correlations for various self-ratings, divided by the within-twin, cross-time (or retest) correlation, so as to estimate the similarity of the genetic set points of each trait.

that the MZ correlations for both Physical and Mental Energy are both fairly high, in the same range as for Neatness, although not as high as for Contentment. This means that half or a little more than half of the variations in these traits, like individual differences in temperament, have a genetic basis.

How well would you expect these self-ratings to correlate with one another? We examined this question on a larger sample of some 4,200 twins. I said earlier that our subjects were able to discriminate between their mental and physical energy levels. The correlation between these two self-ratings turned out to be .27, which is highly significant in this large sample, but it is still a weak relationship; the twins were indeed discriminating. (Mental and physical vigor are not unrelated, of course: Gladstone, when not reading those twenty thousand books or translating Horace, loved chopping down trees.)* Abstract Intelligence correlates .55 with Mental Energy, so these two traits, although fairly strongly related, are not the same thing. Neatness correlates significantly (R = .21) only with Physical Energy, which seems to make sense. It is interesting that Happy Capacity and Misery Capacity are virtually uncorrelated

*See Roy Jenkins's excellent biography, *Gladstone* (New York: Random House, 1996).

(R = −.03) so you can be high or low in both or high in one and low in the other. But these two "capacities" are both related to Contentment; Happy Capacity positively (R = +.56) and Misery Capacity negatively (R = −.27). Moreover, the heritability of both of these "capacities" is on the order of 45 percent.*

Finally, Contentment correlates weakly (.21 to .24) with Abstract Intelligence and with both kinds of energy, which means that only about 5 percent of the variation in Contentment can be predicted from knowing both how smart and how energetic people are. As we saw before, although it may not seem fair that some people are born with more of certain talents and capacities than others are, at least that good luck doesn't guarantee that the smart and lively ones will be any happier.

## Effectance Motivation

This human trait we have of enjoying productive labor, making things, and having an impact on the world around us, was adaptive in the primordial stone-age environment, as it is today. Those ancients who kept busy, both at the routine activities of hunting and gathering and nurturing the young and also in novel ways, developing new ideas, new methods and skills, were more likely to pass their genes along and become ancestors. One sees this effectance motivation even in toddlers, whose ability to impact their world is limited to knocking things over, breaking and banging and making a mess. Why do teenagers break windows, carve their initials, paint graffiti, and commit other acts of vandalism? The "evil demon" theory is wrong, or at least inadequate. Vandalism is a way of having an impact, exerting control, and one reason well-socialized youngsters are less inclined to vandalism is that they are more likely to have developed useful skills and learned that greater satisfactions accrue from making things than from breaking them.

---

*These correlations and heritability estimates are based on estimates of the stable components of Happy Capacity and Misery Capacity obtained by averaging two self-ratings, three years apart, provided by two hundred pairs of MTR twins.

"Doing something constructive" covers a lot of territory, from a ten-minute task such as fixing the loose top on my wife's double boiler, to a long-term project, such as writing this book. Replacing that rusted screw on the top was just enough of a challenge to yield maybe a quarter of a hap; not bad for ten minutes' effort. Long projects can make lots of positive waves because of our uniquely human ability to anticipate the future, discussed in chapter 1. Each portion of this book that I complete makes little waves because it is a problem-solving activity that I enjoy, but the little waves are augmented by the knowledge that the book will be published eventually. How long I can pursue a given activity with enjoyment depends on my reserves of the physical or mental energy required.

Another limitation is more subtle. It happens that I am currently working on two books, this new one and a revised edition of my 1981 book on the lie detector.* To my surprise, I have found that, when I run dry of ideas on one project, I can often work productively for an hour or two on the other one, even though both seem to require the use of the same mental and physical machinery. Apparently, the particular cognitive circuits required for the two tasks are sufficiently distinct so that one can still function even though the other is locked up with fatigue. Maybe I have discovered something useful here for people suffering from writer's block. Start a new book, perhaps a novel if you currently are working on a textbook, or vice versa; at least it works for me.

Perhaps it is this ability to become revivified just by a slight change in the problem that makes it possible for so many people to keep interested, to keep the waves going on their happiness lakes, throughout most of their forty-hour workweeks. I have been watching a woman who clerks at the Northwest Airlines ticket counter at my local shopping mall. She is superefficient, knows all the schedules and when the prices change; she can talk to the customer and, simultaneously, interrogate the com-

*D. T. Lykken, *A Tremor in the Blood: Uses and Abuses of the Lie Detector*, 2d ed. (New York: Plenum, 1998.)

puter with her fingers, sharing eye contact between the two, and never miss a beat. But what is especially impressive is her manner. She makes you feel like a guest in her home. While waiting in line, I've watched her deal with irascible customers, and she rises to that challenge like a queen. She makes me think of the man who ran the local shoe-repair shop when I was a boy; I remember him more clearly than most of the teachers I had then because he was a real *mensch*, outgoing yet dignified, as much a master of his domain as any physician in his consulting room. These two people both put real attention into each brief human interaction so that each customer felt personally recognized. This is not only good for business but it must make each day more varied and interesting and, therefore, more satisfying.

My wife and I have always enjoyed watching the crew who swing by each Wednesday morning to collect our garbage. Those young men do their job with skill and athleticism, and they seem always to be enjoying themselves. They are doing an essential job and doing it with style; why shouldn't they feel good about it? And I always get a lift from visiting my local plumbing supplies store. There one finds several men, all master plumbers, on one side of a long counter, making jokes and solving problems for the customers, either plumbers themselves or duffers like me. These clerks obviously enjoy dealing with the other professionals like themselves; they know each other and exchange stories. But I think they enjoy us duffers even more because we are more of a challenge. We give them a chance to use their knowledge, diagnose our problems, and explain what we need to do to solve them. The cashier at the end of the counter is as skilled and quick at her job as they are at theirs. I firmly believe that the average levels of *amour-propre, savoir-faire,* and *joie de vivre* (the French seem to understand these matters best) at Park Plumbing Supply are higher than in many Wall Street boardrooms.

The Achievement scale of our personality inventory (the MPQ) yields high scores for people who are ambitious, hardworking, and set high standards for themselves; we might say that this scale measures the strength of one's effectance motivation. The heritability of these Achievement scores is substantially higher for males than for females during adolescence, but this pattern reverses in middle age. The seventeen-year-old girls in our Twin/Family Study have lower scores on Achievement than do the boys, lower also than both of their parents. I think what this means is that, in our culture, the typical high school girl is led to believe that her best chances for success will come through being attractive and popular rather than skillful and hardworking. For the middle-aged twins in our Twin Registry, the childless women have higher scores than the men, higher than the scores of their MZ cotwins if their cotwins have children. I think what this means is that many talented adult women regard child rearing as an obstacle to meaningful achievement. If I am correct in believing that this is what our culture teaches women, then I also think that the culture is mistaken. The mothers of our adolescent twins have the same average Achievement scores as their husbands, and I think this is because they have discovered that doing useful things and doing them well is satisfying, whether those useful things are done at home or at the office.

I mentioned in chapter 1 that prisons whose inmates are unable to engage in constructive activity tend to be especially dangerous places. The men "pump iron" to build up their muscles, organize themselves into cliques or gangs, fabricate weapons, compete for position in the inmate hierarchy, connive to smuggle drugs, plan escapes. That is, they inevitably create their own forms of effectance activity and they turn their backs on TV entertainment in order to do these things. If I were to plan an ideal prison, I would put a computer terminal, rather than a TV set, in every cell. Inmates would earn their meals, their treats, their TV time (shown on the computer monitor), the opportunity to play computer games, to work out in the weight-lifting room, to use the telephone and the like, by accomplishing learning tasks set by the implacable, endlessly patient computer. The illiterate would learn to read, the non-numerate would learn basic arithmetic, the ignorant would complete their high school GEDs. A rich variety of more advanced courses would be provided for those capable of mastering them and the computer would unfailingly assess that competence. One of the treats they could work for would be adult, nonviolent, "soft porn" videos, at least until a safe, reversible, implant is invented with which inmates could be desexualized for the period of their incarceration.

My prison would be a busier, more orderly, and safer place. Some may think it inappropriate to go to such lengths to satisfy the effectance motivation of convicted felons and thus to keep them happier and out of mischief. But remember that criminals, too, share the human capacity to adapt to adversity. We know that newly admitted inmates tend to be downhearted, as they should be, but we have to predict that, after the first six months behind bars, most prison inmates now are just about as happy as they were before they got caught. My prison is designed to keep them happy doing harmless and constructive things rather than surreptitious and dangerous things.

## Entertainment

To entertain, for *Webster's*, is *to engage the attention agreeably, to amuse with that which makes the time pass pleasurably, to divert.* We have already seen that many forms of productive work "make the time pass pleasurably," so we need to be a little careful about defining our terms. I'm sure that every employed person, from mechanic to movie actor, experiences periods when the time passes drearily. This is true for self-employed people as well, even wonderfully talented, creative people. Concert pianists and violinists practice four to six hours every day, and they must sometimes glance at the clock in the hope that it is time to quit. Michelangelo, on his back on that scaffold painting the ceiling of the Sistine Chapel, cannot always have felt that his attention was agreeably engaged. On the other hand, we saw that Carl Imhof kept on driving his forklift even after winning the lottery, presumably because he enjoyed it. And he is not an isolated case: national surveys, in 1981[3] and 1989,[4] in which people were asked whether they would continue working if they were to become suddenly rich, 70 percent to 75 percent answered yes. Ticket clerks and grocery clerks, plumbers and police officers, carpenters and garbage collectors—I wonder if there is any occupation in which the time *never* passes pleasurably? In my youth, I had various low-level jobs that I enjoyed. The only really onerous one was a summer spent pulling up wild currant bushes in the white pine forests of Idaho. There was no skill involved, just trudging along endless lanes marked out by string, searching for these intermediate hosts for the blister rust that kills the pines. If the Forest Service bosses had been smarter, they would have given each boy a sack in which to collect the currant plants he'd pulled up, so as to provide a measure of how well each was doing the job and generate some harmless competition. Any job that presents a challenge, that can be done with skill or flair, done well or poorly, can qualify as entertainment, according to *Webster's*.

What is missing from the dictionary definition is that we normally think of entertainment as something we seek in our times of leisure, when we are not working even at jobs we normally enjoy. And it is interesting that many of our leisure-time activities also provide opportunities for the acquisition and the exercise of skill: think of video games, chess and checkers, card games; think of hobbies, collecting things, bird-watching, gardening, not to mention all sports. Even apparently passive entertainment can involve a kind of skill. Think of the sports fans who know all of the players and their records; think of opera fans who could answer the questions on the Metropolitan Opera quiz; think of Shakespeare fans, movie buffs—there may even be people who keep track of the plots of all the episodes of *Seinfeld*. Socializing, certainly entertaining guests at your home, involves for many people elements of accomplishment or skill—fixing up the house, fixing up one's self, choosing the wine, preparing the food, all of the social skills.

Even sex (so I am given to understand) has become a game of skill, and this, too, seems very sensible. When one thinks of the millions (*billions!*) of disappointed, unfulfilling matings, it makes one weep. (What *is* the solution to the problems of cross-gender ignorance in sensual matters? A high school course in precoital technique seems unacceptable. What do the French do? I would devote a whole chapter to this issue if only I knew the answers. I would call it "Happiness Is in Your Jeans.")

Most of us do have some truly passive entertainments, of course. I shall watch *Mystery* on PBS tonight, for example, and at least part of Sunday's Super Bowl, since the Green Bay Packers are playing. My wife and I watch about two hours of television most days, counting the news, and she has kept track of a soap opera, *As the World Turns*, since our children were little and they watched it together at lunchtime. (The acting on this program is uniformly excellent, and the writers confront their viewers with many of the important social problems of our time—terminal illness, abortion, homophobia, parental malfeasance, the American myth of polygraphic lie detection, and so on.) I am old enough to remember when our family listened to the results of the 1932 presidential election over my father's battery-powered radio, the only one on our block. In those days, many children of ignorant parents grew up with no books in the home, no daily newspaper, no radio, and no useful adult conversation. Such children existed with a bleak minimum of intellectual stimulation. Now, thanks to television, almost every child has a window on the world that was unimaginable then.

One fascinating change throughout the Western world over the past sixty years has been the steady increase in IQ scores, at the rate of about three IQ points per decade.[5] It is probable that this increase has been taking place largely at the low end—fewer IQs in the 70s and 80s—thus accounting for the increase in the grand mean. (If the increase had been across the board, we should be seeing several times as many geniuses now as in the 1930s and 1940s, and that is a change no one has been able to document, or even notice.) I think part of this reduction in the proportion of borderline IQs may reflect better prenatal nutrition and the like, but I think part of it must also be due to the richer intellectual stimulation that films and especially television has provided. If you give laboratory rats larger cages with toys and other rats to interact with, their brains grow larger. It seems to work the same way with children.

I read perhaps one mystery novel a month, and my wife and

I go to probably ten movies a year. We go occasionally to the Guthrie Theatre and to a few concerts of the Minnesota Orchestra. We schmooze with our boys and our grandchildren, by mail or telephone or now and then a visit. We listen to a lot of music and I must put in here a plug for ragtime. I have a CD in my car of Claude Bolling playing ragtime piano, and I think it is impossible to listen to this jaunty, strutting music without smiling. Sousa marches are good therapy also, especially when you get sleepy on a long drive. We spend quite a bit of the summer at our cabin near the Boundary Waters Canoe Area Wilderness, but much of that time is working, fixing or improving things. The fact is that *most* of us spend most of our time *working*. My father, who was an inventor-engineer, spent most of his time at the drafting board in our sunroom at home, and there was a family myth that "Father is busy." Sure he was busy—busy doing what he most wanted to do. I do the same thing now sitting at my computer. The only difference is that I cannot sustain the myth that I am doing it because I *have* to—like Dad, I'm doing it because I *want* to. It is better to be honest, at least about the important things.

# 4

# THE EPICURE OF EXPERIENCE

*Epicure.* Formerly, a luxurious sensualist, esp. in matters of
food and drink; now, one who displays fastidiousness in
his tastes and enjoyments; a connoisseur.

—*Webster's*

Remember that the principal way in which the genes affect
the mind is indirectly, by influencing the sorts of things we
do, the experiences we have, and the environments that we
seek out. The average depths of our personal happiness lakes
may be largely determined by aspects of our brain chemistries
that we cannot do much about. But we assuredly can make waves
on those lakes through our own efforts that will keep us riding
higher than we would if we let our genetic steersmen call all the
shots. Neither wealth, nor fame, nor glory will provide lasting
happiness, but trying to achieve these lofty goals may be worth
doing providing that the effort is itself enjoyable. There is nothing wrong with these objectives, but only if we're sure that getting there is at least half the fun—and only if we keep in mind
that, once there, we shall need to set new goals before the satisfaction fades. Bill Gates, the creator of Microsoft, said to be the
richest man in the world, is worth more than $50 billion. Is he
sitting back now, enjoying fame and wealth? No, he is busier
than ever with new projects.

When I was a younger man, I did most of the carpentry, electrical work, minor plumbing, and the like around our house myself and enjoyed doing it. Now that I am a senior and still have to do these things at our cabin in the woods, when something needs fixing, I place a call to Mr. Hemingson. He was here this morning, persuading the kitchen sink drain not to leak all over the floor, and I said, "Your line of work must be very satisfying, Dick, each call a different problem, different place, different people, and you seem to always be able to leave with the problem solved."

"It's funny you should say that," he replied. "For quite a few years I did other things, selling insurance, real estate—the money was better, but I wasn't really happy. I even got some counseling about it. The man asked me what I would like to be doing, and I told him I'd like to have a fix-it business, like I have now. Not a shop where I'd be cooped up all day, but something like this, going out on calls. And so that's what I decided to do, and I've never looked back."

I mentioned an article that had been in the paper the other day about the CEO of a St. Paul company, Green Tree Financial Corporation, a company that sells insurance for "mobile" homes. This man, Leonard Coss, made $67 million last year, but this year he was to get $100 million. (This means that Mr. Coss's efforts were apparently worth more, to somebody, than the combined contributions of my university's arts and sciences faculty.)

"Would you trade places with him?" I asked Mr. Hemingson. After giving the matter some thought, we agreed that we would trade, say, for two months, one to earn $9 million and the second to pay the taxes, but then Coss would have to trade back again. Mr. Coss's life may be rich in other ways than money, but Mr. Hemingson and I have both fashioned lives appropriate to our talents and needs, and we would be foolish to trade permanently with anyone.

We saw in chapter 3 that most of the positive waves that keep the members of our species smiling involve acquiring and exercising skills, doing useful things and doing them well. Imagine a foursome of weekend golfers, teeing off on a sunny morning round. Do they ever play carelessly, indifferently, just to quit as soon as possible and go home? No, they concentrate, think about what they're doing, and play the best they know how. So do we all when we are recreating, playing softball or tennis, hunting or fishing, playing bridge or shopping, bird watching in the woods, or woodworking in the basement. I think that the same rule applies to people who enjoy the work they must do to buy the hamburgers and pay the rent. That man who won the lottery but kept on with his job driving the forklift: would you not bet that he is good at his job? The people I see in their places of work who seem happy are people who are doing their jobs with zest and competence. Do they work well because they are happy? Perhaps, but I also believe that they are happy because they work well; it is called positive feedback.

We have made splendid strides recently in changing transportation and workplaces so that they are more accessible to the disabled, not in order to save money, but rather to make it possible for disabled people to enjoy the satisfactions of doing something useful. There is a lot of talk currently about welfare reform, most of it seemingly motivated to save tax dollars. It seems to me that a principal motivation for getting people off the dole and back to work should be their own personal well-being. Ronald Inglehart asked more than 169,000 people in sixteen countries to rate their "satisfaction with life." One of the only circumstances that significantly decreased satisfaction (which we can take as a proxy for happiness) was being unemployed, as shown in figure 4.1. But notice that our human adaptability shows itself even here. Although the unemployed group were less satisfied overall than those with jobs, more than 60 percent of them rated themselves as "satisfied."

Many welfare recipients will need training to become employable and many will need day care services for their children. By the same token, however, many who have skills can be employed in training those who lack them, and many single mothers currently on welfare could be employed in those new day care centers, under skillful supervision, learning to be better mothers.

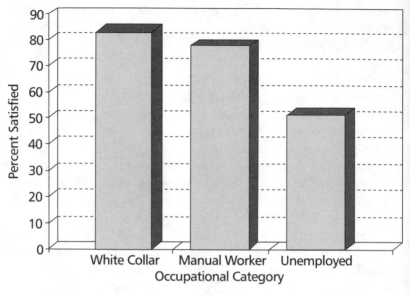

**FIGURE 4.1**

Data for 169,776 people from sixteen countries reported by Ronald Inglehart, *Culture Shift in Advanced Industrial Society* (Princeton: Princeton University Press, 1990).

But let us suppose that you are already usefully employed, at home or in some job, and that you already invest as much effort to be good at what you do as those weekend golfers invest in trying to improve their scores. Let us also assume that you have identified the thieves of happiness that exist in your life, and that you are taking steps to guard against their depredations to prevent them from making all those troughs in your lake of happiness. What then can you do to make some more waves to keep yourself bobbing above the set point of contentment that was established by your genes? We're not talking about tidal waves here. I must leave it to you to win that promotion, that lottery, that election, that lover, that championship, that glory, by your own devices. But remember (as King Solomon discovered) that the joy it brings won't last forever. One needs to cultivate some "happy habits," ways of seasoning one's day-to-day and week-to-week existence with activities that make those little waves that provide us with the little lifts we all need to keep smiling.

Years ago, five or six faculty colleagues and I formed what we called the Wine & Wisdom Society. We met once a month for dinner at my university's Campus Club. One member each time was responsible for bringing the wine and another the wisdom. We all enjoyed those evenings, and one bit of wisdom that I carried away had to do with the wine. The designated sommeliers tended to be a bit competitive in selecting interesting vintages, and we made quite a thing about tasting and rating the wines on a twenty-point scale. I learned a little about wines (not much, because I lack both a sensitive palate and the sort of mind that stores up that kind of information), and I even built a wine cellar in my basement. But the main thing that I learned was how much more one enjoys something pleasurable if one really pays attention! An epicure is not just a show-off but, rather, someone with the good sense to extract the maximum enjoyment from the opportunities afforded him or her by really thinking about and savoring each pleasurable experience.

The first step, it seems to me, in becoming an epicure of experience is to make a list of one's possibilities. What are the things you know you like to do, and what things that other people enjoy might you like to do yourself were you to try them? In making one's list, it is important to remember that variety is the spice of life. (I cannot talk about this most basic of all topics without employing occasional clichés, because most of these truths have been known since language was invented: we know these things, we just don't act on them.) What talents do you have that you could cultivate? What skills might you enjoy acquiring even if you have no special talent? I have no special talent for baking or gardening but, as I explain below, I have derived great satisfaction from both activities. It is a happy fact about our species that many people get real enjoyment from good works, helping their neighbors, mentoring children, doing volunteer work, or just making the effort to be friendly and kind. One small thing I have felt good about over the years is taking the trouble to speak up when someone in authority is guilty of malfeasance. (If no one speaks up, the problem will continue.) But, to compensate for all this complaining, I try to congratulate those who do something well, to write as many complimentary letters as letters of complaint.

I should confess, however, that most of what I know about the savoring of experience consists of chances missed rather than accomplished. One of my fondest memories is of walking through the winter snow with my son, Joseph, then aged about eight, while telling him some hortative parable from my own youth, now long forgotten. When my tale was finished, Joe's comment was: "Gee, Dad, it sounds like you never did anything right!" Ah, but I did learn from all those mistakes. For example, I enjoy toiling away at my computer and, if I am not careful, I will continue long past the point where my lake is becalmed and I need a change to get the waves going again. The last Guthrie Theatre matinee that my wife and I attended came on a day when the work had been going well that morning and, left to myself, I would likely have skipped the play. But, instead, we set forth and saw the best *Midsummer Night's Dream* of my experience. Afterward, however, I resolved always to reread a Shakespearean play prior to the performance so as to retune my ears for the rich language; it took most of the first act before I could easily follow the lines. And what lines they are! "We have laughed to see the sails conceive, and grow big-bellied with the wanton wind." A real epicure of experience would make sure to be ready to hear and appreciate treasures like that. Harriet and I belonged to a duplicate bridge group for several years; it was fun, but it would have been more fun if we had taken the trouble to read a bridge book or two and work systematically to improve our game. Another time we took the family to Western Samoa for a couple of weeks. A memorable trip, but real connoisseurs would have done some prior study in order to know what to look for, to appreciate what one saw. I am sure that the people who most enjoy ball games or concerts, boxing or ballet, are the ones who know the most about what they are watching.

If I were a young man again, I would include on my list some

nonteam sport, like tennis or skiing or golf, that can be continued into one's seniority. I did play squash for years, so I appreciate how oddly satisfying it can be to get breathless and sweaty in
pursuit of a ball, but squash courts are not everywhere available
and, at least in my experience, that game becomes dangerous as
one's reflexes slow down with age. After losing two teeth, and
very nearly an eye, from collisions with my opponent's racquet,
I decided to give up squash. Thus, it will be clear that I do not
claim to be a role model for young epicures of experience, yet I
will mention here a couple of leisure-time activities that I think
everyone should at least sample when they have the opportunity.

## Cooking

I had neither sisters nor daughters and, perhaps for that reason,
my four brothers and I and my three sons all learned at least
the rudiments of cooking. My eldest brother, Henry, now in his
eighties, is a gourmet cook, while Georg, now a widower, is a
good journeyman chef. Two of my sons do most of the cooking
for their families and enjoy it.

   Since my wife became a vegetarian when my sons did, some
twenty years ago, I have cooked whatever meat is served at our
house, but what I really enjoy is making beer bread and pies. I
shall tell you how to make beer bread and also the perfect lemon
meringue pie so that, if you are not already an occasional baker,
you can discover the enjoyment to be found in devoting an hour
to this creative endeavor every now and then.

### BEER BREAD

This is a kind of sourdough bread that fills the house with good
smells while baking, and then makes ideal morning toast. You'll
need a large bowl, two bottles of warm beer, three packets of
quick-rising yeast, and five pounds of unbleached flour.

   The night before you plan to bake, empty one packet of yeast
into one cup of hot water and let it work for ten minutes (this is
called "proving" the yeast). Then mix the yeasted water with the

beer in your big bowl and start adding flour, a handful at a time, while mixing with a whisk or large spoon. When the mixture is about as thick as pea soup, cover the bowl and let it sit overnight in a warm place. Next morning, put the remaining two yeast packets into two cups of hot water and let sit for ten minutes. Add about two tablespoons of salt to the mixture in the bowl (called the "sponge"), which has fermented overnight and is redolent with promise. Then mix in the proven yeast-water and begin to add flour, a cup or double handful at a time, mixing thoroughly after each addition. Your mixing tool will progress from a heavy whisk to a large spoon to your two hands as the batter gets thicker and thicker. When there are perhaps two cups of flour left from the five pounds you started with, the bread dough is ready for kneading. This is a process of folding and working the dough with well-floured hands so as to expose its sticky inner parts, which are then dusted with a handful of the remaining flour. Continue the kneading for about ten minutes or until the flour is all used up and the dough is about the same consistency inside and out. Then cover the bowl again and let the dough rise for an hour or two in a warm place until at least doubled in size.

Now clean off a section of your kitchen counter, dust it with flour, and turn the dough out of the bowl, shaping it into a round mound that you can cut it into four equal parts. With floured hands, manipulate each of the four portions into circular lumps that look like giant mushroom heads, and then let them rest on the counter for ten minutes while you grease the four bread pans. This last is best done with your fingers and a bit of margarine, rubbing vigorously so as to grease all the inner surface of each pan. Then, with your greasy hands, shape your four lumps of dough into oblongs and fit them into the four pans, then set them aside for their second rising. (I let them rise in the cool oven where they will later bake.) In another hour or two, the pans will be full of risen dough, and you should make a shallow lengthwise slice down the middle of each loaf with a razor blade or sharp knife. Then turn on the oven to 425° and set your timer for 45 minutes. You can use one of your four dough lumps to make into three baguettes, a foot long and about half an inch in diameter before rising, which are superb when eaten hot with butter or cheese, but not worth the loss of a loaf if they can't be used within an hour of baking. The bread is best sliced rather thinly and toasted about twice as long as store bread requires.

## LEMON MERINGUE PIE

Making piecrust from scratch is too much trouble, so get a package of Pillsbury piecrusts, let one of them warm up for half an hour so that you can unfold it without breaking, and bake it according to the instructions on the box. Meanwhile, assemble four eggs, one large lemon, and three tablespoons of butter. Put one cup of sugar in a small saucepan and set another one-third cup of sugar aside. Add one-quarter cup of cornstarch to the sugar in the pan and mix with a spoon. Now add one and one-half cups of cold water and mix thoroughly. Before cutting the lemon in half, wash it and scrape off onto a clean plate all of the yellow peel (the "zest") using a food grater or, better, an inexpensive hand tool called a zester. Now halve the lemon and squeeze out all the juice, carefully removing all seeds; this should give you about one-quarter cup of juice. Separate the egg yolks into one small bowl and the whites into another. Beat the yolks vigorously with a fork for a minute or so, then add to the sugar mixture in the saucepan. Add the lemon zest and butter as well.

At this point, your piecrust will be done and cooling nearby. Turn the oven down to 350°. Begin cooking the sugar mixture over moderate heat, stirring constantly. When the butter has melted and the mixture is just about to bubble, it begins to thicken. Keep stirring for one full minute after the first bubbles of boiling appear; this is the key, because if you don't allow the full minute, the pie will end up mushy. Then turn off the heat and add the lemon juice, mixing it in well. Pour this mixture into your baked piecrust, which by now is cool enough. Get out the eggbeater and beat the egg whites until the peaks hold their shape. Beat in the reserved one-third cup sugar plus one teaspoon vanilla. Sculpt this meringue on the top of your pie; I like to leave a hole in the middle showing the lemon-yellow filling. Carefully put your creation into the 350° oven for about fifteen minutes or until the meringue is streaked with brown. Remove, cool, and consume with gusto.

## Growing Vegetables

Cicero discovered "the pleasures of agriculture, in which I find incredible delight," and Diocletian came to realize that being emperor of Rome could not compare to the satisfactions of raising vegetables with his own hands. Voltaire's Candide and his companions, after many disappointments, discovered the same thing: "We must cultivate our garden." Perhaps because of its endless variety and annual renewal, gardening was both a solace and delight to the ancients, as it is to many still today, a source of subjective well-being that does not wear out. Try it; you'll enjoy it, too.

My parents never gardened, and neither did I until my wife and I changed houses when the boys were about four, six, and eight and the small backyard of our "new" house was a disaster area. I fenced it in, dug it all up, laid out a brick patio, and then, on impulse, planted some vegetables in the now rich-looking dirt: tomatoes and corn, squash and onions, lettuce and green peppers. We thought the kids would enjoy watching the developments, but we enjoyed them even more. We left that house within two years because it proved to be in an upper-Yuppie, cocktail-party neighborhood where children were alternately ignored and indulged, and not the kind of peer group we wanted for our sons. But, having belatedly made Cicero's discovery, we dedicated the small, south-facing side yard of our third house to a vegetable garden.

Because space was limited, I found a book by Mel Bartholomew called *Square Foot Gardening* to employ as a basic guide. Using two- by eight-inch boards, I constructed seven four- by eight-foot rectangles for raised beds with narrow paths between. During one rather strenuous week, I dug up all the dirt within each rectangle, then filled each one to the top with good black dirt hauled from a truckload I had ordered dumped nearby. Now, some thirty years later, those beds are still doing their summer's job, reinvigorated every spring with cow manure. We grow strawberries, raspberries, gooseberries, and currants, several varieties of tomatoes and lettuce, snap peas and cucumbers, green beans and carrots, sweet and hot peppers, red cabbage and broccoli, onions, squash, and herbs and catnip for the cats. We always have several Brussels sprouts plants that are left until Thanksgiving, when they are cut down with an ax and the frozen sprouts picked off to be part of that family feast. Another academic gardener, Carl Klaus, a professor of English at the University of Iowa, is more ambitious than I am, both as a tiller of the soil (he digs and plants and harvests three-quarters of an acre) and as a writer. His recent book, *My Vegetable Love: A Journal of a Growing Season*, is both an inspiration and a delight.

Harriet and I are neither sophisticated nor indefatigable gardeners, and I suspect that our produce ends up costing about twice as much as it would have at the supermarket. (The truth is that most supermarket produce is ridiculously cheap; our market this week was selling lovely big heads of lettuce, individually wrapped, for 25 cents—how can that be possible?) But there is such an elemental wonder about seeing things sprout and grow, such a welcome feeling of renewal or rebirth every spring, and everything seems to taste so much better from our own garden! Moreover, it is organically grown and free of pesticides and other poisons, including the really dangerous ones that we Americans sell to other countries to use in growing the fruits and vegetables they then ship back for us to eat. All three of our sons love to grow vegetables in their own yards now, as we do, and I suspect our grandchildren will follow suit.

## Chemical Happiness

There are numerous ingestible chemicals, some legal and some not, that can enhance the activity on one's lake of happiness. Some, such as alcohol and the tranquilizing drugs, affect one's feelings of well-being primarily by reducing tension and anxiety, which have an inhibiting effect on the happiness machinery. Those of us who are able to use alcohol in moderation are fortunate. I must say that I look forward to the cocktail hour as a predictable interlude of relaxed conversation; even Willie, the bull terrier, understands this tradition and climbs up companionably into his chair. I think I was lucky in that, when I first experimented with alcoholic drinks in my late teens, I didn't like them at all, forced them down in order to appear grown up and got violently ill on several occasions. I believe that people who react this way as youngsters are least likely to abuse alcohol as adults. It is the "champagne responders," whose first drinks in adolescence seem delightful, who will need the most self-discipline later on because their innate turn-off mechanism does not activate as readily as mine does. Marijuana, with which my personal experience is very limited, seems to work rather like alcohol as a relaxant and a disinhibiter of the pleasure centers. One virtue of such compounds, used in moderation, is that they do not exact a price later. They do not make happiness waves but, rather, just allow them to happen.

On the other hand, the stimulant drugs, such as the amphetamines and especially cocaine and its derivatives, are very different. They make waves directly, but those waves have troughs. Every stimulant-produced "up" seems to be followed by a compensatory "down," and the net effect is usually negative. Years ago, my complaisant physician prescribed for me an amphetamine compound that I took two or three times a week when I had a particularly demanding day ahead. But I felt less than myself the next day, and my wife pointed out that I was becoming irritable, so I gave it up. Adolf Hitler is said to have abused amphetamines more and more as the war turned against him.[1]

Most middle-class, law-abiding citizens regard illegal "happiness drugs" as ipso facto dangerous and applaud government's efforts to suppress them. Without thinking it through, we suppose that, had it not been for the "war on drugs," drug addiction would be rampant and our children and grandchildren all would be at risk. The fact is, however, that the American war on drugs, which consumes tens of billions of dollars annually, has been a loser from the start. In 1995, at the FBI laboratories in Washington, D.C., I was shown a regulation plastic and metal-grid cage of the type used for dogs in transit. What was unusual about this cage was that the plastic surround was compounded of cocaine that could be easily extracted in a simple laboratory once the cage (and dozens of its fellows) had passed through customs. Because so much money is involved, the other side is always one or more jumps ahead of the enforcers.

The war on drugs has had two important effects, both of them bad. First, American prisons are filling up with drug traffickers, many of them nonviolent lower-level smugglers or distributors seduced by the large profits. In some states, prisons are so crowded that one hundred felons must be given early release in order to accommodate each one hundred new admissions. At least 346 homicides in Florida from 1988 to 1991 were committed by felons after early release. Patsy Jones, the twenty-year-old who became a celebrity in 1993 for shooting a German tourist on a Miami expressway, had been released from jail five days earlier. She had pulled a gun when arrested for shoplifting but, due to the press of more serious offenses, the charges were dropped.[2] The second bad effect of the war on drugs is that every tax dollar expended in this futile fight probably puts two dollars into the pockets of the drug lords and their minions, at home and abroad.

Suppose we were to admit that the "war on drugs" has been lost. Suppose we decriminalize drug use and then nationalize the importation, packaging, and sale of the more popular street drugs in liquor stores or drugstores. Anyone aged twenty-one or over could get a special photo-ID credit card with which to buy small quantities for personal use. A central computer operated by the Drug Enforcement Agency could easily keep track of usage. This would free up one-fourth to one-half of the current beds in the U.S. prison system. It would save the billions of dollars that the DEA is now spending each year on the wasteful "war" and make that money available for something useful, something like drug treatment, for example. And it would also take billions of dollars away from the criminals and gangs, who do bad things with the money, and make it possible to do good things with it instead.

And, perhaps most important, it would eliminate what is now a very tempting career option for urban youth. Instead of working for $300 a week at McDonald's, they are offered a tax-free $1,000 a week with great opportunities for advancement—a temptation that many of the brightest, most energetic and entrepreneurial of underclass youth find hard to resist.

Would your children or grandchildren all become addicts under such a system? If they are in the age of risk now, they already know where to get the stuff. Easy availability of drugs is not the problem. The problem, I believe, is inadequate parenting. For more than ten years, my colleagues and I have been researching the risk factors for substance abuse, supported by grants from the National Institute on Drug Abuse (NIDA) and the National Institute on Alcohol and Alcohol Abuse (NIAAA). Our research subjects are a representative sample of twins born in Minnesota—same-sex twins aged either eleven or seventeen when they first come with their parents to our laboratories—whom we are following with annual contacts and repeat visits every three years as they grow into adulthood. I believe we shall be able to show that substance abuse seldom happens to well-nurtured, well-socialized youngsters reared by both biological parents sharing this most important of human responsibilities as a cooperating team. Unhappily, however, children thus blessed are becoming rarer with every passing year. Due to rising rates of illegitimacy and divorce, they are already in the minority in the black community and may be also among Minnesotans generally by the year 2000. We already know that substance abuse is just another component of what I have called sociopathy,[3] along with crime, violence, teenage pregnancy, school dropout, and welfare dependency. Computed separately for both blacks and whites, a boy reared without his father in the home is *seven times* more likely to end up in reform school and, later, in prison, than a boy reared by both parents.[4]

There seems to be no doubt that some people, however they

may be reared, have an innate physiological vulnerability to alcohol abuse and this may be true also for some street drugs.[5] But even as a youngster with early-onset diabetes will have a better chance if he comes from a stable, two-parent home, so will he, too, if his physiological vulnerability is alcohol- or drug-related. The vast majority of drug abusers, however, began life as normal infants who, due to the lack of sharing, caring, competent parents, never learned to obey the rules of social living. They are children who never transmuted whatever talents they were born with into useful skills, who never discovered the satisfaction of doing something constructive and doing it well—and whose birthright of life, liberty, and the pursuit of happiness was thus abrogated.

Child psychiatrist Jack Westman has estimated that children like this cost society on average about $50,000 for each year of their lives.[6] To reduce the current high rate of production of such expensive social liabilities—and, much more importantly, for the sake of the children themselves—we shall have to make some extensive improvements in our current social infrastructure. We shall have to provide parental training and support and an adequate system of professionalized foster parenting for those many cases in which the birth parents are beyond redemption.[7] This will be very expensive, but it would be a far better way to invest those billions now being wasted on the futile "war" on drugs.

# 5

# HAPPY IN ONE'S LABOR

As Studs Terkel has written, work is also a search "for daily
meaning as well as daily bread, for recognition as well as
cash, for astonishment rather than torpor; in short, for a
sort of life rather than a Monday through Friday sort of
dying." Through our work we define ourselves, even leave
a legacy that adds meaning to our living.

—DAVID G. MYERS[1]

I n a remote valley on the California-Nevada border, there is an
isolated cattle ranch called Deep Springs College. It really *is* a
college, with a student body of twenty to twenty-four very
bright young men from all over the United States. Although
largely unknown to the general public, admissions officers of the
better U.S. universities are all familiar with this two-year junior
college whose annual graduating class of about ten generally find
easy entrée to the college of their choice. I first learned of Deep
Springs in 1975 when my youngest son, Matthew, graduated
from a Minneapolis high school. Because he was a Merit Scholar,
Matt got numerous invitations to matriculate at various colleges,
including an invitation to apply to this unknown school in California where the tuition, board, and room were free. Our first
thought was that this must be some sort of cult endeavor, an Ayn
Rand training program possibly, but when we looked in *American Colleges and Universities* at the library, there was Deep
Springs, right next to Dartmouth. But the median ACE or SAT
scores of its freshman class were higher than Dartmouth's,

higher than Harvard's or MIT's, or any other college in the book. The centerpiece of the application form consisted of ten challenging essay questions and, because he had put off applying until the last minute, Matt had a busy couple of days. Matt's efforts were successful, and he soon set off, only sixteen years old, for two of the most memorable years of his life.

Deep Springs was founded in 1917 by Lucien L. Nunn, a pioneer of the West's electric power industry, for the purpose of training "leaders of tomorrow." Deep Springs really is a cattle ranch as well as a college: a 3,500-acre spread with grazing rights on another 295,000 acres, managed by a professional cowboy but with students doing most of the work. It is also a farm, growing hay for the cattle and vegetables for the Boarding House, where students and staff have their meals family-style. Those meals consist largely of provender made or grown on the ranch: the milk, the meat, the honey, the home-baked breads and pastry, as well as all those good fruits and vegetables. In addition to herding the cattle and working in the fields, students help in the kitchen, run the library, milk the dairy cows, care for the pigs and the horses, and do needed mechanical or other repairs, according to job assignments made by one of their number elected to be "labor commissioner." Each job is essential to the community, and each newly assigned student learns his responsibilities from a "passover" document created by prior incumbents of that position. (One of these responsibilities is updating and improving the information in the passover.)

From the beginning, the Deep Springs student body has been largely self-governing, making the rules, selecting each year's entering class, voting on curricula and faculty replacements. The half-dozen faculty members live in modest houses on the ranch and provide a high-level liberal arts curriculum. Class sizes are typically five or fewer, and teaching is mainly tutorial. The only required classes are composition and public speaking, Mr. Nunn having believed that leaders need to be able to express their thoughts clearly in print and effectively in person. The school year consists of six seven-week terms, from late June through the next May. There is a month's holiday around Christmas and another two-week break in June. Students often spend the short between-term breaks camping in the Sierras or hitchhiking up and down the West Coast, alone or in small groups. Surrounded by the White and Inyo mountains, with no TV and negligible radio reception, with just one party-line telephone, sharing its four- by twelve-mile valley only with the cattle, a few snakes, and other critters, Deep Springs is truly isolated from the madding crowd. Only the designated driver travels weekly the twenty-eight miles through the narrow Westguard Pass to Big Pine, California, the nearest town. Yet the students are not cut off intellectually, because the reading room in the main lodge contains a wide selection of the best newspapers and magazines, in several languages, and the library is accessible twenty-four hours a day.

The volumes in that library include quite a few written by Deep Springs alumni who, though relatively few in number, are among the best educated of any institution in the world. Three-fourths of them have gone on to advanced degrees, mostly doctorates of one kind or another, whereas fewer than 8 percent of Ivy League graduates end up with Ph.D.'s.[2] When I spent three months of a sabbatical there in 1980, teaching a psychology course in exchange for room and board, another volunteer faculty member was a retired professor of electrical engineering at Yale who had been part of Deep Springs's first class in 1918. The library includes a selection of his books, plus nearly twenty thousand more.

This caliber of student would accomplish a good academic education in nearly any college he might choose. What students acquire uniquely at Deep Springs, just as Mr. Nunn intended, is the discovery of the satisfaction that comes from accepting responsibility, from doing a necessary job and doing it well, not for pay or promotion but because the job needs doing. I think part of the power of the place comes from its resemblance to our human "environment of evolutionary adaptation." The Deep Springs community is rather like the self-sufficient extended-family groups in which our ancestors lived, and in which each member needed to pull his weight in the group effort for survival. I think we are adapted to respond appropriately to such a setting because those ancients who did not pull their own weight were less likely to become ancestors.

One interesting phenomenon at Deep Springs is the absence of cliques or pariahs. Some of those very bright young men are highly individualistic and eccentric on arrival and might easily be shunned or made fun of in other settings, but a small, isolated community cannot afford to be exclusionary. A report of the Western Accreditation Commission perceptively observed that Deep Springs students "have palpable evidence of the need to assume responsibility, to be a contributing member of the community." Far from being intellectual snobs who consider manual labor beneath them, the students at Deep Springs take pride in doing any task well, from washing the dishes quickly and efficiently to learning to call the pigs at slopping time. In an environment where the value of every job is obvious to all, the students are able to see that the important thing in life is not what you do, but rather how you do it.

The subsequent success of Deep Springs alumni might be attributed solely to their innate high ability, but I believe that it is more than that. At the same time in their development when ancestral boys were learning to be men, Deep Springs scholars are making the same elemental discoveries, learning the gratification of doing the job for its own sake, helping themselves by helping the community. After making their place in the world, these alumni contribute to Deep Springs at three times the rate of the alumni of other California colleges. This testifies, I think, not only to their appreciation for their own Deep Springs experience, but also to what I believe is their characteristic tendency to want to give more than they take, to do their part and better. Although we know that happiness is only weakly correlated with status or income, with educational attainment or IQ, what would you guess might be the mean score of Deep Springs graduates on our Well Being scale? I would expect it to be higher than for men in general (or than, say, for the average Harvard alumnus) because most of these Deep Springs graduates learned early on to live according to the ancient rules, expressing in their lives and work the innate talents for socialization that Nature instilled in our species, and receiving in turn the rewards of self-esteem and satisfaction that Nature uses to lead us to do her bidding.

Some support for these ideas can be found in a study of another group of young people, who were selected for their high intelligence to participate in L. M. Terman's famous *Genetic Studies of Genius*.[3] When these gifted children were followed up at age forty, it was possible to select a subgroup of 150 who were conspicuous achievers (Group A), comparable to the Deep Springs alumni in being highly educated, listed in *Who's Who* or in *American Men of Science* or the *Directory of American Scholars*, as academics, scientists, statesmen, novelists, inventors, and the like. Terman and Oden also selected a comparison group (Group C) of low achievers, equally promising as children but who had not attained much success either educationally or vocationally. Ratings of personality traits were obtained on both groups from their parents and spouses, as well as self-ratings, and most of them were also visited by Terman's field assistants, who rated them as well. The personality differences between these two gifted groups were striking. The high achievers were much higher than the others in self-confidence, in perseverance, in "integration towards goals," in poise, alertness, curiosity, originality, in common sense—and they were significantly higher in happiness as well.

The hypothesis that I advance in this chapter is that Deep Springs can be regarded as a prototype of an ideal work environment that, in spite of its unique peculiarities—its young and very brainy work force, its isolation—can provide object lessons for both workers and managers in the real world of business and industry. I am convinced that, as a result of their two years in the high desert, most Deep Springs alumni were more effective in their later lives, able to make more productive use of their native talents, than they might have been had they spent those two years at Stanford or Yale or Dartmouth. I think the Deep Springs experience put them in touch with ancient instincts that our ancestors evolved over hundreds of millennia because those instincts made them contributing members of the interdependent hunter-gatherer communities in which they lived. It is reasonable to assume that most ancestral children grew up to accept adult responsibilities and carry their share of the load in these extended-family bands because that is the kind of community to which we are attuned by natural selection, that is, the "environment of evolutionary adaptation" to which our "ancient instincts" resonate. It is reasonable to assume that the members of those ancestral communities were mostly well socialized because that is true today in those remaining traditional societies that are organized along ancestral lines.

Because it is our nature to be responsible, contributing members of a community, I believe that we are happiest when we follow these ancient instincts. But modern society is vastly different from the kind to which we are adapted. We moderns cultivate individualism, self-striving, competition, and self-indulgence. Many young people, even some with special talents, never learn that doing the job and doing it right is the sine qua non of human happiness. Some student athletes find that being "a member of the team" taps these ancient instincts and, for some, this discovery carries over into the world of work. Some employment settings manage to create a communitarian atmosphere in which workers feel themselves to be a significant part of a social organism whose survival and success is interrelated with their own. If I were a manager, this is the model I would strive to emulate.

## The Productive Worker → The Happy Worker → The Productive Worker

The recursive formula that I have used for a heading here says it all. This is what students learn at Deep Springs and what some employees and some managers never figure out. There is an assistant whom I see at the supermarket once a week, busily replenishing and straightening the shelves; as he hustles past, he always smiles and says something cheerful, and if you ask him where some item is in that vast store, he is delighted to take you to the spot. By the same token, nearly every interaction that he has with customers must provide positive feedback for him because (1) he knows the stock and can answer any question, and (2) he is so pleasant about it that he must elicit agreeable responses from all but the worst grouches. Being a stockman in a supermarket is a relatively low-level job but, like almost every job that one can think of, it is a necessary job, and it can be done really well or just well enough to get by. I mentioned earlier the men who collect our garbage weekly, another low-level but essential job, and how our crew does it athletically and with style. We know from the research that garbage collectors and grocery clerks are just as happy on average as their bosses are, but these examples illustrate that *some* garbage collectors and *some* grocery clerks do their jobs unusually well and seem to be unusually happy. Which direction does the causal arrow point? Does a good-natured attitude produce good work or the other way around? How might we explore that question experimentally?

## A Happiness Experiment

Let us select a random (and therefore, we hope, representative) sample of two hundred male and two hundred female seniors from next year's graduating classes in, say, Minnesota high schools. They are recruited with the incentive that we shall pay to send them to a good two-year junior college. Now we split each gender group in half, being careful to match the halves on IQ, grade point average, and Well Being score. One group of one hundred males and one group of one hundred females is sent to the junior (or, for the first two years, of a four-year) college of their choice at our expense. The remaining two groups are each split up again, this time at random, into four groups of twenty-five students each, and these lucky ones are sent off to eight newly formed colleges built on the Deep Springs model. These would have unisex student bodies and be located in some isolated place where the students make the rules, do the work (which could include operating a farm or ranch or, possibly, an orphanage or some sort of business venture), and at the same time pursue a good junior college curriculum appropriate to their interests and abilities. Ten years later, we do a follow-up assessment of all four hundred of our original subjects. We find out how far each one went in school and how well they did. We learn their work histories, promotions, accomplishments, we solicit performance ratings from their supervisors or employers, and we measure their happiness levels. What do you predict that we should find?

The most confident prediction, I think, is that the two hundred whom we sent to the Deep Springs clones (I'll call them the "DSC students") will have high performance ratings, on average, higher than the junior college (JC) group obtains. This follows fairly directly from the fact that the real Deep Springs alumni (the DSAs) perform like the Terman high achievers, rather than, say, midway between the two groups of Terman gifted children who were *selected* at age forty because they were either high or low achievers. The DSAs were all gifted children, too, but nearly all of them became high achievers and that, in turn, suggests that the Deep Springs experience made a real difference in their lives. The hitch in this argument is that the DSAs were already high achievers before they got to Deep Springs; all had been Merit Scholars or the equivalent. Our experimental subjects, in contrast, will not be selected either to be gifted or to be exceptional students; all they have to do is to graduate from high school to be a part of our experiment. Therefore, one's confidence in my prediction, that the DSCs will perform better than the JCs (although not so well as the DSAs, who were selected to be gifted), depends upon whether you think as I do that learning to play your part in a team effort—having your "ancient instincts" elicited and shaped—during late adolescence can have important lasting effects.

But the point of our experiment is to answer the following questions:

1. Is worker happiness correlated with worker productivity? That is, do happier people tend to have the better work habits that make for greater productivity and better supervisor ratings? We have seen that happiness is *not* strongly correlated with in-

come or status; does that imply that happiness is also unrelated to the quality of one's work? Not at all. It indicates that garbage collectors, as a group, are about as happy as, say, dentists as a group. But some garbage collectors, like some dentists, are really good at what they do, while some are marginal and most are average. What we want to know is whether happy garbage collectors and happy dentists both are better and more productive than their less-happy colleagues. We know that IQ scores and years of education correlate negligibly with subjective well-being, but what we want to know is whether a student of average ability who is happy does better in school than another of similar ability who is less happy. We can't answer question 1 by comparing the subjects' happiness scores with their subsequent academic or professional achievements; we already know that correlation will be negligible. But we can ask instead: Do the happier people do better in college than their IQs would predict? And rather than ask whether the engineers, architects, and lawyers are happier than the clerks, janitors, and mechanics, we can ask whether the effective, highly rated people in each of these professions are happier than those with average ratings or below.

2. Assuming that the answer to question 1 is yes, then we want to know whether it is doing good work that is conducive to happiness or the other way around. Do the people who were happiest in high school, before plunging into the great world of work, turn out to be the more valued employees later on? I think the answer to this question would turn out to be yes. This is the result that would be useful to employers: in addition to assessing the talents of your job applicants, try to get an estimate of their levels of subjective well-being, and then pick the happy ones.

3. But the answer that would be useful to employees (and to parents, teachers, and to people in general) is whether the DSCs will turn out to be both more highly rated and also happier than the JCs ten years later. If I am right in thinking that learning teamwork and the satisfaction of doing one's job right for its own sake—by or during late adolescence—tend to make people more productive, better citizens, and also happier in their later lives,

then that is something worth knowing. And, taking questions 2 and 3 together, I think that the outcome of this Gedanken experiment would be to confirm the truth of the heading above: The Productive Worker → The Happy Worker → The Productive Worker. Happiness makes for employee effectiveness *and* the other way around as well.

There is a voluminous body of research showing that the best performance on complex or creative tasks, whether in academics or in the workplace, is produced by people motivated by intrinsic interest in the task rather than by contingent rewards. In fact, when employers focus attention on rewards for performance, it is likely to *decrease* performance and be counterproductive.[4] Employees who are interested in their work, who enjoy it, do a better job, and it appears that extrinsic motivators cannot substitute for the intrinsic satisfaction of work well done. Moreover, high performance—the exhilarating sense of mastery and "flow"[5]—enhances the value and interest of the task. Hence we have another recursive formula: Performance → Interest → Performance. And the important point is that it is possible to develop a habit of mind by which one may find interest in almost any task. Recall the memorable line from the Mike Nichols film, *The Graduate*, when a friend of his father's tells the young Dustin Hoffman, sententiously, "I have just one word to say to you, Ben—*plastics!*" The line is funny because, like young Ben, we do not share this man's enthusiastic interest in the plastics business. But remember those four young men I mentioned in chapter 1 who, in just the few years since their high school graduation, had developed a consuming fascination with *linoleum*? Think of it this way: Each of us, *if we are fortunate*, will have one or more strong interests in topics or activities that engender only puzzlement or yawns in lots of other people. What was dumb (and funny) about Ben's father's friend was not that that plastics made his eyes gleam (since that was apparently his life's work, he was lucky that he loved it), but, rather, that he naïvely thought this young Yale graduate could be so easily seduced by the same siren without hearing her song.

## Some Advice from the Real World

Academics like me are not really employees—we have salaries but no real bosses—nor do most of us have any real managerial experience. But I know a DSA (my son Matt) who has accumulated some twenty years of experience in the real world, both as an employee and as a manager, since his two years at Deep Springs, and he was kind enough to give me some of his ideas on the subject of this chapter. I cannot do better than to pass along his thoughts with minimal editing.

It has come to the attention of management that employees are not happy campers these days. People spend a great deal of their time at work, and job satisfaction for most of them is problematic. They may get raises and promotions from time to time, but they remain unsatisfied and they think that they need to advance still further. A number of books on the "take charge of your career" theme suggest that promotion, climbing the ladder of success, should be the goal and that workers ought to focus on that one objective. I think, to the contrary, that one should regard promotion as a by-product of one's enthusiastic performance on the job, not as a goal in itself. As someone who has been promoted four times in two years, it doesn't bother me that the "experts" advise a different approach, because I think that approach is calculated to produce mainly angst and stress. Employees who choose to focus on the job itself find that it is a great stress alleviator because, first, it permits them to attend to the things in their work that they enjoy rather than fretting about disappointments or what other people think. Secondly, they actually do better, both in the work itself and, eventually, in the regard of management. Managers desperately want to see enthusiasm, to see employees seeking to do a great job just because they *want* to. The rising stars in my department tend to be people who fundamentally don't give a damn what the company thinks; they just want to do a good job for the fun of it.

It is important to focus on your current function (broadly defined, because doing a good job may require procedural improvements that alter that function), even if that particular function is not very glamorous or exciting. Glamour always fades on close examination, so pursuit of that phantom is futile. When you stop getting "ups" from doing your prescribed job, then it is important to reach out to develop new skills and attack new problems and, thus, to renew the highs. In jobs that involve dealing with people, there is almost unlimited scope for developing new skills, getting better at sizing people up so that you can choose the most effective way of dealing with them. In many jobs it may mean taking on new tasks, enlarging and improving your own job description. It is important to see that this sort of job development is not a thing that is given from above, but rather something that you take on yourself. Think of it as a video game where reading the hint book and winning that way is boring. Learning on your own by playing is exciting and fun. A good employee is one who learns by playing, seeking advice and mentoring when needed to avoid screwups, and not one who says, in effect, "Train me to perform this task by rote." Similarly, just sticking to what you have done well previously is not always a good idea, if the result is a loss of challenge and enthusiasm. Once you have conquered one video game, you want a new one, and we should recognize that same impulse in the work situation.

It is hard to overemphasize the importance of human interactions. If everyone is trying to do their job well, rather than just to succeed by hook or by crook, work should be a warm and cooperative environment, and supervisors and those they supervise should be on friendly terms. Friendliness is a happiness-maker, and mutual recognition of good performance is a powerful reinforcer. Supervisors can critique and give advice without impairing the friendly relationship. I've given my employees very direct criticism without creating hard feelings because they know that I genuinely value them and want to help them to do better. That's an important atmospheric, and it makes the difference between changing just to placate the boss and actually rethinking one's behavior with a view to improvement.

Money—salary, bonuses, promotions, etc.—really isn't (or should not be) the main motivator. But, if money is the only way you have of saying "well done," then failure to give it is grating. Person-to-person expression of respect and appreciation, if genuine and sincerely given, is a better currency and one that does not foster counterproductive competition and jealousy.

One needs to resist the "winning is the only thing" mentality. How you play the game really is the central issue; if you enjoy the game you are more likely to excel at it. In my experience internationally, this is a very American idea and I think it explains why we do so well in international competition, because, ironically, we think less about competing and more about the quality of the product or the service or the job itself. We don't want to be Number One so much as we want to do the job better than it has ever been done before, at least by us. My son's Little League coach understood this. He didn't scold the team for losing, but he didn't hand out "Good job" comments indiscriminately, either. When they played badly, even if they won, he'd say, "What happened? You guys did better than that in practice." And when they played well he was proud of them even if they lost. He got them to focus on their performance, not on the score. I think that's why his eight- and nine-year-olds managed to beat the ten- and eleven-year-olds at the end of the season: they were focusing on performance, and the score took care of itself.

I try to get my people to regard mistakes as problems to be solved rather than as things to be ashamed of. Feeling bad is useless. Asking, "Why did this happen? What can I change to avoid similar mistakes in future?" is useful. I don't want to see remorse, I want to see improvement. I've made my own share of mistakes, in part because I've been willing to take risks, to try something new. In many jobs that is the only way to improve, to make progress. But I focus on the improvement, not on the mistakes, and that makes what I do fun and satisfying. Sometimes I've found that an employee and I have different ideas about what constitutes good performance—different models or different objectives in mind. This is a recipe for real misunderstanding and dissatisfaction on both sides. I think a manager owes it to the employee to be straightforward and clear about what he is looking for, what she thinks is important. Beyond that basic task definition, though, the employee should be encouraged to do the work in a way that gives him or her real satisfaction. The motivation that flows from that intrinsic satisfaction is invaluable to all concerned.

## The Peter Principle

One fact about the real world of work that I have had a chance to observe directly is the sad truth described in a very funny book, *The Peter Principle*, some thirty years ago: "People tend to rise to the level of their incompetence."[6] Good university professors become department chairs or deans, good teachers become principals, good salesmen become sales managers, good researchers become heads of departments, good machinists become foremen, and so on and on. Sometimes it works out well, of course, and the impulse is perfectly natural.

> "Fisbee is retiring, as you know. Who shall we put in his place?"
> "Well, we need someone who knows the situation over there and the best [teacher, salesman, researcher, machinist] person in Fisbee's unit is Ignatz."
> "All right then, offer Ignatz the job."

Ms. Ignatz now is looking at a significant boost in salary, welcome recognition of her good work, and a *promotion*! It is hard to resist. Quite naturally, not having read this book, she assumes that more money and higher status will mean a permanent up-tick in her feelings of well-being. But she ought to understand that the only thing that would really make her happier in the long run would be a shift into a job that she can perform at least as well as she does the job she has now, *and* that she thinks is at least as important as the job she has now, *and* which pays more and includes a key to the executive washroom. The trouble is that very often these sorts of promotions provide only the latter perk and not the former ones, which are much more important in the long run. Even if Ms. Ignatz turns out to be a perfectly competent manager, that position may not be as challenging, as interesting, as the one she left. And all too often the best worker in the department turns out to be a washout as department head, not because he or she is lacking somehow in human value or quality but simply because the two positions require different talents. My English-teacher brother always knew enough to avoid this trap, although friends thought that a teacher as successful as he was ought to aspire to be principal. No one ever invited me to be the department chair or the dean of the college; either my friends were wiser than my brother's, or my limitations were more apparent. We were both wise (or lucky) to hew to what we enjoyed and were good at, rather than attempting to "rise" to the level of our incompetence. I hope this book helps at least one person to avoid the same mistake.

## Upstairs, Downstairs

Human status ought not to depend upon the changing demands of the economic process. . . .
—ARCHBISHOP WILLIAM TEMPLE

One of the most considerable advantages the great have over their inferiors is to have servants as good as themselves. . . .
—CERVANTES

Many readers will recognize in the heading of this section an excellent television series from the 1970s, presented in the United States on public television's *Masterpiece Theater*. The series portrayed the continuing adventures of the Bellamys, an upper-class, Edwardian, English family residing (upstairs) in a fine (but not *grand*) London house on Eaton Place, and of their modest staff of five or six servants who spent most of their time downstairs in the kitchen and servants' quarters (although the junior staff slept in small, cold rooms at the very top of the back stairs). Richard Bellamy, the master of the house, was a Member of Parliament and his wife, Lady Marjorie, was the eldest daughter of an earl whose estate was known as Southwold. Their two rather spoilt grown children, James and Elizabeth, both were handsome and feckless and would have profited from reading this book, or at least from finding useful work to do. The butler and pater familias downstairs was a dour Scot named Hudson, an upright, capable, and proud man, at least as good at his job as Mr. Bellamy was at his. The cook, Mrs. Bridges, ruled in the kitchen and could proudly say that many notables had admired her cooking, including once even His Majesty, Edward VII himself. Rose, the head parlormaid, also knew her job and took pride in it. Edward, the young footman, and Ruby, the simple scullery maid, rounded out the household.

One reason why *Upstairs, Downstairs* was so popular was that it conveyed a strong sense of verisimilitude. Even those of us who have never mingled with the upper crust or dwelt in a house with servants found it easy to believe that there were, in that time and place, houses like this with characters like these living lives very much like those portrayed. I have been reviewing the videos of a selection of these episodes (I would not otherwise have remembered all those names!) and what has impressed me most is that the general level of subjective well-being downstairs was at least equal to that of the Bellamys in the drawing room and salons up above.

In fact, I will go so far as to outline a plot for a new episode. The time is twenty-some years earlier, just after the birth of James Bellamy. Mr. Hudson and Mrs. Bridges have jointly produced a baby boy at the same time, and he and infant James look much alike. Somehow (I haven't worked out all these details yet), the opportunity arises for Hudson to exchange his own son for baby James with no one the wiser. The drama centers upon Hudson's dilemma: wanting only the best life for his own flesh and blood, should he let him grow up as James Bellamy or should he raise him belowstairs to aspire to a butler's station like his own when he grows up? In real life, of course, Hudson would suppose the upstairs position to be somehow superior to the one below, and only his Calvinist conscience might prevent him from making the switch. But what should he do if his sole consideration is his own son's future happiness? Were he to grow up like Richard Bellamy, with important responsibilities and the talents to discharge them competently, that would be a tempting prospect. But Hudson would know that many young gentlemen in James's set grow up as James did, as decorative drones without a real function, gentlemen playboys. The son that Hudson raised himself would be more likely to find a useful niche, to develop useful skills and well-founded self-respect. What would you do in Hudson's place?

The Bellamys would certainly have assumed themselves to be better off than their servants downstairs, as indeed they were, in wealth, possessions, and in social status. But we know now that their responses on the MPQ's Well Being scale would have shown that they were not, in fact, any happier. In this more egalitarian age, we think it sad that Hudson and Mrs. Bridges were foredoomed by their lower-class origins to aspire no higher than butler or cook, but why should that be sad if they were good at those jobs and happy in consequence? In personal terms, it seems to me more sad that the Bellamy children should have been foredoomed to become social parasites, vain and stylish, yet with no useful function through which to garner satisfaction and real self-respect. James might have made an excellent butler and Elizabeth a fine lady's maid, and both might have been happier in consequence.

This is not a defense of that master-servant caste system, now happily abandoned. It was too bad that people like Rose, Edward, Hudson, or Mrs. Bridges could not have aspired to Parliament or to professional careers, but not because this barrier prevented them from leading a happy and fulfilling life. It was too bad for the community in general to waste that much human potential. There are so many different jobs that need doing in our complex, interdependent society that it is in everyone's interest to make it possible for each individual to seek out and find that niche that suits him or her the best.

In the United States, the profession of baseball (in Europe, soccer) seems to me to provide an ideal prototype. Virtually every American boy has enough experience of playing baseball to learn whether he enjoys and has a knack for it. Those who do are likely to graduate from backyard and sandlot games to Little League; the best of the Little Leaguers play on their school teams; the best of those may later become minor league professionals; and the very best of all end up in the major leagues, the "bigs," whose rosters can truly be said to constitute the cream of the crop. Would it not be a fine thing if our political leaders were selected in a similar fashion? Yet no one I knew in high school aspired to a political career, and the only aspirant I knew in college was considered eccentric.

It is unfortunate that, even in the United States, enough remains enough of the *Upstairs, Downstairs* attitude that too many parents are determined that their children should head Upstairs even when it seems clear that this child would be happier Down. A distinguished Professor of Educational Psychology at my university, a pioneer in the measurement of high-level academic talent, had such a child, a boy whose only interest was in cars and engines. Many fathers in this man's position would have dragooned his son through college and into some white-collar job for which he was ill-suited and in which he was miserable. This father, happily, supported his son's decision to study automotive mechanics at a local technical school, and helped him to establish his own filling station and garage near the university campus. The young man (now retired) soon had a flourishing business as the word spread through the faculty about what good work he did. Mr. Bellamy was not as wise as this other father, but then Bellamy was not a psychologist.

# Flow

Happiness isn't something you experience;
Happiness is something you remember.
—OSCAR LEVANT

Psychologist Mihaly Csikszentmihalyi has spent years studying a phenomenon familiar to all of us, the experience he calls "flow."[7] To be in flow means to be absorbed in what you are presently doing, focused, unselfconscious, like a chess master planning his next move, a skier making a fast run down a challenging slope, a writer managing to find the right words—or lovers making love. It means doing something that you feel is important, worth doing, something that is challenging but for which you have the skills and energy to meet the challenge so that the process flows and the goal draws ever nearer. When a great athlete, like Michael Jordan or Tiger Woods, is having a good day, he is in flow. When a concert artist is fully absorbed in the music, his or her fingers finding the right notes without conscious attention, and when Luciano Pavarotti manages to sing the tenor aria the way he hears it in his head, they are in flow. And what is interesting is that none of these people tend to be smiling at the time.

Sky divers do not tend to grin while standing in the plane's open doorway at five thousand feet. Tower hands, those "adrenaline junkies" who erect two-thousand-foot radio or TV broadcast towers, tend to look rather grim while bolting each new section into place, and they swear a lot. But they also tend to feel that "Every day's a good day. A good day to be alive."[8]

We saw in chapter 3 that Archimedes would "forget his food and neglect his person" while absorbed in calculation, and that Isaac Newton often became so caught up in cerebration that he would forget to eat or sleep. Edwin Land, inventor of the instant Polaroid camera and of a sophisticated computational theory of color vision, sometimes worked at his desk for thirty-six hours or more, unaware of the passage of time until he felt faint upon standing up. Similar stories were told of Thomas Edison. But when we imagine any of these geniuses, absorbed in the flow of their thought, we do not picture them as joyful or exhibiting any of the usual symptoms of happiness. Indeed, if we were to interrupt the performer, the lover, the athlete, and the thinker in the midst of their flow and ask them to rate themselves as to how happy they feel at the moment, they would likely be enraged, while we, on our backs, noses bloodied, would not feel very happy either. But if we wait considerately until the game, the match, or the concert is over, until the problem has been solved, then we are likely to get a much happier response.

We ordinary folks are in flow whenever we are truly absorbed in an activity—driving in traffic, playing tennis, dealing with a customer, repairing something broken, giving a lecture—that commands our full attention and that challenges our abilities. Even very ordinary, simple tasks can keep us in flow at least long enough to finish them.

I have been arguing that constructive activity and the exercise of skills comprise the principal and most dependable sources of human happiness. Because we are the most productive, our skills manifesting themselves most fluidly, when we are in flow, then it would seem to follow that the experience of flow should be an ideal generator of feelings of well-being. According to Csikszentmihalyi, however,

> It is the full involvement of flow, rather than happiness, that makes for excellence in life. When we are in flow, we are not happy, because to experience happiness we must focus on our inner states, and that would take away attention from the task at hand. If a rock climber takes time out to feel happy while negotiating a difficult move, he might fall to the bottom of the mountain. The surgeon can't afford to feel happy during a demanding operation, or a musician while playing a challenging score. Only after the task is completed do we have the leisure to look back on what has happened, and then we are flooded with gratitude for the excellence of that experience—then, in retrospect, we are happy.[9]

My only problem in accepting this perceptive analysis is with Csikszentmihalyi's implicit definition of happiness. Because persons in flow do not smile, are not aware at the time of how they feel, and would be unlikely to report "I feel happy!" if we were to interrupt their flow to ask for their introspections, Csikszentmihalyi concludes they are not happy. This is the reasonable "If it doesn't walk or talk like a duck, it ain't a duck" form of inference, but I think it is wrong in this case. Anyone who has seen a Border collie herding sheep, his attention absolutely focused, believes that animal is happy in his work, even though his tail may not be wagging. The essential thing about flow is that it is an experience that we avidly seek and, once in flow, we stay there as long as the task or our energies last. If Nature controls our behavior with the stick of pain and the carrot of pleasure, if we seek to avoid pain and obtain pleasure, then surely that hardworking Border collie—crouched, quivering with excitement, ready to leap into action at her master's call—is a happy dog? And so, I believe, we should conclude that Pavarotti and Itzhak Perlman are happy during the performance, even though the smiles come later in response to the applause.

Now, of course, the mere fact that we deliberately undertook some experience, like going to the dentist, does not mean that the experience itself is something we enjoy. Many performers feel quite miserable while waiting to go on. Sir Laurence Olivier is said to have had periods of almost paralyzing stage fright. When that fear, self-consciousness, and self-doubt persist after the curtain rises, the performer never achieves flow and the only reinforcement comes when the ordeal is over. But I believe that even a boxer, like Muhammad Ali—facing an elemental struggle with even his life on the line—will be able to say, "I felt good out there!" once the bell rings, and his focus of attention narrows to the task at hand, and the muscles and the reflexes ripple and flow.

# PART THREE

<sub>⁕</sub>

# HAPPY FAMILIES

Put all your eggs in one basket and—*watch that basket.*
— MARK TWAIN

One of the more startling findings of behavior-genetic research has been that raising children together in the same family does not tend to make them more alike as adults, either in their IQs or in their personalities. This has been taken to mean that parents, as long as they are not abusive, corrupt, or crazy, are essentially interchangeable. The only special part your parents played in making you what you are today was completed at the moment of your conception. Had you been adopted at birth by the parents of any of your friends, the chances are that you would have developed very much as, in fact, you did. Therefore, if you have been in the habit of blaming certain of your problems or faults on the way you were brought up, you ought to reconsider. Moreover, if you have been possessed by doubt or guilt about your own failures or inadequacies as a parent, put your mind at rest. The way your children will turn out (or have already turned out) will depend on the interaction of two sets of causal factors, and you aren't one of them. The first set of influences is their genetic makeup (you did play a role in that, of course, but your part was just an early walk-on, and it's over). The second set of influences that makes a difference in how children develop is their peer group, their schools, and other experiences outside of the home. Two eminent psychologists, Hans Eysenck (about forty years ago) and Thomas Bouchard (only yesterday) have told me that this is exactly what they think, and most behavior geneticists agree with them.

By far the strongest case for this provocative hypothesis was made by Judith Rich Harris in her *The Nurture Assumption\**, a fascinating work that I have been privileged to read in manuscript. In this scholarly, funny, and important book, Harris manages to relegate to the myths of folk psychology most of what developmental psychologists believe about the importance of parenting. Harris's arguments have compelled me to conclude that, apart from their genetic contributions, most parents (she would say *all* parents) have a negligible lasting effect on their children's adult personality and behavior patterns. Nevertheless, I will try to show in the next three chapters that parents *can* make a real difference, that skillful parents (with a little luck; luck always plays a role in human affairs) have happier children than less skillful parents.

---

*J. R. Harris, *The Nuture Assumption*. (New York: The Free Press, 1998.)

# 6

# HAPPY PARENTS

Wait. Are they going to let me just walk off with him? I
don't know beans about babies! I don't have a license to
do this. . . . I mean you're given all these lessons for the
unimportant things—piano-playing, typing. You're given
years and years of lessons in how to balance equations,
which Lord knows you will never have to do in normal life.
But what about parenthood? . . . Before you can drive a car
you need a state-approved course of instruction, but
driving a car is nothing, nothing, compared to . . . raising
up a new human being.

—ANNE TYLER, *Breathing Lessons*

The fact that identical twins reared apart by different families, even in different countries, are found to be so similar
as adults—as similar in most respects as identical twins
reared together—is part of the evidence for the claim that parents are *fungible*.* Another kind of evidence comes from pairs of
unrelated children adopted and reared by the same parents. Most
studies of these pairs have been limited to measures of IQ, and
they indicate that such unrelated pairs are no more alike in IQ
as adults than are random pairs of strangers. A third kind of
evidence involves studies of twins reared together. If differences
in parenting were important, then fraternal twins, who share half
their polymorphic genes on average, should be more than half as
similar as identical twins are;[1] this is true, for example, for birth
weight. The correlation in birth weight for some 600 MZ twin
pairs in our Registry is .71, while the value for 450 pairs of DZ

---

*"*Fungible*. Of such kind or nature that one specimen . . . may be used in place of
another in satisfaction of an obligation." (Random House Dictionary of the English Language, Second Edition, Unabridged.)

twins is .69. Body size later on will depend strongly on genetic factors, so that the DZ correlation for height, for example, will be about half of the MZ correlation. But birth weight depends most on gestational age at birth, and both MZ and DZ twins, because they share that same first home in the mother's womb, tend to be born at the same time.

This is true also for educational attainment. Parents with the resources and the desire to have their children go to college are likely to send both sons or both daughters, even though only one or neither of them is strongly motivated by talent or interest. The MZ correlation for years of education is .70, while for same-sex DZ twins the correlation is .50, more than half the MZ value, thus indicating the influence of having the same parents. (The correlation for 380 pairs of opposite-sex DZ twins is .42, probably because parents are less likely to set the same educational objectives for twins who differ in gender.)

This effect of shared rearing environment is also seen on certain adult interests. For male twins in our Registry, for example, the DZ pairs are two-thirds (rather than one-half) as similar as the MZ pairs in their interests in church work, in hunting or fishing, and in farming or ranching. The women show more family influence on their interests in gambling or in careers as scientists; the female DZ pairs were more than 80 percent as similar as the MZs in respect to these interests. But, for most psychological traits, the DZ correlations are half or less than half the MZ values. And for happiness, in particular, we have already seen that fraternal twins are hardly similar at all as adults, while MZ twins are very similar indeed.

Thus, none of my scholarly colleagues would be shocked if I concluded here that we have nothing useful to say about rearing happy children, no good advice for parents on how to maximize their offsprings' chances of realizing or even exceeding their genetically determined happiness potentials. But I should hate to pass up an opportunity to shock my colleagues, and I do, in fact, believe that there are some useful things to say in this connection. First of all, I think there is no doubt at all that many parents would be happier themselves if they were more skilled in matters of discipline, just as I feel certain that dog owners are happier if they have taken their pet through a course of obedience training—where the first thing explained is that it is the owner rather than the dog that is the target of the training. And I believe that the dogs whose masters know how to get them to sit, stay, and down are happier in consequence themselves.

In a book about antisocial personalities,* I wrote about Susie, a middle-aged bull terrier (BT) female, whose middle-aged permissive owner brought her to a gathering of owners and dogs who were meeting for a kind of BT beauty contest. Susie was uncontrollable, barking and lunging on the end of her chain—Susie bit through ropes or leashes in a hurry—while her poor owner strove to hang on and maintain her balance. In the end, she had to lock up Susie in the car and wistfully depart because there was no way that Susie could be taken into the show ring with the other dogs. Canines and, I believe, all social animals, including *Homo sapiens*, tend to form dominance hierarchies. Every dog trainer knows that it is essential to establish and maintain an ascendant position; either the human or the dog will be dominant, and it is in both their interests for the human to assume that role. Susie's owner failed that test and they both suffered for it. About 25 percent of human children have the potential to develop oppositional-defiant disorder or, worse, conduct disorder during childhood, and this is the group from whom the adolescent delinquents and the adult criminals (i.e., the antisocial personalities) are recruited. If your child is counted among either of these candidate groupings, you will not be a happy parent, and yours will not be a happy family.

But I think that parents who *enjoy* their children, who like doing things with them, who like having them around, meeting their friends, and taking them along on trips, are happier themselves, have happier households, and have happier children. Not only does this seem eminently plausible, but I even have some data to support it.

*D. T. Lykken, *The Antisocial Personalities*. (Mahwah, N.J.: Lawrence Erlbaum Associates, 1995.)

Remember that happiness is a lake with waves, and if you are measured high on a wave while your twin is measured deep in a trough (a "slough of Despond"), then your scores will be more dissimilar than you two really are. When we measured happiness levels on twins some nine years after they were first measured, the 131 pairs of MZ cotwins correlated with each other over this long interval about as strongly (R = .54) as they correlated with themselves over that period. The DZ pairs, however, were not very similar in Well Being score, not over nine years (R = .05) and not even when measured on the same occasion (R = .08; see table 2.4). This is why we say that the happiness set point is an "emergenic" trait, strongly genetic but running in families only very weakly.

We have also measured well-being or happiness on a large sample of seventeen-year-old twins and their parents as part of our Minnesota Twin/Family Study. Those results, given in table 6.1, indicate that adolescent fraternal twins who are still living at home *are* nearly half as similar as their MZ counterparts. The data also show that the parents of these twins are about as similar in happiness, spouse to spouse, as the DZ twins are to each other, and that the happiness scores are modestly correlated between parents and offspring (the "midparent-midtwin" correlation). We need to collect more data to be sure how to interpret all this, but here is what I think it means:

| | Number of Pairs | Correlation |
|---|---|---|
| Seventeen year-old-twins | | |
| Monozygotic | 349 | .47 |
| Dizygotic | 192 | .22 |
| Family correlations | | |
| Midparent : midtwin | 447 | .20 |
| Spousal pairs | 447 | .18 |

TABLE 6.1

Within-pair correlations of MPQ-WB from the Twin/Family Study.

When these adolescent twins are ten or twenty years older, most of them married and long out of the parental home, I believe that their similarity in happiness will be as predicted from our large samples of middle-aged Registry twins. The MZ pairs will still be quite similar, and the DZ pairs will be hardly more alike than random pairs. Currently, however, because they are living together in the same family milieu, the DZ twins now in happy families both feel a bit happier with their lot than DZ pairs living in fractious or unhappy families. There is really nothing wildly speculative about this: some households *are* happier—less stressful, more interesting, more loving and supportive—than others, and each of their current residents is likely to feel better on average than he/she would feel if the family atmosphere were gloomy or argumentative or mutually estranged. But when those children move away and form their own households, the atmosphere will be determined more by their own genetic makeup than by that of their parents. And it is important to remember that these correlations were based on single measurements of subjective well-being. If we could have measured the *average* happiness levels of the members of these families of adolescent twins, then all the correlations would have been considerably larger than those shown in table 6.1.

This means, I think, that your children will be happier, at least while they're at home, if their parents are happier, and any parent knows that parental happiness is much affected by the behavior of their children. If they are like Susie, out of control, sullen, argumentative, and disobedient, then family tranquillity and parental peace of mind goes out the window. Some parents, like some schoolteachers, have an innate gift for discipline. I can still name teachers I had more than fifty years ago that possessed this gift, and others that did not. The good ones were not domineering or punitive, yet they could quiet a disturbance with just a reproving glance. My brother Georg was such a teacher, and I have had many university students volunteer that "I had your brother for English in junior high, and he was the best teacher I ever had!" His classes were fun because the students respected him and, since discipline was not in doubt, everyone could relax and enjoy talking about the reading assignment.

Parents who have this knack must be happier and have hap-

pier homes than those who don't. But many parents whose instinct for discipline is defective could repair that deficiency with
training and practice. If I were in charge, young couples could
not get a license to have children unless *either* (1) they had completed a course in parenting at a local community college *or* (2)
they had each successfully taken a puppy (preferably some sort
of terrier) through obedience training. In my experience, the gift
for working easily with children seems to be an innate special
talent, rather like having perfect pitch, and largely unrelated to
how good or smart or well-educated you may be. There is no
shame involved in not having the gift but, if you plan to be a
teacher or a parent, then both for the children's sake and for
your own, you should accept the responsibility of acquiring the
ability to be *authoritative* (not *authoritarian*) so as to command
the children's respect. We shall discuss this further in chapter 8,
"Happy Children."

## Working Mothers

Did you know that the Hallmark Company has introduced a new
line of greeting cards "for parents that are too busy to see their
children," cards that say things like "Sorry I can't be there to tuck
you in"? I first heard about this depressing development from a
recent book by sociologist Arlie Russell Hochschild, *The Time
Bind: When Work Becomes Home.*[2] Researching the modern family
in which both parents tend to be employed, Hochschild finds
that the reasons are not exclusively economic necessity. More
and more modern-day parents, both fathers and mothers, are
finding that they are happier, less stressed, more fulfilled, and
more satisfied at work than they are at home. Yet evolutionary
psychology (not to mention sheer common sense) tells us that
our species is adapted to a child-rearing environment in which
an extended family—grandparents, uncles, aunts, older cousins,
always on hand, always helpful—participated in guiding and socializing youngsters. Children need *more* parent figures, not
Hallmark cards and an empty house. We cannot reasonably re-
vert to the extended-family system of ancestral times, and at least

one parent, in most cases, has to go out each day to earn the money for the rent and the hamburgers. But parenting is *the* most important and most difficult job most of us will ever undertake. At least one parent needs to be there when the kids are home, and that parent needs to know that the spouse will be there at least on evenings and weekends, to provide the full-time parent some relief and free time and also to talk things over with, to help resolve problems.

It is a long-standing tradition in all cultures that have abandoned the extended-family system that it should be the father who ventures forth to earn the bread while the mother stays home with the children. I think we should be flexible about this tradition; most of us can think of couples in which it is the dad who nurtures best and the mom who has the most earning potential. As a general rule, however, in most happy families it will be the mother who becomes the full-time parent and the father who is the breadwinner and the substitute and supporter and consultant. But many modern women find this tradition to be deeply offensive and unfair. Why should it be always the man who gets to show what he can make of himself? Why must it be the woman who is saddled with the tiresome, low-status responsibilities of homemaker and resident parent?

I offer my own family as a counterexample. My wife, Harriet, went to college, then worked as a social worker for eight years before our first child was born. That opportunity to prove herself in the world of work was assuredly important. When Jesse and then Joseph and Matthew came along, she accepted full-time motherhood as a new and even more challenging job at which she expected to do as well as she had always done in her previous undertakings. I don't think it ever occurred to Harriet that what I was doing at the university was somehow more important than what she was doing at home, and of course she was entirely right. It turned out that, by good luck, she had a gift for parenting but, had there been problems, I am sure she would have done the same thing she did when she wanted to learn how to deal with the plumbing: she would have taken a course. When the boys were all in school, the Vietnam war was in progress, and

Harriet became active in antiwar politics. After she ended the war, she became an environmental activist and a lobbyist on wildlife issues. It is hard to imagine a more useful and fulfilling career for any person, and her years as a full-time mother may have been her most significant accomplishment. I know it was the happiest time of her life. I wish more of this generation's mothers could see the issues and the values as clearly as Harriet did.

But what about all those data showing that being reared by the same parents in the same household does not make pairs of children more alike (except, perhaps, in their religious beliefs, their years of education, and their interests in gambling or blood sports)? Does this not prove that parents have little lasting effect on their offspring other than their initial genetic contribution? In an important and fascinating new book, *The Nurture Assumption*, Judith Harris argues that the nurture component of the nature-nurture construction process consists primarily of influences experienced by children outside of their homes, in their neighborhoods, and with their peers. Young children, she points out, are inclined to be drawn to and to interact with other young children, rather than adults. Young children, along with their age peers, tend to emulate older children and so on upward toward the ultimate role models, the adults of the community. The children of immigrant parents, Harris reminds us, may speak Polish or Vietnamese at home, but they rapidly learn their neighborhood's version of English outside the home, and the neighborhood's standards and values as well. Harris emphasizes children's capacity for context-dependent learning, for being able to adopt one set of behavior precepts in the home environment, but quite a different set in the broader community environment. And it is the latter set of values and behavior tendencies, rather than the ones modeled and shaped within the narrow confines of the home environment, that gradually evolves into that child's adult personality and behavior patterns.

In ancestral times, when all these behavior dispositions were laid down by natural selection, it truly did take an entire village to raise a child. That is to say, the children of those extended-family groups of hunter-gatherers learned to behave, not like their parents, but like the other children of their age and gender, while all the children looked to the example of the older children who, in their turn, emulated the community adults. The biological parents took primary responsibility for the feeding, care, and shelter of their offspring, but the socialization of those children was a community function.

So is it in modern times, Harris insists. Most parents provide the basic nurturing that is necessary for their child's survival, but beyond that, the only contribution that the biological parents make to their offspring's individuality is completed at the great genetic lottery that takes place at conception. Notice that Harris is not saying that parents do not influence their children's behavior. We all know that cannot be true, although our conviction may be stronger when we remember our own parents' influence on us than when we contemplate our influence on our own offspring. Harris's claim is that parents have little differential effect on how children "behave the way they do in the world outside the home—the world where they will spend the rest of their lives."

I think Harris makes a very powerful case, one that cannot be refuted on the basis of evidence collected so far. Yet I do not believe that all parents are fungible in respect to the socialization and adult adjustment of their offspring. I believe that some parents play an important role in either maximizing their children's good qualities and chances for success, or in helping their disadvantaged children to overcome those disadvantages. And I believe that some parents are truly bad—incompetent, uncaring, or downright malignant—so those children in their feckless care are at great risk to become unsocialized adults. In particular, I believe that good parents do not *try* to make their children more alike, to fit them all into some common mold. Apart from those six kids in every one thousand who are MZ twins, every child is unique, a different package of strengths and weaknesses, a unique mix of talents and potential problems. A sensible gardener does not try to make her tomatoes resemble her carrots or to turn her rutabagas into raspberries.

Psychologists are not necessarily good at parenthood, but if they are any good as psychologists, they should at least be good observers and able to appreciate the way in which those who have an innate gift for this endeavor—people like my wife, Harriet—go about it. Harriet raised three well-adjusted sons who were happy children and are now successful family men raising children of their own. We always took them with us on our travels, all around the United States, to Europe, even to exotic places like Western Samoa and East Africa, and I know they were happy because we enjoyed our travels more for having them along. Our first long trip was by car to California when they were aged four, two, and six weeks. Our old car broke down in Last Chance, Nevada, on the edge of the Mojave Desert, and we had to put up in a ratty old motel while I fixed it, but somehow that only added to the fun. If every family's kids were as happy as ours were growing up, the world would be a better place. In the next two chapters, I propose to tell you how we (Harriet) did it.

# 7

# HAPPY BABIES

We haven't all had the good fortune to be ladies . . . (or)
generals, or poets, or statesmen; but when the toast works
down to the babies, we stand on common ground.
—MARK TWAIN

A baby is an inestimable blessing and bother.
MARK TWAIN


Parenting, this most important and difficult responsibility
most humans ever assume, Harriet and I undertook for the
first time (and inadvertently) in 1955. What's more, we
began this project far from home and families, in what was to us
a foreign country where I had a fellowship to spend a year at the
University of London. The English obstetrician Grantly Dick-
Read had rediscovered natural childbirth not long before and
was then practicing at University College Hospital, a Victorian
pile in central London.[1] Harriet, who has always had a deep suspicion of modern medicine, liked Dick-Read's ideas, so I called
the hospital soon after we arrived.

"I'm afraid we're always booked up nine months in advance,"
was the response when I reported that Harriet was five months
along in her pregnancy.

"But, you see, we just arrived from the United States."

"Well, then, you couldn't have booked earlier, could you?"
came the astonishing reply. Here we were, foreigners, asking to
have our baby at public expense on the then-new National

129

Health Service, at what many thought to be the finest obstetrical hospital in the world, where openings were so much in demand that they took only first births on the principle that, after you learned how to have a baby properly with them, you could have subsequent babies anywhere. And this paragon of a kindly bureaucrat bent the rules to make an exception for us—amazing!

The hospital provided superb antenatal care and training. The entire staff participated in convincing all the new mothers-to-be that "this will be the happiest experience of your lives and you will want to be wide awake so that you can treasure it all!" In the first lecture for prospective parents, the midwife explained, "Baby is the most sensible little chap in the world and he knows just how to be born. Right now he's curled up like a little kitten, taking up as little room as possible." There were no private rooms-with-bath in University College Hospital but, rather, twelve-bed wards with real central heating—that is to say, there was a coal-burning fireplace situated in the center of each ward. With the other new mothers, Harriet remained in hospital for ten days (unlike our HMOs, the National Health Service was not devoted to shareholder profits), resting and learning how to breast-feed and care for her new baby boy. It was indeed an experience full of wonders and she came home rested and well-acquainted with little Jesse and his needs.

Jesse's bed, called a "carry cot," sat upon a rather rickety stand that was easy to agitate back and forth with one's hand, and we quickly found that such movement was soothing, that it prevented the usual twitches and dysrhythmic breathing that Jesse showed when first put down to sleep. The cot had cloth handles on each side that could be gripped in one hand and the whole cot swung, as on a pendulum, in a head-to-toe motion. This more vigorous stimulus feeding was effective on those occasions when mere jiggling of the cot stand proved inadequate. The head-to-toe motion prevented Jesse from rolling from side to side and it never failed to lull him into sleep, however fretful he might have been to start with.

We did quite a bit of traveling the next few months, visiting points of interest in England and Scotland and staying nights in

**FIGURE 7.1**

Jesse in his carry cot.

local inns. I have at least one vivid memory of swinging Jesse vigorously up and back on the landing outside our small room in one such inn, as several parties of bemused but polite British guests made their way down to dinner, trying not to notice the outlandish American. It was thus that, like Dr. Dick-Read rediscovering natural childbirth, I rediscovered baby rockers.

## Baby Rocking

> Is rocking necessary? By no means. It is a habit easily acquired but hard to break, and a very useless and sometimes injurious one.
>
> —L. EMMETT HOLT, M.D.

Dr. L. Emmett Holt was the Dr. Spock of the first part of this century. His little book, *For Mothers and Nurses*, revolutionized

infant and child care in the United States. It was Dr. Holt who
put American infants on schedule:

*"It is rarely advisable to feed any infant, except one seriously ill,
oftener than the time put down in the schedule."*

When should regular training be begun?

*"During the first week of life."*

To reluctant mothers whose babies seemed unhappy under
Dr. Holt's strict regime, he explained, *". . . Crying is normal for a
very young child. What is the nature of this cry? It is loud and
strong. Infants get red in the face with it; in fact, it is a scream. This
is necessary for health. It is the baby's exercise."*

Dr. Holt was ruthless in his determination that American
children should not be "spoiled." Not only must baby sleep, feed,
and bathe on a strict schedule, and be left to "cry it out" when
his schedule conflicts with Dr. Holt's, but neither should the
mother try to make it up to baby by expressions of affection. To
the rhetorical question, "Are there any valid objections to the
kissing of infants?," Dr. Holt gives this firm reply: *"There are
many serious objections. . . . Infants should be kissed, if at all, upon
the cheek or forehead, but the less often the better."*

In the fourteenth and last edition, published in 1929, he extended these restrictions to youngsters of eight or ten: *"Expressions of affection should be limited to a pat on the head at bedtime
and a firm handshake in the morning."*

The extent of Dr. Holt's influence on American mothers was
dramatically evidenced by the disappearance, almost within a
single generation, of the rocking cradle from American homes.
Before World War I, rocking cradles or rocking chairs or both
were essential items of furniture in homes where an infant was
in residence. In larger families, rocking the baby was one of the
more pleasant chores commonly assigned to the older children.
American inventors busily applied themselves to the design of
improved, labor-saving cradles. A search of U.S. Patent Office
records reveals a stream of proposals for automatic rocking cradles, a stream that dried up suddenly in the early 1930s. There
were spring motors and escapement devices with weights like a
grandfather's clock. One patented baby rocker *was* a clock; the

idea was to swing the baby's bed like a pendulum and, since the weights and escapement were already in place, this inventor threw in a two-sided clock at the top of his six-foot contraption. Although rocking baby "is a habit easily acquired, but hard to break," Dr. Holt managed to put a stop to it in middle-class America within a decade or two by telling mothers that this "habit is a very useless and sometimes injurious one." Americans find it hard to resist supposed experts who speak emphatically and with great certainty, even when they're talking nonsense.

Anthropologist friends tell me that all traditional cultures whose child-rearing practices are known provide their infants with some form of motion stimulation for extended periods each day. Babies are carried on the mother's back or chest or hip as she goes about her daily activities. Or the baby's hammock is suspended from a nearby sapling and swings in the breeze ("Rockabye baby, in the tree top, when the wind blows, the cradle will rock"). Or the baby lies on an animal skin in the center of the family group and is intermittently played with by older siblings or cousins or aunts, held or dandled whenever it fusses. Among traditional Ashkenazim, the infant "is placed in its swinging crib near mother's bed. She may hold a string attached to the baby's cradle which she rocks incessantly, even in her sleep."[2] Unlike our primate cousins, the gorilla and the chimpanzee, whose infants are never left "to cry it out," we humans are capable of developing perverse and unhealthy practices, often as the brainstorm of some self-important shaman like L. Emmett Holt, M.D. But practices that are common across cultures—from the Australian Aborigines to the Maoris of New Zealand to the many native peoples of North and South America and to those of Africa—are likely to represent a kind of evolutionary wisdom that we would be foolish to ignore. "Is rocking necessary?" Perhaps Dr. Holt's answer should not be taken as the final word on this subject.

The infant nervous system, although it is responsible for all the vegetative functions essential to life, from breathing to digestion, is incomplete at birth. The nerve fibers of an adult are sheathed with myelin, an insulating coating that, in effect, prevents short-circuiting of the nerve impulses. Myelinization is incomplete during the first few months of infant life. Erratic nerve functioning, interruptions, and dyssynergies can disturb or prevent sleep, cause gastric upset and other discomfort, and can even interrupt breathing. Such glitches in the smooth rhythmic functioning of the infant nervous system are probably responsible for some instances of sudden infant death syndrome (SIDS).

When the heartbeat or breathing stops, normal function can sometimes be restarted by external stimulation. Even the adult nervous system often seems to benefit from external "stimulus feeding," especially in the form of rhythmic stimulation, most especially rhythmic *motion*. Anyone who has slept soundly on a train or ship appreciates this truth. Every parent knows that baby is likely to sleep happily in the baby carriage or the car seat, lulled by the motion of travel. The fetus experiences similar rhythmic stimulation as its mother walks and breaths. Perhaps stimulus feeding, especially the stimuli that are imparted by passive movements of the body, is a natural anodyne for infant distress. Providing stimulus feeding for babies seems to be a universal practice that may have evolved to compensate for the delayed maturation of the infant human nervous system. Motor development is so much faster in the other primates that "monkey cradles" are not necessary; infant apes and monkeys cling to mother's fur and share her motion almost from the moment of birth.

Watching little Jesse at two months, all fed and dry and tucked on his tummy in his carry cot, one could actually observe the periodic misfires of his nervous machinery; he would twitch, sometimes actually "jump" as if startled. After a period of regular breathing, the next inspiration would sometimes be delayed and then come with a gasp and his eyes would open in alarm. More often than not, although he was obviously sleepy when first put down, there would be a crescendo of twitches and starts leading to a period of active crying. On the one occasion when we left him for three hours with a reluctant baby-sitter, we came home to find him exhausted, sobbing uncontrollably, and damp with perspiration. The inept woman had left him in his stationary bed to "cry it out."

Our second son, Joseph, exhibited classic infant colic during his first few months. His face grew red and his little legs strained up against his hot, hard abdomen while he screamed bloody murder, usually between 2:00 and 5:00 A.M.—and Joey had the loudest voice I've ever heard in a child. Fortunately, by then, I had asked a local sheet metal shop to build me a sturdy rocker consisting of a frame bent out of pipe with a metal pan suspended at the corners by four arms some twenty inches long with bearings at both ends. The baby's cot fit snugly on the pan, which could then be swung back and forth by hand in a head-to-toe movement, the vigor of the swings being determined by the degree of Joey's obvious distress.

It was like a miracle! By the second or third surging swing, the screaming would stop, the little eyes would open as if in wonder, and the legs and body would gradually relax. In a minute or two, Joey would be stretched out prone again, the eyelids would flutter and close, and the swinging could be tapered off to a stop. It never failed!

Dr. Holt's babies had colic, too, of course. Here is the advice he offered mothers in the 1920s: *"First, see that the feet are warm. Place them against a hot-water bag. If the colic continues, a half cupful of warm water containing ten drops of turpentine may be injected into the bowels with a syringe."*

My rocking cradle never failed with Matthew, our third son, either, nor with the children of our friends to whom we lent the cradle when Matt no longer needed it. When Matt fathered our first two grandchildren, our original cradle had long since disappeared, so I sent him a commercial rocking cradle powered by a spring motor; it had the correct head-to-toe motion but, alas, it didn't work. The motion was too gentle, and the child was held in a kind of car seat rather than prone in a sleeping position.

For our third grandchild, Jesse's son, Zeke, I had a new cradle made on the original design. There is no motor to drive it. Instead it is easily actuated by hand, with strong, surging swings if little Zeke seemed really fussy and uncomfortable, or gentle

**FIGURE 7.2**

The Lykken nonpatented, never-fail baby rocker.

swings if sleep is near. When he was about one month old, Zeke would wake up every couple of hours through the night like most babies, demanding to be fed. With the cradle conveniently next to the parents' bed (on Dad's side, to share the work), ten minutes of rocking every other time Zeke wakened would help him slide into his next natural two-hour sleep cycle so that Mom could have four hours of uninterrupted rest. If baby is wet or in some real distress that needs his mother's attention—or if it is truly his time to be awake and active—then the rocker will not send him to sleep. It is not a narcotic, but a safe and natural adjuvant, promoting peaceful sleep when sleep is called for.

We made another discovery when Zeke came to spend a night with his grandparents. The wicker bassinet that had been Harriet's baby bed was dusted off and brought down from the attic. This elderly implement rode on four wheels, about ten inches in diameter with hard rubber tires. After Zeke was put down on his stomach for sleep, we could roll his bed forth and back on the hardwood floor, getting the same basic motion as his rocking cradle and with the same effect. It is not quite as easy as swinging the cradle and rather noisier but vastly better (and quieter) than having a fretful, unhappy baby. A child's wagon, with reasonably high sides and equipped with an infant's mattress pad, should work as well as our wheeled bassinet and almost as well as the cradle. And both methods can be used, almost effortlessly, from one's chair while reading or watching television. To really enjoy holding, feeding, and playing with a baby, there is nothing that helps half so much as those hours in between when baby is quietly sleeping.

I have never done a controlled, scientific experiment on the benefits of baby rockers, but there are some truths that do not require such experiments in order to be manifest. As Mark Twain remarked, "How many times do you have to see a two-headed calf before you believe it?" L. Emmett Holt never did a controlled scientific experiment in his life, and we do not require additional research to see that he was wrong. Rocking is necessary, for most babies some of the time and for some babies much of the time.

Controlled experiments could and should be done, to determine whether (as I believe) newborns gain weight faster, cry less, and experience fewer gastric problems when given regular stimulus feeding in a rocking cradle (little Zeke weighed twenty-three pounds at three months and had dimples in his dimples). I hope some enterprising baby-furniture maker will get such a device on the market, simple and sturdy, no motors or monkey business. And I especially hope that pediatricians will come to

realize what our ancestral mothers all understood, that babies
need motion, rhythmic stimulation to keep their nervous machinery in good working order.

One would hope to see such cradles be provided for those
infants thought to be at risk for sudden infant death syndrome.
Most important of all, when we see those all-to-frequent news
reports of infants battered, even killed, by parents driven to dis-
traction by the baby's constant crying, Harriet and I are convinced that many of these tragedies might be avoided if those
parents (or that single mother, already stressed near the breaking
point by the conditions of her life) had possessed an effective
rocking cradle.

## Happy Mothers

Children are what their mothers are. No fondest father's
fondest care can fashion so the infant heart.
—Walter Savage Landor

"Ye know a lot about raising children," said Mr. Hennessy.
"I do," said Mr. Dooley. "Not bein' an author, I'm a gr-reat
critic."
—Finley Peter Dunne

Because Harriet had been a social worker for several years before
we went to England, when she settled down to being a full-time
mom she was secure in the knowledge that she had already
proved her competence as a professional person who earned her
own living. Moreover, she understood intuitively a fairly obvious
fact that many modern women seem to have difficulty grasping.
If parenting is more challenging and also more important than $X$
(where $X$ equals almost any job you care to name), then surely
if you do it well, parenting should be a rich source of fulfillment
and satisfaction.

Baby rockers are all very well for getting the little ones off
to sleep but, when they are awake, babies need stimulation and
maternal contact. Every psychology student has read about those
baby monkeys at the University of Wisconsin whom Harry Har-
low kidnapped from their mothers and reared with two surrogate

"mothers," one made of wire cloth but with a nipple that worked, the other made of soft toweling that was cuddly but provided no nutrition. Those babies spent most of their time with the cuddly surrogates rather than with the wire-cloth mothers that were their source of nourishment, and they ran to their cuddly mothers when they were frightened. In hunter-gatherer societies such as the !Kung, whose infant-rearing practices are probably closer to those to which our species became adapted during evolution, infants are in constant physical contact with their mothers or with a substitute mother most of the day and night. Infants treated this way do not become "spoiled" as Dr. Holt would have expected. On the contrary, they seem more secure and less dependent upon security blankets or the !Kung equivalent of teddy bears.

Moreover, it is important to appreciate the rich sensory and perceptual stimulation that is provided to these much-handled, socially included, hunter-gatherer infants. During those early months, a remarkable amount of perceptual learning is intended to take place. White rats that are housed alone after weaning in bare single cages have brains that are lighter, with fewer cells and many fewer interconnections between their brain cells, than rats housed together in an enriched environment. Little Genie, the thirteen-year-old girl whose parents raised her in isolation, tied to a potty-chair, remained severely retarded in spite of intensive efforts at compensatory training. We cannot be certain that Genie's brain was normal at birth, but it is probable that the development of even Mozart's or Newton's brain would have been aborted by such lack of early stimulation. One reads of ill-equipped, understaffed orphanages in Eastern Europe in which babies are dying of protein-energy malnutrition and neglect, left so long in their cribs, deprived of human handling and contact, that their little nervous systems just shut down.

Harriet nursed her babies, a happy time for both mother and child, and she let each baby decide when he was ready to be weaned to the bottle—twelve months for Jesse, eleven for Joe, but three years for Matthew, who was so attached to his bottles that he didn't give them up until after a thoughtful discussion with his mother of the pros and cons. She also talked to her babies and frequently talked *for* them, explaining to an older child or to me what the baby thought about this or that event. This inclination to talk for animals and babies became habitual in our house. We tended to impute distinctive personalities and often strong opinions to the critters we were speaking for, and I recommend the practice, foolish as it may sound. What baby thinks or what the cat has to say is often amusing, and this give-and-take seems to create a friendly and tolerant atmosphere. Arriving home from the university, I would get the impression that quite a bit had been happening during my absence.

This ventriloquist lark also seems to make it easier to see (and to accept) that each child is unique, a combination of genes never seen before upon this earth. It is as if you two parents had set off on a years-long spaceship trip to somewhere and that just a few (in our case, three) random seeds had been included for your ship's small greenhouse. How eagerly one would await each sprouting, wondering what kind of plant this would turn out to be. Nature equips most parents with feelings of love and nurturance toward their babies, but I think it is wise also to sustain and encourage an appropriate sense of wonder. If a new $10 million Cray supercomputer had been delivered to your home, you would be awed by its complexity and the things it can do, yet your infant is vastly more complex than any supercomputer and can already do many things the Cray will never accomplish.

When I was still doing psychotherapy, spending hours listening to people who were somehow damaged, I discovered that something about the therapeutic relationship made it possible for me to appreciate how truly remarkable each patient was and to feel a respect that is harder to feel for just a casual acquaintance. Listening to their dreams was especially impressive, discovering that this insecure, inarticulate person had a creative surrealistic playwright inside her head, churning out new dramas every night. If you look at your baby with the kind of appreciation he or she deserves, you will enjoy him or her all the more, and your enjoyment will lead you naturally to spend the time and do the things required for the little one to thrive and be a happy baby.

# 8

# HAPPY CHILDREN

. . . continue to make glad the heart of childhood.
— FRANCIS PHARCELLUS CHURCH

Children begin by loving their parents; as they grow older,
they judge them; sometimes they forgive them.
— OSCAR WILDE

Happiness is an imaginary condition, formerly attributed
by the living to the dead, now usually attributed by adults
to children, and by children to adults.
— THOMAS SZASZ, M.D.[1]

When baby Joe was imminent, Harriet made a point of
getting two-year-old Jesse to understand that the three
of us—Mom, Dad, and Jesse—were expecting a new
baby. When the time came to collect Mom and Joey from the
hospital, Grandma went inside while Dad and Jesse waited in the
car so that, after this first separation, Mom could appear unen-
cumbered and be able to hold Jesse in her lap while Grandma
held the baby. From the beginning, Jesse was proud of and un-
threatened by his younger brothers, and he still is.

Harriet thought that each of her children was remarkable
(they were, actually), but each in his own way. She delighted in
their individuality, and they grew up feeling that each had his
own space in which to be himself, not being compared with or
competing with his siblings. She enjoyed talking with them and
treated what they had to say with interest and respect. Starting
school was an exciting adventure, and the younger ones could
hardly wait their turns. Our boys grew up before the foolish and
counterproductive practice of bussing for integration was im-

posed, so they were able to walk to their neighborhood school and race home at the lunch break to tell Mom what had happened that morning.

The boys helped their mother around the house. One simple trick Harriet learned from her own mother was to say, not "I want you to set the table" but, instead, "Jesse, I'm going to let you set the table." (Jesse claims now that he saw through that all along, but the fact is that it worked.) Mealtimes were fun because the menu was presented with genuine enthusiasm: "These little Brussels sprouts are *so* good and they're even better with a little butter and salt and pepper!" The children got small initial portions but were encouraged to ask for more. They were not made to eat anything but were not allowed to say "I don't *like* that!" because it was offensive to the cook. On the other hand, a good appetite was commented on favorably and finishing (and enjoying) one's vegetables was made to seem a source of pride and adult status. Once leftovers had accumulated in the refrigerator, Mom would serve "blue plate specials," each one a different assortment, and they were always eagerly received because they were presented as a special treat and because they became a kind of periodic ritual. Kids love rituals.

Bedtimes were fun, too, and therefore not resisted. Father put all three in the tub at once and there were songs and foolishness. Then came the lineup to have their teeth brushed, which also was enjoyable, so that their self-care later on was thorough. They grew up with only one small cavity among the three of them. Finally came the bedtime stories. Usually Mom had finished the dishes by then and came up to read to them. Each boy collected his "guy" or stuffed animal and then they climbed on the double bed with their mom, who let them each choose a story. They were all tucked up by nine o'clock, and their parents had some evening to themselves, but without feeling harassed, because the hours with the children were quality time and fun.

The importance of birth order in explaining why children raised in the same family can turn out to be so different, one from another, has been documented by Frank Sulloway in his fascinating book, *Born to Rebel: Birth Order, Family Dynamics,*

*and Creative Lives.*[2] Children presumably have always had to
compete for parental favor and resources and, over the aeons,
human children have evolved a strategy of carving out separate
and distinctive niches for themselves. Instead of competing head-
on in the same race—which is hard when elder brother is bigger
and stronger than you are and already knows how to do long
division—later-born children tend to enter different races, cultivate different talents and qualities. I think an important part of
Harriet's success as a parent resulted from her natural delight in
each boy's uniqueness; they were each special to her in their own
special ways. She felt that each one was a champion in his own
separate field of endeavor, and she seemed to communicate that
feeling to each boy.

Harriet's guiding principle in matters of discipline was "If you
act like that, no one's going to want to see you coming!" On
rare occasion, a swat on the behind was required to get a child's
attention. Jesse, the most "hyper" of the three, got more than his
share. Matthew, on the other hand, got only one swat. He was
about three at the time, and he looked reproachfully at Harriet
and said, "Why did you do that? All you had to say was 'Matthew,
please stop doing that' and I would have stopped." Thus can
parents learn from their children as well as the other way
around.

An important and continuing activity in childhood is the formation of a self-concept. Harriet and I both helped to write the
scripts. "One thing I especially like about you, Jesse, is that
you're always fair and reasonable." "Matthew, Mrs. Holte says
that she knows how smart your big brothers are, but she thinks
you may be the smartest one of all." These script suggestions
seem to work even better when they are reports of what someone
else has said: "Joey, your father said he'd never known a boy that
was as good a block builder as you are." I cannot recall ever
having to scold our boys for littering, and I think that was because we implanted early an antilittering self-concept: "Did you
see that stupid kid toss his candy wrapper out the car window?
What a twit!" The implicit message, of course, is: "I'm glad you
boys aren't litterbugs like that." One has to be careful not to

stretch the truth too much with such remarks, or they will back-fire. We always kept a litterbag in the car, and our kids used it as we did.

When the boys were still quite young, we moved into and, within a year, out of, a rather posh neighborhood. We found it full of upper-middle-class kids whose parents assuaged their guilty dislike of their children by permissiveness and indulgence. This vicious circle could not be more obvious. A child neglected, inconsistently disciplined, talked down to rather than conversed with, a child not treated with real love and respect and genuine interest, will not be a very lovable or interesting child, and thus will tend not to elicit love and respect from anyone.

But it is not just the self-centered and neglectful parents whose children can be hard to love. It is an important but widely unrecognized truth that many parents, including devoted, car-ing, highly responsible parents, simply lack the kind of instinc-tive parental competence that is natural to some people. I am convinced that many children of the middle class would become serious delinquents, unsocialized and unlikely to make the most of their abilities and opportunities, were it not for their generally well-socialized peer group. As I will argue below, the influence of the peer group in determining the values and behavior of most children is inversely proportional to the quality of the parent-child relationship.

This family idyll I have been describing came about in part because we were lucky in our children's innate temperaments. Jesse had the potential for being a bit of a hellion but, fortunately, he was the firstborn, and firstborns tend to identify with the parents, as Sulloway points out. (Jesse remembers every family member's birthday, for example, as did his mother, another firstborn. I, being a last born, remembered only my own until I started my own family.) Therefore, our children readily acquired the traits necessary for socialization, an effective conscience, the ability to empathize with others, and feelings of altruism and personal responsibility. They each developed a distinctive self-concept that they valued and that was incompatible with break-ing the house rules. For that reason, we enjoyed doing things with them and they, in turn, enjoyed doing things with us. When they were ten, twelve, and fourteen, we spent two weeks in East Africa, visiting the game parks in Kenya and Tanzania with a group of British tourists. A middle-aged English couple found themselves assigned to the same nine-passenger minivan with us, much, I am sure, to their initial dismay (three small boys, and Americans at that!). At the end of the trip, however, they made a point of telling us how much they had enjoyed our boys. We were even more impressed by a similar compliment from a retired British schoolmaster, who was also touring with us.

I am sure, of course, that our children would have turned out much the same had they been raised by many other pairs of parents, and even by a few star-quality single parents. I feel confident that the boys would have become successful adults reared in almost any nest. Yet I am certain that even our sweet-tempered children could have been turned into whining, dissembling, quarrelsome, irritating kids by the kinds of parents who do not have an instinctive sense of which buttons to push or who are too self-occupied to bother to find out. I would be fascinated to know whether, with such parents, they would have become such loving, dedicated fathers to their own children, as they have done. If there is a heaven for psychologists, it will provide machinery for replaying lives under differing circumstances to see how they turn out (but without anyone actually suffering the consequences). One thing we can be sure of, however, is that happy children make for a happy family, and happy children are socialized children.

## Happy Children Are Socialized Children

At the Oregon Social Learning Center, psychologist Gerald Patterson has for many years been studying the parenting of children with conduct problems, and he has discovered that these children's willful and aversive behavior is often shaped by the reactions of their parents. Suppose you want to train a laboratory rat to press a lever ten times in rapid sequence. You begin with a hungry animal and a device that dispenses a small food pellet either when you press a button outside the cage or the rat presses the lever inside. At first, you press the button each time the rat turns toward the lever. Then, once he is hanging out in the right area, you wait to press the button—you withhold the *reinforcement*—until he rears up, as he will need to do to press the lever. Once he's rearing up consistently, you require him to rear up right beside the lever in order to get a pellet. Before long, he will be pressing the lever accidentally as he rears and sniffs around it, and he will hear the dispenser eject a pellet whenever the lever moves sufficiently. If you are skillful, you will soon have your rat very deliberately pressing the lever, eating the resulting pellet, then pressing again in a workmanlike fashion.

But you want him to press the lever ten times in succession, not just once. Nothing could be easier. Your "Skinner box" (this lever-pressing apparatus is named after the late, great Harvard psychologist, B. F. Skinner) is electronically equipped so that you merely throw a switch to make the pellet dispenser work only after every second lever press. At first, your rat will appear surprised, even irritated, when the first press fails to deliver, but even as you or I would do at the candy machine, he will bang it again and the pellet appears. By the time we have a cup of coffee and return, your rat is very purposefully pressing the lever *once, twice,* then turning to retrieve his pellet. Now we set the machine to reinforce only every third time, then every fifth time—well, you get the idea. Skinner and his many students and disciples showed that you can train rats to press levers, pigeons to peck at illuminated panels, dolphins and circus animals to do sophisticated tricks—you can even train your average house cat to shake hands—by this sort of systematic behavior shaping, using reward or "reinforcement" provided in a judicious manner to "shape" the behavior in the desired direction.

What Patterson discovered is that many parents nonjudiciously and inadvertently shape the behavior of their own children in the direction of willful disobedience. Suppose you tell your child to stop what he's doing at the moment, because it is aversive or messy or whatever: many children (not all, it depends upon temperament) will resist. They will whine or object or pretend not to hear. They were doing whatever it was because they wanted to at the time and no one likes to be at someone else's command. Think of it as a laboratory rat turning toward the lever. How do you increase the probability that the next time you say, "Stop that!," your child will whine or object or ignore you? You give him a pellet for doing it this time. *You let him get away with it!* Being able to do what you like, to have your own way, to be in control, is as reinforcing as any old food pellet. Most parents will try again. "Bobby, I said you should stop that!" The next response from many children will be a somewhat stronger refusal, a louder whine, perhaps a wail, even a tantrum. How do you train a child to have tantrums? By making them pay off, that's how; by *reinforcing* them.

For years, Patterson has been observing mothers of high-risk kids doing what he calls this "three-step dance"—make the request, receive an aversive response, back off—with predictable results. Most parents don't always back off, of course. Sometimes the matter is too important or the parent gets too irritated to let the child get away with refusal. Therefore, what the child experiences is what Skinner called "aperiodic reinforcement" of the aversive refusal or tantrum. Aperiodic reinforcement is what has made the Mafia rich in Las Vegas; it is the principle that distinguishes between the slot machine and the coffee machine or the ATM. When we trained that rat to press the lever ten times running, we worked up to it gradually, first reinforcing every press, then every other one, every third press, every fifth press—and we did that because if we had jumped suddenly from continuous reinforcement, a pellet for every press, to requiring ten presses per pellet, the rat would have almost certainly quit pressing when the pellets stopped coming, before he ever got to ten.

It is easy to terminate or *extinguish* a response habit that has been getting reinforced continuously. But once we have our rat pressing ten times per pellet, suppose we reset the controls so that sometimes it takes twelve or thirteen presses to produce a pellet, while other times seven or eight will do it. The rat will accommodate to that schedule readily. And now we can begin to stretch out the maximum number of presses that are sometimes required. As long as he sometimes gets a pellet after only five or ten or fifteen presses, our rat will keep working away even if, sometimes, he has to bang the thing one hundred times before the pellet is dispensed. By making the reinforcement unpredictable, we have made the lever-pressing habit extremely resistant to extinction or change; we have created a kind of rat slot machine.

Patterson's troubled mothers were reinforcing their child's disobedience by not *enforcing* their requests or commands and they were making their youngster's aversive or disobedient response as resistant to extinction as a slot-machine habit by backing off sometimes, but not always, and doing this unpredictably. I acknowledged in chapter 6 that my wife had an instinct for parenting that I could only observe and admire. I must now admit, however, that Harriet's instinct for dealing with four-legged animals leaves much to be desired. A true-blue animal person, she chairs the Wildlife Task Force of our chapter of the Sierra Club and is the CEO, office manager, and everything else for an organization called Help Our Wolves Live (HOWL). She is one of a handful of people responsible for the preservation of the only safely viable population of timber wolves in the contiguous forty-eight states—but she gets poor marks for shaping the behavior of our three cats and a dog.

At Sunday breakfast, I dawdle over the paper and a second cup of coffee while Harriet drinks hers standing up. She does this because Willie, the bull terrier, keeps dumping tennis balls in her lap while she is sitting down. Willie does this to her but not to me because she sometimes picks up a ball and throws it for him to chase. I never do, not at mealtimes. The cats rouse Harriet from her bed before dawn each morning, wanting their breakfast, never me. Why? Because eventually she gives in and gets up and gets it for them; I never do.

I don't recall this ever being a problem with our children; they didn't tease or whine. Probably this was because Harriet (and I) did not tolerate teasing. But animals only stop teasing when it really never works, and I think some children are that way, too. Our kids knew that they got treats predictably when they could look forward to them. Matthew, when he was three or four, would go shopping with his mom and bring home a dozen doughnuts. These were "Matt's doughnuts" which he could pass out to his older brothers after lunch, a predictable treat. Sometimes they got treats as surprises. But they never got treats by saying, "Mom, I want . . ."

The children Patterson was studying were considered to be at "high risk" for delinquency for two main reasons. First, they had the sorts of temperaments that made them hard to discipline. Some were unusually aggressive, some impulsive, some were relatively fearless and not easily intimidated. Shy, diffident children or loving, warm-hearted children are unlikely ever to get involved in those coercive cycles of the three-step dance. Secondly, most of Patterson's harried mothers were single moms, trying to do this most demanding of jobs alone, with no father present to help exert authority, to share the load and assist in setting clear and definite limits. By patient training and practice, many of these mothers were gradually able to reassert control, but it is not an easy job.

Those who dropped out of Patterson's program were likely to end up with children whom modern psychiatry would classify as having oppositional defiant disorder. American psychiatry's official *Diagnostic and Statistical Manual, 4th Edition* (commonly known as *DSM-IV*) provides admirably clear criteria for making this diagnosis.

## Diagnostic Criteria for Oppositional Defiant Disorder[3]

A pattern of negativistic, hostile, and defiant behavior lasting at least six months, during which four (or more) of the following are present:

1. Often loses temper
2. Often argues with adults
3. Often actively defies or refuses to comply with adults' request or rules

4. Often deliberately annoys people
5. Often blames others for his or her mistakes or misbehavior
6. Is often touchy or easily annoyed by others
7. Is often angry or resentful
8. Is often spiteful or vindictive

Does this describe any child you know? If it does, we can be reasonably sure that this is not a happy child, and that the home in which this child resides is not a happy place for anyone. And unless appropriate remedial steps are taken soon, the condition is likely to get worse. Remember, we are talking about rewards here (positive reinforcement), not punishments. The oppositional child got into that fix by being rewarded for disobedience, and now it is necessary to reward him instead for doing what he's told. This means that when the child fails to do what is asked, the parent has to get up and go over and make him do it. That sounds scary and punitive, but it need not be at all. "Toby, when I say 'Stop bouncing the ball in the house,' you must do what I tell you. I'll take the ball now; why don't you play with your game?" If Toby tries his tantrum maneuver, then he gets carried to his room because "No one wants to hear all that noise." If Toby kicks or hits, then he may need a quick swat on his bottom to get his attention. Good parents learn to distinguish readily between "mad howls" and "sad howls." The former should be ignored or get the "time-out" treatment, while the latter may require a reassuring hug. After all, you are bigger and smarter than he is, so all it really takes for you to be the boss, rather than the child, is endless patience, persistence, and determination (who said it would be easy?)—and the sense to reward the desired behavior rather than the tantrums.

Psychologist Judith Harris argues persuasively that *socializing* children, getting them to accept the norms and rules of society, is determined largely by their interactions with their peer group.[4] I think, however, that peer group influence varies inversely with parental skill and competence. Effective parents develop relationships with their children that enable the parents to be admired role models, teachers, and counselors, and most children of such parents are not attracted to antisocial peers. Good parents will not attempt to rear their offspring in neighborhoods where most potential peers are antisocial. The values and behavior patterns of the children of ineffective parents, on the other hand, will be determined primarily by the peer group. I believe that this is why most middle-class children do manage to become socialized, even though many middle-class parents lack parenting skills: because most middle-class children *are* tolerably socialized.

I once observed a young couple I know hovering about their two-year-old, who was seated fretfully in her high chair, the father attempting to engage the child's attention with a picture book while the mother watched for chances to pop spoonfuls of baby food into the little girl's mouth. These two were both highly educated, intelligent, well-socialized, loving parents, but in spite of those credentials, they were ineffective parents to whom the most elementary principles of behavior modification were terra incognita. Between the ages of one and six, their child was a small tyrant who kept them on the jump—the behavior-shaping was all working in the wrong direction. Once in school, however, the youngster began, ineluctably, to behave as her little friends did, to become socialized. Surely, this is a common pattern. It is also an indictment of our failure, as a society, to appreciate the need for formal training in parenting skills.

In ancestral times, the precarious period of adolescence began later and ended sooner than is true today. Just since the early 1900s, youngsters in developed countries are attaining puberty nearly three years earlier, due to improved health care and nutrition. During the same period, educational requirements for entry into the adult world of work have greatly increased, trapping today's adolescents in a "maturity gap, chronological hostages of a time warp between biological age and social age."[5] When our ancestors lived as hunter-gatherers, the transition from childhood into man's (woman's) estate was accomplished relatively quickly after that late puberty, probably marked by a rite of passage of the sort observed by most traditional societies of today. These newly accredited adults then took their places as apprentices in the adult community, learning adult ways and skills by imitating and being guided by their elders.

Today's adolescents, in contrast, are required to remain for as long as ten years in a "time warp," in which they are adult in physique and inclination but not in occupation or status. During this period, most important, their social community consists largely not of adults disposed to teach them the ways of the larger community, but of their adolescent peers, from whom they are likely to learn less useful and constructive lessons. As psychologist Terrie Moffitt has pointed out, the risky and antisocial behavior of some adolescents tends to be mimicked by others because it gives the *appearance* of adult status. Moffitt argues that youngsters are programmed to imitate the behavior of their associates because that was how our ancestors of that age learned adult ways. Because this protracted and insular adolescence was not a feature of ancestral life, our species has not evolved foolproof adaptive ways of accommodating to this interlude.

I think my own family was fortunate in that we did a lot of traveling when the boys were young and, moreover, they spent the summers at the lake cabin with their mother. Instead of becoming tied to their respective peer groups, this periodic uprooting helped lead them to become best friends with one another and close to their parents. Parents who are not so lucky and who lack the knack for dealing with recalcitrant children have a harder time than we did, yet most of their youngsters do tend to "turn out all right" as they become socialized in their neighborhoods and in their schools. But as Moffitt points out, sometimes they happen to get in with the occasional wild child whom they find attractive because he makes his own rules, just as the adults seem to do. Then, absent competent parenting, the next step may be the one known to psychiatrists and juvenile corrections workers as conduct disorder. Now the chaos and distress spreads beyond the family to the school and to the neighborhood. The vast majority of serious delinquents and adult criminals were classifiable as having conduct disorder in middle childhood.

# Diagnostic Criteria for Conduct Disorder

A repetitive and persistent pattern of behavior in which the basic rights of others or major age-appropriate societal norms or rules are violated, as manifested by the presence of three (or more) of the following criteria in the past twelve months, with at least one criterion present in the past six months.

AGGRESSION TO PEOPLE AND ANIMALS
- Often bullies, threatens, or intimidates others
- Often initiates physical fights
- Has used a weapon that can cause serious physical harm to others
- Has been physically cruel to people
- Has been physically cruel to animals
- Has stolen while confronting a victim (e.g., mugging, purse snatching, extortion, armed robbery)
- Has forced someone into sexual activity

DESTRUCTION OF PROPERTY
- Has deliberately engaged in fire setting, with the intention of causing serious damage
- Has deliberately destroyed others' property (other than by fire setting)

DECEITFULNESS OR THEFT
- Has broken into someone else's house, building, or car
- Often lies to obtain goods or favors or to avoid obligations (i.e., "cons" others)
- Has stolen items of nontrivial value without confronting a victim (e.g., shoplifting, but without breaking and entering; forgery)

SERIOUS VIOLATIONS OF RULES
- Often stays out at night despite parental prohibitions, beginning before age thirteen years
- Has run away from home overnight at least twice while living

in parental or parental surrogate home (or once without returning for a lengthy period)
• Is often truant from school, beginning before age thirteen
  years

   However, conduct disorder is a reversible condition provided
that professional help is sought in time and that the parents are
willing and able to implement that help by changing their parental tactics and investment. A child with unremediated conduct
disorder is a child whose birthright to "life, liberty, and the pursuit of happiness" may rapidly be lost forever. Because I believe
that the rights of the child outweigh the rights of the parents,
whose feckless ways have produced the problem, I would advo-
cate removing such children to foster care or boarding schools
when the parents (usually a single parent) will not or cannot
adequately cope.[6]

## The Psychopath

All too many children graduate from conduct disorder to the
adult classifications of psychopathy or sociopathy. In another
book I distinguished between psychopaths and sociopaths: A
psychopath is someone who is born with an innate temperament
that makes him (or her, although males outnumber females as
psychopaths several times over) unusually difficult to socialize.[7]
A sociopath is someone who grows up unsocialized primarily
because of parental malfeasance. It should be obvious to anyone
who wears shoes that people who have difficult temperaments
*and* incompetent parents are especially likely to grow up to be
unsocialized. (I put it this way because some of my colleagues,
who do wear shoes but are encumbered by Ph.D. degrees, find
this concept difficult to grasp.) This means that there will be
people who are difficult to classify because they meet criteria for
both psychopathy and sociopathy.
   A variety of temperamental peculiarities can produce a psychopath. Hypersexuality is one example. Judging from the accounts in his biography, the serial rapist-murderer known as the

Boston Strangler seems to have been in such a state much of the time every day.[8] It seems necessary also to identify a subspecies of psychopath consisting of persons at the high end of the normal distribution of rage readiness or rage intensity. Worse yet, there is no doubt that violent aggression is an essential or, at least, a preferred accompaniment to sexual expression in some men. It is likely that this association can be learned, perhaps in the same way that sexual fetishes become conditioned. Consider friendless, lonely Thomas Schultz who, in 1993, murdered the woman he had met through a lonely hearts ad and then spent two hours mutilating her body. Even in grade school, he said, "I'd get attracted to a girl and for some reason even without knowing them I'd want to hurt them." His sexual appetites grew increasingly violent, finally demanding murder and mutilation for satisfaction.[9] But the most interesting—and probably the most numerous—psychopath of all is not obsessed with unusual cravings, nor overcome easily by emotional storms. The *primary* psychopath is simply someone who is not much affected by punishment, who does not worry as you and I might do about the consequences of his actions (most primary psychopaths are males).

An example of a primary psychopath is "Monster" Kody Scott, also known as Sanyka Shakur.[10] Kody was a fearless boy,[11] initiated at age twelve into the Eight-Tray Gangster Crips in South Central Los Angeles, and he shot his first victim that same night. Kody never knew his father, who is said to have been a professional football player. On the other hand, another fearless psychopath, Christopher Boyce (the Falcon in Robert Lindsey's *The Falcon and the Snowman*),[12] was the son of a retired FBI agent with a large, well-socialized family. After being sentenced to a long prison term for selling secrets to the Soviets, Boyce managed a daring escape from a high security prison and remained at large, robbing a series of banks, for more than a year in spite of the most vigorous manhunt in the history of the U.S. Marshall's Service.[13]

In his classic monograph, *The Mask of Sanity*, psychiatrist Hervey Cleckley illustrated the problem of understanding the primary psychopath by means of a collection of vividly drawn case histories from his own practice. Here were people from good families, intelligent and rational, sound of mind and body, who lied without compunction, cheated, stole, and casually violated any and all norms of social conduct whenever it suited their whim. Moreover, they seemed surprisingly unaffected by the bad consequences of their actions, whether visited upon themselves or on their families or friends.

Cleckley also cited several examples from literature of the kind of individual he had in mind, including Shakespeare's Iago and Falstaff, Ibsen's Peer Gynt, and Molnar's character Liliom, the prototype of Billy Bigelow in Rodgers and Hammerstein's musical *Carousel*. Unaccountably, however, Cleckley neglected the Shakespearean character who best epitomizes the primary psychopath, Richard III, who, in the first speech of scene 1, declares himself bored, looking for action: "Now is the winter of our discontent . . . Why, I, in this weak piping time of peace,/ Have no delight to pass away the time."

In the next scene, Lady Anne enters with the corpse of her husband, Henry VI, borne by servants. It was Richard who killed Henry, and Anne fears and despises him, yet he commands the bearers to set the coffin down while he proceeds to make love to the grieving widow! Richard talks her around in just three pages—surely one of the greatest tours de force ever assayed by a dramatist or by an actor—and then he gloats:

> Was ever woman in this humour woo'd?
> Was ever woman in this humour won?
> I'll have her, but I will not keep her long.
> What, I, that kill'd her husband and his father,
> To take her in her heart's extremest hate,
> With curses in her mouth, tears in her eyes,
> The bleeding witness of my hatred by,
> Having God, her conscience, and these bars against me,
> And I no friends to back my suit withal
> But the plain devil and dissembling looks?
> And yet to win her—all the world to nothing!

Some female psychopaths in literature include Mildred, in Somerset Maugham's *Of Human Bondage*; Sally Bowles, the heroine in *Cabaret*; Ibsen's Hedda Gabler; and Bizet's Carmen. We can see primary psychopathy in the character played by the actor Jack Nicholson in numerous movies, including *Five Easy Pieces, Chinatown, The Last Detail*, and especially in *One Flew Over the Cuckoo's Nest*. Harry Lime as portrayed by Orson Welles in the film *The Third Man* conveys the eerie combination of charm and menace found in some of these individuals. The character played by child actress Patty McCormack in the film *The Bad Seed* and the eponymous hero in Thomas Mann's *The Confessions of Felix Krull, Confidence Man* are contrasting portraits of the psychopath as mendacious manipulator. The brother in Graham Greene's novel *The Shipwrecked* is a good example of the feckless, self- and other-deluding, poseur type of psychopath, as is the protagonist's father in John Le Carré's *The Perfect Spy*, a character said to be based on the author's own father. The psychopath in youth can be found as the hero of E. L. Doctorow's book *Billy Bathgate*, which also provides a more dangerous version in the character of the gangster Dutch Schultz.

As used by the media, "psychopath" conveys an impression of danger and implacable evil. This is mistaken, however, as Cleckley made very clear. Like the unsocialized sociopath, the psychopath is characterized by a lack of the restraining effect of conscience and of empathic concern for other people. Unlike the ordinary sociopath, the primary psychopath has failed to develop conscience and empathic feelings, not because of a lack of socializing experience but, rather, because of some inherent psychological peculiarity that makes him especially difficult to socialize. An additional consequence of this innate peculiarity is that the psychopath behaves in a way that suggests that he is relatively indifferent to the probability of punishment for his actions. This essential peculiarity of the psychopath is not in itself evil or vicious but, combined with perverse appetites, or with an unusually hostile and aggressive temperament, the lack of these normal constraints can result in an explosive and dangerous package. Examples of such combinations include the serial killer Ted

Bundy;[14] Gary Gilmore, described in Norman Mailer's excellent *The Executioner's Song;* Diane Downs, who tried to murder her three children because her boyfriend didn't want them;[15] and the sex-murdering RAF officer, Neville Heath.[16] *Without Conscience: The Disturbing World of the Psychopaths Among Us*, a recent and highly readable book by R. D. Hare, the leading researcher in this area, provides numerous sketches of real-life criminal psychopaths.

In marked contrast to these dangerous characters, and illustrative of why psychologists find such fascination in the psychopath, is the case of Oscar Schindler, the savior of hundreds of Crakow Jews whose names were on *Schindler's List*. He was an opportunist, bon vivant, ladies' man, manipulator—a man who was unsuccessful in legitimate business by his own admission but wildly successful in the moral chaos of wartime. And his rescue of those Jews can be best understood as a thirty-five-year-old con man's response to a kind of ultimate challenge: Schindler against the Third Reich. Any swine could kill people under the conditions of that time and place; the real challenge—in words that his biographer may have put in his mouth, the "real power"—lay in rescuing people, especially in rescuing Jews. Some parts of Steven Spielberg's film do not fit with my diagnosis of Schindler as a primary psychopath; in particular, the scene near the end in which Schindler breaks down in tears while addressing his Jewish workers. British filmmaker Jon Blair, whose earlier documentary film, *Schindler*, was truer to history than Spielberg's feature film, noted this same discrepancy. "It was slightly out of character, and, of course, it never actually happened," Blair said.

Some other biographies of colorful primary psychopaths include Nicholas von Hoffman's *Citizen Cohn*, Neil Sheehan's *A Bright Shining Lie: John Paul Vann and America in Vietnam*, and Daniel Akst's *Wonderboy: Barry Minkow, the Kid who Swindled Wall Street*. Some historical figures who, I believe, had the "talent" for psychopathy but who achieved great worldly success include: Lyndon Johnson,[17] Winston Churchill,[18] the African explorer Sir Richard Burton,[19] and Chuck Yeager, the first man to break the sound barrier.[20]

The fact that many of these illustrative characters were not adjudicated criminals reminds us that we are talking here about a class of actors rather than a pattern of actions. Psychopaths are at high risk for engaging in criminal behavior, but not all of them succumb to that risk. Even the identical twins of criminal psychopaths, with whom they share all their genes and many of their formative experiences, do not necessarily become criminal themselves. To mention Churchill, Johnson, Burton, and Yeager in this context may seem especially surprising, but all four set out as daring, adventurous, unconventional youngsters who began playing by their own rules early in life. Talent, opportunity, and plain luck enabled them to achieve success and self-esteem through (mainly) licit rather than illicit means. Johnson and Burton were at least borderline psychopaths, if we can believe their biographers, while Churchill and Yeager seem merely to have shared what I call the talent for psychopathy. I believe the nature of this talent may be nothing more exotic than an innate, relative fearlessness.

## Preventing Primary Psychopathy

By definition, the child whose innate temperament makes him or her a potential psychopath will remain at high risk unless the parents are unusually skillful or have skillful help. On the other hand, I believe that the principles involved in the successful socialization of "difficult" children are the ones that also work the best with children of average temperament. The rules for training a bull terrier are the same as those that work with beagles; the task of rearing a bull terrier is merely harder and more demanding and the price of failure greater. In the early years, the main objective in rearing any child is the creation of a strong and loving parental bond. Unless the parents can genuinely enjoy holding the toddler, feeding her, playing with her, and reading her stories, then they should seek professional help, because that

early emotional relationship is the basis on which later successful parenting depends.

As the child's behavioral repertory expands, the potential
primary psychopath will not be shy or timorous but, on the contrary, venturesome and sometimes aggressive. Careful monitoring then is required as well as patient and consistent intervention
whenever necessary. A good parent will not rely heavily on punishment (and not at all on heavy punishment) because it does
not work with the potential psychopath and can have bad side
effects with most children. Sometimes a hard swat on the behind
may be necessary to get the youngster's attention, but that is
about all that corporal punishment is good for. Whether the
child seems to have the "talent" for primary psychopathy or not,
he or she must learn that tantrums do not work and that disobedience costs more than it pays. In addition, the good parent tries
to develop in the child the self-concept that he or she is the sort
of a person who does the right thing and is therefore deserving
of love, praise, and respect. While they are still bigger and
smarter than their youngster, parents should be able to accomplish this or, if their efforts seem not to be working, to seek help
before it is too late.

I think that, whether their child is "difficult" or not, parents
should make a conscious effort to treat their youngster with respect, to really listen to what he or she has to say, and to be
responsive, to treat him or her like a person and not like a "dumb
kid." Many adults shift into a patronizing or condescending
mode when they interact with children and this does not help to
sustain a strong parent-child bond. To the infant, the parent is
the source of all good things; to the older child, the parent
should continue to be the principal source of interest, support,
encouragement, affection, information, admiration—that is, still
the source of most of the good things that the youngster wants
and needs. To the extent that such a relationship exists, then the
parent's values will tend to become the child's values.

A venturesome and relatively fearless child can and will do
some things—things he finds gratifying and fun—that the average child is too timid to attempt or carry off successfully. Many

of these attractive temptations will be illicit or dangerous. The challenge to any parent of such a child is to direct his interest toward exciting activities that are also constructive. Suppose that Kody ("Monster") Scott's biological father, had started teaching his daredevil son the rudiments of that game when Kody was very small. Suppose Dad had enrolled him in a Little League team and shared his triumphs and disappointments with him. What committed Kody to a life of crime early on was his discovery that he was *good* at it, he could dominate other boys, beat people up, become feared and respected by his peers. What if he had learned instead that he could dominate and be respected on the football field? What if he had learned in that context that it is more gratifying to win within the rules than by flouting them?

I believe that pride can be an effective antidote to psychopathy. Winston Churchill was a fearless boy and a bad student who seldom did anything right until he finally (on his third attempt) got admitted to the military college at Sandhurst and began playing polo, for which he had a gift. His heroics on horseback, in polo and later in battle, gave the young Winston status among his fellows and a sense of pride and accomplishment that undergirded his later political career. As was true for many upper-class Englishmen of his generation, Churchill's nanny, Mrs. Everest, and his strict schoolmasters were effective substitute parents, while the remote Lord and Lady Randolph Churchill were more like dreams of glory, incentives to great accomplishment that, happily, Winston had the gifts to achieve.[21]

## The Sociopath

An example of a sociopath, and of the sociopath's tendency to produce sociopathic children because they are such dreadful parents, is Rosa Lee, the subject of a Pulitzer prize–winning series by *Washington Post* reporter Leon Dash.[22] Rosa Lee, the youngest child in a large, fatherless family, began stealing at age nine, quit school in the seventh grade, married at sixteen, left her abusive husband soon after, then proceeded to have eight children by five different men. Rosa Lee worked as a waitress, a prostitute, and a small-time drug dealer. She had shoplifted since age ten and taught her grandson to shoplift when he was about the same age. She introduced one daughter to prostitution at age thirteen and several of her children followed her example of heroin addiction.

Two of Rosa Lee's eight children, however, raised under the same squalid conditions as the other six, were boys with easily socialized temperaments. They were repelled by chaos and violence, and attracted to stability and order. Somehow they stayed out of trouble, found socialized masculine role models outside of the home, and became self-supporting family men. Reversing the current trend, in Britain and especially in the United States, in which increasing proportions of young people are growing up unsocialized, is a major—I would say *the* major—social problem of our time. Solving this problem will be difficult and expensive, yet not nearly so expensive as not solving it. If my analysis is correct, the essence of the solution is to reduce the numbers of youngsters being reared by incompetent or indifferent or unsocialized parents. I discuss how this might be accomplished in another place.[23] It will require establishing the infrastructure needed to provide worthy substitutes for all these malfeasant parents: a system of trained, licensed, foster parents paid in accordance with the importance of their job; many more group homes; single-sex boarding schools—all very expensive but not nearly so expensive as not doing it because we know that every child rescued from a life of sociopathy will save the taxpayers at least $3 million.[24] The only real solution, I believe, will be to require of persons who wish to raise a child of their own the same minimal standards we demand of someone proposing to adopt someone else's baby: grow up, get a job, and get married.

## Single Parents

Nearly four out of ten American children today are being reared by single parents, almost always by single mothers. Because the responsibilities of parenting are so difficult and so unrelenting, we applaud those single parents who do manage to socialize

their children and start them on their way to a happy and productive life. Because our species is adapted to the extended-
family method of child rearing, even the traditional two-parent
team is not always successful. When the biological father merely
plants his seed and goes on his merry way, the consequences are
too often grim indeed. In 1992, of the juveniles incarcerated in
the United States for serious crimes, about 70 percent had been
reared without fathers.[25] This 70 percent figure seems to be a
magic number for much social pathology. Of the antisocial boys
studied at the Oregon Social Learning Center, less than 30 percent came from intact families.[26] Of the more than 130,000 teenagers who ran away from home in 1994, 72 percent were leaving
single-parent homes.[27] A 1992 study of "baby truants" in St. Paul,
Minnesota elementary school pupils who had more than twenty-
two unexcused absences in the year found that 70 percent were
being reared by single mothers.[28] Nationally, about 70 percent of
teenage girls who have out-of-wedlock babies were raised without fathers.[29] All of these youngsters had been victimized by the
inadequacy of their rearing. Such children are also at much
higher risk for being victimized more violently. Some 1,300 children died in the United States from familial abuse in 1993, and
only a small fraction while living with both biological parents.[30]
Of the sixty-one children murdered in Chicago in 1993, for example, fifty-one (83 percent!) were being reared by unmarried
teenage mothers.[31] A recent survey by the county attorney in
Minneapolis of 135 children who had been referred for crimes
ranging from arson, vandalism, and theft, to assault, burglary,
and criminal sexual conduct—youngsters *aged nine or younger*—
found that 70 percent of these children were living in single-
parent (almost always single-mother) homes.[32] According to the
administrators of juvenile corrections facilities, family problems
are the most common type of problem among juveniles in cus-
tody, affecting at least 76 percent, more common than substance
abuse, peer problems, learning problems, or gang involvement.[33]

The postlude of this sermon goes like this: If you don't enjoy
your child, if you would prefer to take your summer vacation

when he or she is at camp rather than with you, then I strongly suspect that you have been pushing the wrong buttons (or not enough buttons) and that you would be smart to get some professional help. If you do not truly enjoy having your child around (not every minute of every day—let's be reasonable about this), then it is likely that yours is not a happy child or, at least, that he/she will not be happy later on. And remember who it is that needs the counseling. If you take a young dog for obedience training, the instructor always makes it clear that it is the one on your end of the leash who is the student. If you need help in choosing a parental adviser, ask whether he or she is familiar with the works of the late B. F. Skinner, a psychologist who knew a lot about which buttons to push.

# 9

# Happy with One's Pets

Let your boat of life be light, packed with only what you
need; one or two friends worth the name, some one to love
and some one to love you, a cat, a dog, and a pipe or two.
—Jerome K. Jerome

If you pick up a starving dog and make him prosperous,
he will not bite you. This is the principal difference
between a dog and a man.
—Mark Twain

A mericans spend billions of dollars each year nurturing animals: dogs, cats, birds, and a variety of more exotic species.
Not everyone is what my wife calls an "animal person," but
many of us are and, in our millions, we can testify that our furred
or feathered friends play an important role in our sense of subjective well-being. Why this is, and how those of us blessed with
this "critterphilia" can make the most of our gift, is the topic of
this short chapter.

Unless we are ecologists looking at the global picture, we
think of trees as sources of lumber and shade and as things of
beauty. Why do many humans not regard animals of other species in a similar way, as sources of food, as beasts of burden, as
things of beauty, or as scientific curiosities? Why do so many of
us tend to *care* about animals? One plausible explanation goes
like this: We know that female mammals of most species can be
persuaded under special circumstances to adopt the young of
other species: a brood mare may adopt a baby goat, or a nursing
bitch may let a foundling kitten scrabble with her pups for suste-

nance. In the Maine woods this winter, a mother bear, denned up snugly with her pair of eight-week-old cubs, adopted a lost beagle dog that happened to be wearing a radio collar. When the dog's owner tried to coax it out of the den, Mama Bear gently pulled it back again. The mothering instinct was plainly an essential part of Nature's plan, because it made possible the survival of those young who need parental care and feeding for a time. But Nature creates by natural selection mechanisms that are only complex enough to serve her purposes. The mothering instinct is triggered not just by her own offspring, but also by young, helpless creatures roughly similar to the young, helpless creatures that Mother is likely to produce herself. Thus, many nesting birds will accept a cuckoo's egg and feed that alien chick when it hatches.

Our primate ancestors did not pair-bond, and it was the rare baby chimpanzee that knew his own father or vice versa. As will be explained in chapter 11, it was when our ancestral grandmothers began producing big-brained, helpless infants that romantic love evolved to keep the daddies involved in nurturing those vulnerable offspring. Thus Nature had also to evolve a fathering instinct, already found in many birds and in pack animals, but only very weakly in our immediate ancestors, the primates.

And, like the mothering instinct, the tendency for males to feed and protect their own young was nonspecific and easily generalized to other infants or to other species, and even to adults of our mammalian cousins, who seem relatively young and helpless to our eyes. For more than forty years, I have been observing Harriet's and my behavior toward a succession of hamsters, dogs, and cats who have been members of our household, and there can be no doubt that we have felt toward these creatures an only slightly attenuated version of the feelings that we had toward our own children. Harriet is the more nurturant. She does almost all of the feeding, for example—while I am more inclined to set limits.

But if some vandal were to torment one of our cats or the dog when my shotgun was near to hand, I wouldn't hesitate to deal roughly with the villain, just as I would had my child been the victim. The Humane Society of America refers persons anguished by the loss of a pet to support groups that exist for that purpose in many communities. I find it curious that the law still regards a pet as having only a monetary value. If you carelessly or deliberately kill my child, you will be subject to both criminal and civil penalties, each of them serious. But if you kill my dog, the only serious penalty would be the one I might administer myself. If I did not already have more "causes" in hand than I can do justice to, I would be lobbying my state legislature to make cruelty to animals a felony.

This affectionate regard for animals, like all human traits, varies in intensity from person to person. Among Bouchard's 250 twins who were separated in infancy and reared apart, only two were dedicated "dog people"; one entered her pure-bred dogs in shows around the country, and the other taught dog obedience classes; they were a pair of identical twins. But many of the other twins had pets, like the "Jim twins" who had both grown up with dogs they each had named "Toy."

As I write, Bouchard is trying to track down what we think may be another pair of reared-apart MZ twins who both are "dog people." A 1996 issue of the *Smithsonian* magazine contained an article about a veterinarian service catering to the pets of the poor in New York City. A full-page photograph displayed one happy client cuddling his little dog, which had been injured in an accident but now, leg freshly splinted and bandaged, was on the mend. Within a few days, a man in Las Vegas, known to his friends as a dog fancier, found himself being congratulated on being pictured in the magazine. Bouchard has a photograph of the Las Vegas man and he is indeed the smiling image of the man in the *Smithsonian*, holding his Chihuahua. He is not the same man, however, but was himself adopted, and the possibility seems irresistible that he has an MZ twin living in New York! Unhappily, the photographer who took the *Smithsonian* picture did not get the name of his subject, so the search is on. Bouchard has encountered two other pairs of unrelated persons who look very much like twins but are not, and this may prove to be a third such instance; yet the fact that they are both dog people increases the odds that they are indeed twins.

My rule of thumb for deciding whether one should undertake the responsibility of a pet (other than a bowl of goldfish, perhaps, or a singing bird) goes like this: Can you imagine not only giving the animal free run of your living quarters, but also talking to it, and even talking *for* it: "Willie says it's time for his ball game" or "Socks says he's glad he's not out 'on the bum' this winter!" A pet should become a member of the family; otherwise, neither your responsibility to him nor his contribution to your life will be realized.

Animals repay their cost in time, trouble, and veterinary fees with a commodity that is hard to come by if your only friends are other featherless bipeds—namely, unconditional love. One of our cats, Desi, likes to watch me take my shower. Forty years ago, it is possible that certain humans might have enjoyed watching me in the shower, but now the bathroom mirror tells me that the scene would be of interest only to gerontologists and Desi, who loves me and thinks I look just fine. I may smell rankly of pipe tobacco, yet Desi, Socks, and Sidney all like to sit, purring, in my lap, and so would the dog, Willie, if I would let him (and if he could purr). Progressive nursing homes are learning to include an animal or two in their dayrooms to help provide a kind of solace and tranquillity.

Animals also add something useful to a home with children. One has to set limits with animals, as with children, and I think it is useful for Johnny occasionally to see Mom or Dad get angry over a serious infraction and scold the pet, with Johnny knowing all the while that the animal is still loved and will be fed and petted in the future just as before. When the shoe is on the other foot and it is Johnny who has sinned, I think that it is good for him to see Mom or Dad treating the family pet in a loving way; it softens the atmosphere and facilitates reconciliation. And children, too (perhaps *especially*), benefit from a relationship of unconditional regard and love. A child's human talents for empathy and altruism need to be elicited and practiced, and this also is more easily accomplished when a pet animal is a part of the family.

I think that most married couples, both before any children arrive and after the nest is empty once again, would benefit from having an animal around the house, but only providing that they both willingly share responsibility for its care. In some odd way, rather like a friend in common, a dog or cat can act as a kind of mediator in territorial disputes. If the atmosphere is a bit tense, if the parties are not currently speaking to each other, it seems to help if both at least are speaking kindly to the dog. The rest of the time (let us say, hopefully, almost all the time) that unconditional love and regard continue to pay dividends. I am more of a dog person, perhaps because I enjoy Willie's uninhibited enthusiasm when I come home from the university, when he does his leaps and twirlies in the driveway and follows me, tail fiercely wagging, into the house. Harriet is more of a cat person, perhaps because she prefers the more sedate demonstrations of affection provided by a cat in her lap while she reads or watches television, or on her stomach when she takes a nap. I sometimes complain about the after-dinner walks, especially if the wind chill is 40 degrees below 0, but the fact is that Slick Willie, and Polly Peachum before him, have induced me to take at least six thousand miles of healthy postprandial exercise I would otherwise have missed.

An important source of the satisfaction one derives from having pets is the opportunity they provide for exercising our instincts of nurturance. Just as I complain sometimes about having to take Willie on his walk or out for his afternoon ball game, Harriet sometimes complains about having to feed the critters, especially about having to get up at 5:00 A.M. to get the cats' breakfast in order to stop them dashing around the bedroom. But the fact is that she enjoys feeding them, especially Willie, because dogs, being omnivorous, provide greater scope for culinary innovation. Chicken necks with cabbage, for example, is a dish that Willie says he really likes, or so I am told. Pets aren't for everyone, but those of us who enjoy them find they make more waves than troughs on our happiness lakes.

## Postscript on Behalf of the Critters

If you wish to brighten your days by keeping a pet, it is reasonable that you should repay the enjoyment that you get from them by following a few simple rules. Any real pet lover of any experience will agree on the following precepts:

1. Do not patronize pet stores. It would be far better for our animal friends if all pet stores (and all their suppliers) were to go into another line of work. The best purveyors of pet food and other supplies and equipment do not run a sideline in live animals. Do not plan to keep exotic pets, because this encourages a cruel and often illegal trade in threatened or endangered species.

2. Remember that mixed-breed animals, the kind you are likely to find at the local animal shelter, tend to be smarter and healthier than pure-bred specimens.

3. Unless you have definite plans to enter your pet in dog or cat shows, be sure to have it spayed or neutered. If your animal participates in producing a litter of kittens or pups, some of them are almost certain to end up homeless or abused.

4. If your pet is a dog, sign up for obedience training. It is work, but it is fun and satisfying, and life will be better both for you and your dog. If your pet is a cat, keep your fingers crossed.

5. When you need to board your pet while you're taking that vacation trip, don't let it be caged for days on end in your veterinarian's basement. Find a pet lover, either a friend or a professional, who will let your pet have some fun while you're having yours.

6. When your pet can no longer enjoy life, put it peacefully to sleep. Some vets are prepared to keep your pet alive no matter how much it costs you in money or the animal in misery.

# PART FOUR

## PROBLEMS OF GENDER

> Just as a cautious businessman avoids investing all his
> capital in one concern, so wisdom would probably
> admonish us also not to anticipate all our happiness from
> one quarter alone.
>
> —SIGMUND FREUD

Ever since Adam lost a rib and gained a wife, relations between the sexes have been somewhat dodgy. If we can believe Tom Wolfe,* "The most prominent feminist in America, Gloria Steinem, in a television interview with John Stossel of ABC, insisted that studies of genetic differences between male and female nervous systems should cease forthwith." But men and women *are* different, one from another, radical feminism to the contrary notwithstanding. The sexes are different in their interests, in their values, in their talents, in their ways of thinking. From the genes' point of view, men and women are the two parts of a fallible mechanism for the genes' immortality—we provide temporary housing while we construct the little vessels that will carry those genes on their next lap round the track. But even in this most basic of functions, men and women make different contributions and have slightly different agendas.

These differences between the sexes we sometimes celebrate and at other times lament, and they include differences in the

---

*T. Wolfe, "Sorry, but Your Soul Just Died," *Forbes ASAP* (December 2, 1996).

171

male and female recipes for happiness, which, while similar in outline, differ in their details. The institution of marriage is at the same time a principal source of, and yet obstacle to, human happiness. Our research with twins has allowed us to discover why couples fall in love and cleave together and also why, too often, they later cleave apart.

# 10

# SEX DIFFERENCES

A pretty foot is a great gift of nature.

—GOETHE

Down by the salley gardens my love and I did meet;
She passed the salley gardens with little snow-white feet.
She bid me take love easy, as the leaves grow on the tree;
But I, so young and foolish, with her would not agree.

— YEATS

For an aging university professor who has been admiring female bobby-soxers during nearly fifty years of perambulating about the campus, the current fashion of unisex dress and bodily adornment poses a real problem. In all that time, I've never tried to pick a boutonniere, much less a bouquet, yet one does enjoy a stroll along the garden paths. But this young person now approaching with the shoulder-length auburn hair and the golden earring, is this a boy or a girl? (I have learned to refer to young men and young women in this fashion only in the privacy of thought.) What is the gender of that young strider ahead of me in the short hair, pants, and boots? The ratio of waist to hip circumference is a useful cue but not wholly reliable (and not always detectable). There is another clue that I have recently confirmed experimentally and am now ready to announce to the waiting world. *The female of our species has smaller feet, relative to her height, than does the male.*

This discovery is a (perhaps minor) fruit of a serious and important scientific project, started by myself but now in the

173

charge of two younger colleagues, Bill Iacono and Matt McGue, who will carry it into the next millennium, the Minnesota Twin/Family Study that I referred to in chapter 6. Two cohorts of same-sex twins, aged either eleven or seventeen when first brought to our laboratory with their parents, are to be followed for (at least) nine years from that initial visit, coming back to the university every three years for further testing, a total of some 1,300 families, 5,200 people, and about 20,000 person-visits. Of the many tests and interviews conducted during their first visit were a series of anthropometric or bodily measurements, including stature and foot length. With all these numbers in the computer, it dawned on me that here was an opportunity to test my conjecture that the ratio of foot to body length is smaller for women than for men. Figure 10.1 shows the distribution of this ratio for the twins' mothers and fathers and confirms my thesis.

It was natural, then, to wonder whether this sex difference, like so many others, manifests itself at puberty. If so, then the corresponding distributions for the seventeen-year-old twins should show the same sex difference that the parent data evidence, while the distributions for the eleven-year-olds should overlap completely. Figure 10.2 demonstrates that this prediction was mistaken. The prepubescent boys' feet are as much longer than the girls' relative to their height, as was true for the older twins or for the parents. But figure 10.2 does show one interesting difference: Youngsters of both sexes have "puppy feet," considerably longer for their height than is true for their elders. Perhaps, when they are learning, as all children must, to "stand on their own two feet," Nature kindly provides them with a sturdier platform.

Before you conclude that it was a criminal waste of federal research grant funds to generate such foolish findings, let me give assurance that the data were collected for good and different reasons and that this particular bit of data analysis was conducted one Saturday on my own time. Moreover, these results do validate a suspicion that many people have expressed: namely, that those who design women's fashions don't like

## FOOT/HEIGHT RATIO: PARENTS

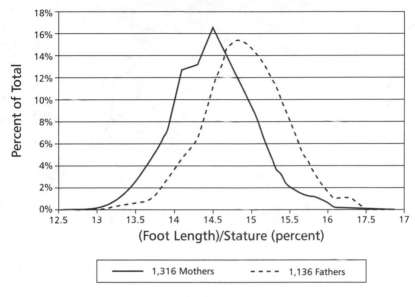

**FIGURE 10.1**

Distributions of foot length (x100) divided by height for a representative sample of middle-aged male and female residents of Minnesota. While there is considerable overlap (as in most gender comparisons), the average woman of any given height has a smaller foot than the average man of that height. Warning: this clue to gender status is insufficient as a basis for romantic overtures.

women very much. Since long before Goethe or Yeats, male poets have celebrated the attractions of little female feet. Therefore, it follows, as the night the day, that the modern designers of those currently fashionable great clunky women's shoes either do not know what most men like or else they do not care.

However, it is not only in these and other physical character-istics that the sexes differ. In respect to temperament, for exam-ple, our studies indicate that the average man is more aggressive and also less fearful (less harm-avoidant) than two-thirds of all women; no surprises there. Women are much more sentimental than men, much more nurturant, and have stronger feelings of empathy for other people. Men and women are about equal, in-terestingly, in their degree of empathy for animals. And men and

**FOOT/HEIGHT RATIO: 11 YEAR-OLDS**

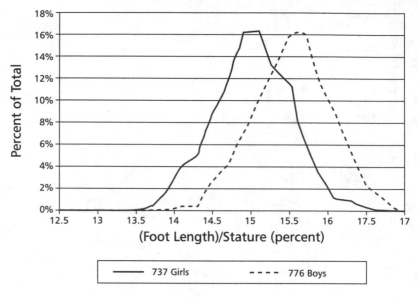

FIGURE 10.2

Distributions of foot length (x100) divided by height for representative samples of 11-year-old male and female twins. Because the sexes differ as much at this age as they did for the parental sample in Fig. 10.1, the difference cannot be attributed to pubertal changes. Note, however, that children of both genders have bigger feet for their heights than do the adults in Fig. 10.1

women are also about equal, at least in Minnesota, in their average ponderal index, which is to say, in how fat they are.[1]

## Sex Differences in Interests

We asked more than four thousand middle-aged twins to indicate their degree of interest in 120 different leisure-time activities. Table 10.1 lists the interests in which the sexes differed the most; for example, the average woman enjoys dancing more than at least 70 percent of men. Men and women differ significantly in their interest in 62 of the 120 recreational activities, and they differ substantially in those listed in table 10.1.

| Women Prefer | Men Prefer |
|---|---|
| Work with fabrics, yarns | Rebuilding boat or car |
| Weaving or rug making | Hunting small game |
| Working with flowers | Hunting ducks |
| Working with food | Hunting big game |
| Going shopping | Watching boxing |
| Watching TV soap operas | Target shooting |
| Writing letters | Rebuilding, repairing things |
| Live theater, musicals | Watching TV sports |
| Cultivating looks, dress | Watching pro wrestling |
| Reading current novels | Inventing things |
| Phoning friends or family | Building a workshop, darkroom, etc. |
| Dancing | Fishing |
| Creative artwork | Risky pastimes (e.g., bungee jumping) |
| Doing crossword puzzles | Trading, speculating |
| Sitting or lying in the sun | Trail bikes, snowmobiles |
| Doing amateur theater | |

**TABLE 10.1**

Sex differences in leisure-time interests. To be listed here, the average person of the given sex must indicate a stronger interest in the given activity than at least 70 percent of the opposite sex; the items are listed in order of decreasing sex difference. Data are based on middle-aged twins from the Minnesota Twin Registry, 1,778 men and 2,338 women.

It is interesting to look at these differences from an evolutionary perspective. During Neolithic times, there was a division of labor by gender. The men made things, mainly weapons, they went trekking off on hunting expeditions, and probably played some rather physical games. The women made things, too, but different things, they fixed up the cave, did a bit of gardening ("gathering"). They gossiped with one another, perhaps while fixing themselves up in preparation for the men's return, they cooked what the men brought home from the hunt, and, most important of all, the women took care of the little ones. Those boys and girls who were not interested in gender-appropriate activities would have appeared strange to their peers and would have been less likely to find mates, have babies of their own, and thereby to become ancestors.

The sex differences in occupational interests are *not* differences in status; men and women express roughly equal interest in most professions, for example. But there are substantial sex differences in which professions they find appealing: engineering *versus* pediatrics, for example. Men and women differ in what they like to do for fun and also for a living and, although these differences are surely influenced by cultural traditions and expectations, it is also true that interests, like all psychological traits, have strong genetic roots. But the main thing to realize is that that there is substantial overlap between the sexes—some women want to be astronauts, truck drivers, or engineers, while some men want to be nurses, psychologists, or potters.

What do interests have to do with happiness? Come on, now, pay attention! Happy people either have many interests or, at least, they have a few strong interests that keep them involved, productive, active, and, well, happy. At least some unhappy people have been neglecting their own innate interests, either because they thought they weren't appropriate for someone of their gender or someone in their position (dumb reasons, both) or because they were too busy doing things they were not interested in, doing them because they thought they had to.

Operating above your innate well-being set point is a bouncy business because you will quickly adapt to anything you do that gives your happiness a lift, and then your well-being will sink down again to your natural average. That means you have to vary your diet of happy-making activities, a little of this and then a little of that, if you want to keep the ball bouncing. I love to work on this book, for example, because I think it is interesting, but when my enthusiasm begins to wane, I click the "save" symbol on the computer and turn to something else. But the first requirement is to have a reasonably clear idea of what your own real interests are.

| Women Prefer | Men Prefer |
|---|---|
| Child care: nursery or day care center | Heavy construction: bridges, etc. |
| Office worker, clerk, secretary | Professional athlete: box, wrestle |
| Hairdresser, barber, cosmetician | Driver of emergency vehicles |
| Care of the elderly | Racing driver, sky diver, stunt man |
| Homemaker, family caretaker | Railroad crew: engine driver, etc. |
| Retail sales, supermarket checker | Engineer: chemical, electrical, etc. |
| Nurse, paramedic, midwife | Skilled trades: mechanic, carpenter |
| Fashion model: magazine or TV | Sergeant or petty officer in military |
| Social worker, counselor | Coach of a team sport |
| Potter, embroiderer, jewelry maker | Home building: framing, painting, etc. |
| Museum or gallery curator | Commissioned officer: army, navy |
| Production staff: opera or theater | Truck driver, interstate |
| Caterer, manage restaurant, bakery | Airline cockpit crew |
| Bookkeeper, auditor, accountant | Professional athlete: team sports |
| Physician: infants and children | Selling: real estate, machinery, cars |
| Painter, sculptor, designer | Highway patrol officer, police |
| Psychiatrist or psychologist | Janitor, security guard |
| | Astronaut, test pilot, explorer |
| | Elected public official |
| | Factory supervisor, foreman |
| | Agent for the FBI, CIA, or DEA |
| | Forestry, lumbering, forest ranger |
| | Driver: taxis, buses, parcel delivery |
| | Grain farmer |
| | Game warden |

TABLE 10.2

Gender differences in occupational interests. To be listed, one sex had to indicate they "liked" the given occupation at least twice as often as the other sex. The largest sex differences are those at the top of the table.

## Physical Attractiveness and Happiness

The girl that I marry will have to be
As soft and as pink as a nursery. . . .
—IRVING BERLIN (*Annie Get Your Gun*)

Perhaps the best authority on physical attractiveness, both real (that is, rated by impartial observers) and imaginary (that is, one's own self-rating), is a young Yale psychologist, Alan Feingold. In a recent survey of the world literature on this topic,[2] he reports some interesting findings. First, about two-thirds of the studies (or, at least, two-thirds of the 168,000 subjects studied) come from the United States. Second, the average woman is rated to be more attractive than about 60 percent of men in the United States but more attractive than about 70 precent of men in other parts of the world (mainly in Europe). On the other hand, women the world over see themselves as slightly less attractive than men see themselves.

The biggest sex difference, however, is in general satisfaction with one's own body. The average woman, both here and abroad, is less satisfied with the appearance of her salient body parts than are 70 percent of men satisfied with their own bits and pieces. Moreover, this dissatisfaction among women has been growing since at least the 1970s, and Feingold and others believe that this trend helps to explain the current miniepidemic of eating disorders such as anorexia (self-starving) and bulimia (binge eating followed by self-induced vomiting), which affects women almost exclusively. When I was a student, no one had heard of bulimia, and anorexia was rare, but both are commonplace today.

Psychologist David Buss has shown that, across many diverse cultures, men put youth and beauty at the top of their lists of female attractions, whereas women are more intrigued by a man's status than by his looks. This makes good evolutionary sense. It is the woman who carries the baby for nine months and then suckles it a year or more longer; she is the garden in which the seed is planted and Nature leads men to seek out a virgin plot with rich and healthy soil. The man's job is, first, to provide strong seed, and then to care for the garden and its fruit. A man of strength, skillful and responsible, respected by his fellows, is therefore a better prospect than a mere Adonis. As is so often the case, poets have understood these matters sooner than psychologists. For example, consider Ira Gershwin's lyric: *Your pa is rich and your ma is good lookin', so hush little baby, don't you cry.* Woody Allen and Walter Matthau were lucky to have been born with Y chromosomes.

These facts undoubtedly explain why eating disorders, expressing neurotic hyperconcern with physical attractiveness, affect girls and women almost exclusively. In spite of these facts, however, such concern is irrational. Nearly all women who want a mate eventually find one and, before marriage started to go out of fashion in the 1960s, about 90 percent of women eventually married (and about one-third of the never-married did not want a husband). Having once found a mate to father and provide for her children, it behooves a woman to care about her health, but not to fret about her physical attractiveness. That biological imperative having been accomplished, what matters then is the love of her children and the affection and respect of her husband and her friends, and none of these is based on beauty. Yet, all too often, the genes' "prehistoric song" keeps ringing in her ears, and the cosmetics and fashion industries continue to flourish.

## Sex Differences in Happiness

Although men still tend to have better jobs than women do, and get higher pay for the same jobs, we already saw in chapter 1 that not only are most women happy most of the time, but they report well-being levels as high as those of men. And this is true not just in North America but across Europe as well. Ronald Inglehart, at the University of Michigan, gave the same questionnaire, suitably translated, to representative samples of both genders in sixteen different countries. He found that 80 percent of both sexes declared themselves to be "satisfied" with their lives, while 21 percent of the men and 24 percent of the women went so far as to claim that they were "very happy."[3] David Myers[4] reports that only 14 percent of married women held outside jobs in 1890, compared with 25 percent in 1940 and about 60 percent today. Yet working women are neither more nor less contented on the whole than full-time homemakers. Myers wisely points out that it is the challenge and the resulting satisfaction of the work that makes the difference, whether the job is at home or away, whether compensated by a paycheck or by its intrinsic satisfactions.

Professor Myers goes on to review evidence showing that women as a group, while their happiness set points compare favorably with those of men, are inclined to experience greater swings about those average levels than do men. And, contrary to popular belief, this greater emotional ability is *not* attributable to changes in the menstrual cycle.

## Sex Differences in Social Relationships

Another difference between men and women that is apparent in our data, for middle-aged twins, for seventeen-year-old twins, and for the parents of these younger twins, is that women score higher on the trait of social closeness; most women have a stronger need for close, confiding, intimate relationships than does the average man. A family with daughters is more likely to feel the need for a second telephone than is a family having only sons. Men, on the other hand, take more naturally than women do to organized activities and teamwork; the "chain of command" is a male invention. I still remember how much I enjoyed drilling on the parade ground in navy boot camp years ago. It surprised me because I had thought of myself as an individualist, yet there was a strange, elemental satisfaction in becoming, at least for a while, one of a hundred pairs of legs of some larger organism. Enoch Powell, a conservative member of the British Parliament when I was studying in England in 1955, rose from a lowly private to officer rank in World War II, but when asked by a BBC reporter what he had enjoyed most about his army service, Powell said, "Marching in formation."

## HARM AVOIDANCE

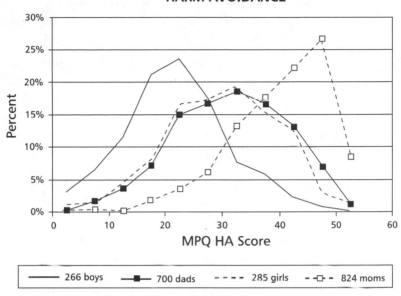

**FIGURE 10.3**

Distributions of MPQ Harm Avoidance scores obtained by 17-year-old male and female twins and by the parents in the Minnesota Twin/Family Study. Most of the mothers score higher than most of the fathers, the girls score higher than the boys, and the adolescents of both sexes are less fearful than the same-sex parents on average.

Another major difference between men and women is in fearfulness, as can be seen in figure 10.3. Most of the moms in figure 10.3 scored higher than the average dad did on the harm avoidance scale of the MPQ. Most of the seventeen-year-old girl twins scored higher than the average boy twin. The origins of this difference are mixed. Although harm avoidance has strong genetic roots, this trait is also subject to considerable modification through experience. Notice that the boys in the figure are much less fearful than their fathers, and the girls less fearful than their mothers. This is the risk-taking propensity of adolescence that grown-ups regard as foolhardy. The MPQ measures fearfulness with items like this:

Of the following two situations I would *dislike more:*
(A) Riding a long stretch of rapids in a canoe; (B) Waiting
for someone who's late.

One alternative is scary, while the other is merely onerous.
Fearful people tend to dislike the scary alternatives more than
the merely irritating or tiresome ones. Are adolescents simply
less able to forecast how unpleasant it might be swooshing down
those rapids in a tippy canoe? Or are they biologically less vulnerable than they will be after the years have worn down their
defenses?

On the other hand, we know that the right kinds of experience can make shy people less fearful than they were at first.
As I shall explain in chapter 13, shyness and fearfulness can be
decreased gradually by a process of systematic desensitization.
Fear of heights, for example, can be reduced by climbing just a
bit higher each day. A child's fear of strangers can be mitigated
by exposing her, gradually and safely, to new people, first one at
a time and then, when one stranger no longer frightens her, to
two, then three, then more. In many human cultures, boys are
expected to be more venturesome than girls, and this puts a
greater pressure on boys to climb a bit higher than they might if
no one was watching—and thus to desensitize their innate fears
more than girls are likely to do.

At least part of this gender difference in venturesomeness is
assuredly innate, however. While sitting in a doctor's waiting
room recently, I watched two siblings, one a baby not yet able to
walk and the other a toddler less than three years old. The older
one had made a game of climbing on to a coffee table and then
jumping bravely down the ten inches to the floor. The younger
watched, entranced, laughing gleefully at each jump. I don't have
to tell you that these were brothers, not sisters. Many well-
intending parents, wanting to avoid cultural stereotyping, try to
provide their children with unisex toys. Nine times out of ten,
however, it will be the little girls who adopt the dolls and the toy
furniture while the little boys will be attracted to toys that lend
themselves to more boisterous ("boy-stir-us") play.

## AGGRESSION

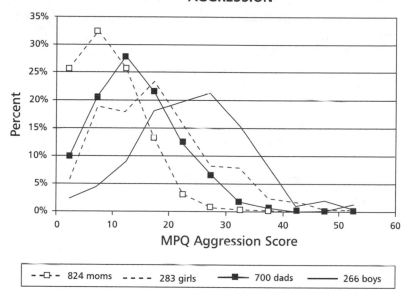

**FIGURE 10.4**

Distributions of MPQ Aggression scores obtained by 17-year-old male and female twins and by the parents in the Minnesota Twin/Family Study. Most of the dads score higher than most of the moms, the boys score higher than the girls, and the adolescents of both sexes are more aggressive than the same-sex parents on average.

We saw in table 10.1 that men are much more attracted to "risky pastimes" than are women, as would be expected from their lower score on harm avoidance. Figure 10.4 shows the scores of the same twin-family members on aggression, a measure of the tendency to strike out or hit back, either verbally or physically. Here the dads are more aggressive than the moms, the seventeen-year-old boys more so than the girls, and the adolescents more aggressive than their parents. These sex and age differences in fear and in aggression help to explain why the vast majority of criminals, particularly those inclined to violence, are men, especially young men and boys. The women, however, are beginning to catch up. One effect of women's liberation has been that young women and girls are now expected to be feistier, more venturesome, less willing to let the men and boys take all the risks. This may have had the unintended consequence of increasing the rate of crime and violence by female perpetrators. Between 1994 and 1995, for example, while the male rate actually declined slightly (because so many men and boys had been imprisoned), the female violent crime rate increased 6.4 percent. Although the male is more dangerous than the female on average, the two figures illustrate that there are a few women and girls who are much less fearful or much more aggressive than the average man or boy.

# 11

# How to Stay Happy Though Married

That state which is a blessing to a few, a curse to many,
and a great uncertainty to all.
    —Rev. E. J. Hardy, *How to Be Happy Though Married*

When our love was new, and each kiss an inspiration:
But that was long ago . . .
                        —Hoagy Carmichael

A t the supermarket, my wife takes note of prices while I take note of people. My wife estimates (and I believe her) that our grocery bill would be at least 50 percent higher if I did the shopping, which means that we are now at least $140,000 richer after forty-six years of marriage because of her clipping of coupons and knowledge of prices. But more important than the money (which seems to have been spent anyway, probably foolishly by me) is the fact that my wife *enjoys* being a good shopper; she is good at it, it is a useful skill, and we humans all enjoy exercising useful skills.

Meanwhile, back at the market, on almost every visit, we encounter at least one sour-faced elderly couple standing by their cart and bitching at each other. One can imagine what their home life must be like, nag and grumble, swear and bang, about as happy as a prison. What is wrong with these people? Once upon a time, their marriage had seemed made in heaven, they had delighted in each other's company; now, all that was positive is negative.

187

Their counterparts in the baby boomer generation have been divorced, of course, long since, often more than once. According to his Boswell, Samuel Johnson once spoke of "a gentleman who had been very unhappy in marriage, [who] married immediately after his wife died [only kings got divorced in Johnson's day]: Johnson said it was a triumph of hope over experience." Many divorced boomers grew up with parents constantly quarreling and had always told themselves that they would never let their own marriage descend to such a state. And, indeed, when the going began to get bumpy, they split. Unhampered by the old taboos against divorce that kept their parents together, will they be better off, happier, when they reach their parents' age? One of the interesting things about those bickering old couples at the market is that they are there together; what are we to make of that?

Perhaps we could make headway in understanding some of these thorny problems if we understood better why people fall in love in the first place, and why they get divorced in the last place. By happy coincidence, recent research with our Minnesota Twin Registry has thrown new light on both of these interesting questions.

## The Psychology of Infatuation

Ah! Sweet mystery of life, at last I've found you!
Ah! I know at last the secret of it all!
—VICTOR HERBERT

In every lasting relationship, except those between relatives, the partners are bonded by shared experience, mutual understanding, and mutual tolerance, and this is a bond that forms slowly, over periods of years. Some other force is needed, like a woodworker's clamp, to hold the partners together until the glue has set. Lasting friendships generally require people to have been thrown together by external circumstance, as schoolmates, coworkers, neighbors, long enough to become accustomed parts of each other's lives. The relationships that produce good marriages sometimes begin the same way, but most often they begin sud-

denly, and some other force or "clamp" is required to give enduring companionate affection time to develop. That clamp, that
centripetal force, is infatuation.

In a fascinating discussion of the evolution of love, Mellen
attempts to account for the fact that, unlike our primate cousins,
except the solitary gibbon, we are a pair-bonding species.[1] No
baby chimp or bonobo knows its own father, or needs to.[2] It
matures quickly and can cling to its mother's fur as she climbs
about in the pantry of the forest, a "single mother" fully capable
of feeding and rearing her baby with just the routine assistance
of the troop. But when our ancestors came out of the forest onto
the savannas and began producing babies with big brains, babies
who were altricial, or slow to develop, that posed a problem.
Now that early hominid mother needed assistance in watching
over and nurturing that helpless babe, who better than the other
adult who had the same genetic investment in her child that she
had?

These pairings of mates are not always exclusive, nor do they
always endure for life, but pair-bonding is characteristic of our
kind across cultures and since before there were cultures. Therefore, the fact that pair-bonding (sometimes polygynous pair-
bonding) is universally supported by cultural institutions, such
as marriage and sanctions against adultery, attests to its adaptational importance without denying that its primal roots are in
the human DNA. And that adaptational importance, of course,
derived from the need for the shared efforts of a male and female
parent to provide for the nutrition and protection of the uniquely
altricial human infant.

The bond to which Mellen refers, the capacity for which
evolved during the late Pleistocene, motivated those ancestral
fathers to stand between their families and danger, and to trek
home from hunting expeditions carrying heavy loads of meat
instead of merely consuming their fill on the spot. And these
impulses had to be sustained at least through the mate's pregnancy and the early infancy of the offspring of that bond. This
pair-bonding, which was adaptive during the evolution of our
species and thus became a species-typical human tendency,

should be distinguished from what Berscheid and Walster, among others, refer to as *companionate* love, "the affection we feel for those with whom our lives are deeply intertwined."[3] In ancestral times—and often in modern times as well—companionate love developed *after* mating or marriage, and there is a large literature concerned with those factors that determine whether companionate love blossoms or withers.[4] But companionate love takes time to leaf out and blossom, time for mutual adjustments, the sharing of experiences, for the forging of the ties that bind. One universal of human culture is the institution of marriage, which has the effect (and was presumably designed for the effect) of providing the time for pair-bonding to mature into a more stable companionate relationship.

But it is necessary to ask: What effected this result during the Pleistocene? What served to bind the mated pair together until the glue was set? This is where we need to invoke the concept of infatuation or romantic love. The time course of romantic love is opposite to that of companionate affection, the first peaking early and then tending to subside while the second more gradually matures. Young lovers generally feel an intense and exclusive commitment to one particular beloved, often after only months or even weeks of acquaintance. Berscheid and Campbell describe the state of the young lover as one "of heightened and intensified positive emotional experiences perhaps unmatched by any other period in most people's lives."[5]

Some empirical support for this characterization of the early stages of romantic love can be found in the responses of hundreds of young lovers who filled out a forty-two-item Love Attitudes Scale.[6] Among the items most strongly endorsed by these subjects were: "My lover and I have the right physical 'chemistry' between us"; "I feel that my lover and I were meant for each other"; "My lover fits my ideal standards of physical beauty." Among the students studied by Hazan and Shaver, some 85 percent rejected the statement: "The kind of head-over-heels romantic love depicted in novels and movies doesn't exist in real life."[7] Fisher, in a study of fifty-eight contemporary societies, finds a remarkably consistent tendency for the first divorce, if divorce occurs at all, to happen after a modal period of four years.[8] This, she believes, "reflects an ancestral strategy to remain pair-bonded at least long enough to raise a single infant through the period of lactation." Liebowitz contends that romantic infatuation is associated with increased specific neurotransmitter activity,[9] which creates the sensations of euphoria and optimism that characterize this state, and that this biochemical process is self-limited to two or three years, the same interval that others report to be characteristic of romantic attachment.[10] Tennov, who coined the term "limerence" specifically to distinguish romantic delirium from the more sober and stable companionate love that limerence ideally will presage, provides many case histories illustrating the phenomenon.[11] Tennov also provides examples of "nonlimerent" people, both from her researches and from the literature (e.g., Richard Wagner, Lord Byron), people experienced in sexual relationships yet who had never been "in love."

## Why Do People Fall in Love?

Well, you'll know in your heart if it's so,
In spite of how little we know.
—HOAGY CARMICHAEL

Wagner and Byron are the exceptions. Most young couples, when the wedding march is playing, are under the illusion that they have found their one and only (and isn't it remarkable that he/she lived on my block or went to my school or my church?). But what are people looking for when they get in line at the mating cafeteria? The most popular theory is that people look for someone like themselves. This "similars attract" idea gets superficial support from the fact that spouses tend to be more like one another than random pairs of people on nearly every characteristic that has been studied, from age and stature to IQ and years of education, to their interests and religious attitudes. But most people are nearly as similar to their friends and associates as they are to their spouses. Moreover, there are lots of dishes in the mating cafeteria that are as much like you as most spouses are to one another, so that does not help explain why you chose the one (and only) that you did.

It occurred to Auke Tellegen and me that we could investigate this curious problem of mate choice using again our large and representative sample of middle-aged twins. Even if we were to suppose that each Chooser employs idiosyncratic criteria in making a selection, identical or MZ twins, who have the same DNA and who were reared together in the same family and neighborhood, ought to have very similar criteria. We know, in fact, that MZ twins are similar in most of their choices: they like the same cars, the same recreations, the same clothes, the same movies. Even Bouchard's twins reared apart often used the same brands of cigarettes or cosmetics, chose the same names for their children, had similar jobs or hobbies, and so on. Therefore, it seemed reasonable to suppose that MZ twins would choose (that is to say, fall in love with) similar spouses. We already had scores for hundreds of the spouses of Registry twins on seventy-four psychological and demographic variables, so we could do a preliminary test of this conjecture. To our surprise, we found that the spouses of MZ twins are no more alike than the spouses of DZ pairs and, at least on our set of measures, hardly more similar than random pairs of people of that age and sex.

We needed to collect more data. A confidential survey was mailed out to 125 pairs each of male and female, MZ and same-sex DZ twins, 500 pairs or 1,000 individuals in total, all of whom had been married. More than two-thirds (734) of the surveys were filled out and returned.[12] The first few questions were intended just to confirm that MZ twins tend to have similar tastes. The twins were asked to rate their cotwin's choices of clothes, household furnishings, vacation plans, and jobs and, indeed, from 64 to 80 percent of the MZ twins liked their cotwin's selections, compared with 40 to 61 percent of the DZ twins. (On the jobs question, however, only 54 percent of the female MZs liked their cotwin's job, compared with 64 percent of the males, which probably means that women still are less able than men to get the kind of job they like themselves.) Figure 11.1 shows that, indeed, MZ twins tend to approve of, for example, their cotwin's wardrobe choices, and that DZ twins, in contrast, are less enthu-siastic about each other's clothes.

The bottom-line question was different. After an extra pledge of confidentiality, we asked each twin to think back to the time when the cotwin first decided to marry and to describe his or her feeling at that time about the cotwin's choice of mate. The alternatives were:

1. I felt that I'd rather stay single than marry my twin's fiancé;
2. I would not have chosen my twin's fiancé;
3. I had no strong feeling one way or the other;
4. I really liked my twin's fiancé;
5. I could have fallen for my twin's fiancé.

On this question, the results were entirely different. For both MZ and DZ twins, about as many disliked as liked the mate that

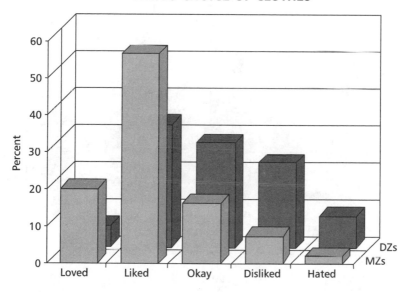

**FIGURE 11.1**

Responses of 545 twins when asked whether they approved of their cotwin's wardrobe clothes. As expected, the MZ twins display more similar tastes than do the DZ twins.

their cotwin had selected and was about to marry! In fact, as figure 11.2 shows, when we asked these twins to rate their own attraction to the person that their cotwin had found irresistible, they produced the same distribution of responses that we might expect if we asked them to rate, say, their next-door neighbor.

Now, there is one question mark about these results: When twins meet their cotwin's beloved, perhaps they feel a bit jealous of the person who has intruded into that formerly exclusive twin relationship. Or perhaps some twins underrate their attraction to their cotwin's choice in order to avoid potential competition with their twin. Happily, Tellegen and I also sent questionnaires to the spouses of these twins and asked them to tell us how they felt when they were first in love and had that initial meeting with their beloved's twin. Figure 11.3 shows the results.

### TWIN'S CHOICE OF SPOUSE

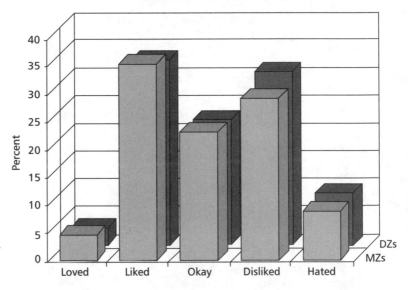

**FIGURE 11.2**

"When you first met the person with whom your twin was in love and eventually married, how did you feel about that person? Were you attracted, too, or actually repelled, or just neutral?" Both MZ and DZ twins seem to have reacted to their cotwin's choice of mate about as they would to some random person of that age and gender.

## FEELINGS FOR SPOUSE'S TWIN

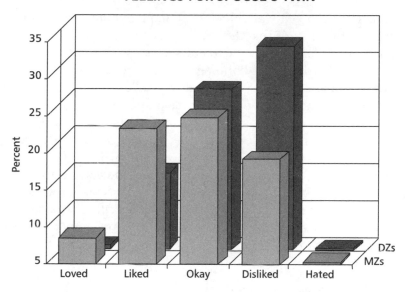

FIGURE 11.3

"When you first met the twin of the person with whom you were in love and eventually married, how did you feel about his or her twin?" DZ twins, for some reason, tended to be rather negative in their reactions. Among the wives of MZ twins, the same proportion (37 percent) reported positive as negative reactions. But the husbands of female MZ twins were biased in the positive direction, 53 percent "liked" or "loved" while only 32 percent "disliked" or "hated." This may be because men, shallow creatures that we are, are more influenced by physical appearance than are women.

The first time we were asking whether the clone of a lover was also attracted to that lover's beloved, and the answer was no. This time we were asking whether the lover is attracted to the clone of the beloved and, once again, the answer was no. This means that we cannot predict who will fall in love with whom, *either* from the characteristics of the Chooser (since the Chooser's MZ twin is unlikely to make the same choice) *or* from the characteristics of the Chosen (since the lover of that Chosen is unlikely to be attracted to that Chosen's clone). This is very curious indeed! My colleague Auke Tellegen suggested what I think is the correct (albeit still mysterious) explanation.

If the tendency for pair-bonding evolved in our species to enhance the viability of vulnerable hominid young, it seems reasonable to conclude that the related capacity for romantic infatuation, which may be unique to our species, evolved concurrently because it enabled pair-bonding. Within broad limits, it would not have mattered who paired with whom; as long as the female was young and healthy and the male strong and an attentive provider, the evolutionarily important goal—the bearing and rearing of offspring—would have been achieved. Ancestral pairings need not have been any more selective or predictable from the individual characteristics of the male and female involved than modern matings appear to be. But the infatuation-induced ancestral pairings would have had to be specific and singular, bonding a specific male to a specific female long enough to get them through that vulnerable early period (and, perhaps, for a more permanent relationship to develop).

> . . . And maidens call it love-in-idleness.
> Fetch me that flower, the herb I shew'd thee once.
> The juice of it, on sleeping eye-lids laid
> Will make or man or woman madly dote
> Upon the next live creature that it sees.
> —OBERON TO ROBIN GOODFELLOW

> Lord, what fools these mortals be!
> —ROBIN TO OBERON, *A Midsummer Night's Dream*

Imprinting evolved among precocial birds (like ducks and geese, whose chicks can run about almost as soon as they hatch) because it tied the newly hatched but mobile ducklings by invisible bonds to their mother, who could thus lead them to food and to safety. Romantic infatuation, Tellegen suggests, like imprinting, forms an initial bond almost adventitiously and then sustains it long enough, in most instances, for an enduring bond to be forged by the slower processes of learning and adaptation that result in companionate love.

Ducklings are equipped with a species-specific "search image" that, in the presence of two moving objects at the critical time, causes them to imprint on the more ducklike.[13] But the ducklings' search image is only schematic. Any mother duck as well as many quite unsuitable surrogates (not normally present in the wild) can serve as releasers of the imprinting instinct. By confining the mother goose and then approaching her nest himself soon after hatching, Konrad Lorenz managed to have broods of goslings imprint on him.[14] The data reviewed herein suggest that the search image for human mate selection is similarly schematic; nearly any opposite-sexed individual of roughly siblinglike similarity might serve as a releaser. What we do not understand is the mechanism of human sexual imprinting or infatuation.

Do humans have critical periods for infatuation? If we do, they are plural. Monogamous nonhuman animals like geese, wolves, or gibbons pair up again when a mate dies. In our species also, an existing relationship seems to inhibit infatuation, and it may be that termination of a relationship initiates a period of renewed responsiveness. Unlike ducklings, however, even during a period of susceptibility we do not imprint romantically on just any passing individual who falls within the range of our search criteria. Adolescence is assuredly a critical period, yet even adolescents do not become infatuated with every potential releaser. Having been reared together seems to inhibit romantic imprinting, but what affirmatively triggers the response?

Usually (although, alas, not always), we do not become infatuated with targets that are altogether beyond our grasp. Such evidence as the modest correlation between spouses for physical attractiveness suggests that we tend to focus our search on individuals whom we perceive as being in the same class of "mate worthiness" as ourselves and, thus, as potentially available. I suspect that attraction is often transmuted into genuine infatuation when it is reciprocated, that "I love you, too" or its equivalent is an important trigger mechanism (cf. Victor Herbert's lyric, "I think I could love someone madly, if someone would only love me!"). I shall not speculate further; it is an intriguing problem for more research.

## So What Does All This Mean?

Well, first of all, we have some very strong, persuasive, scientific evidence that the poets have been right all along. Whom you fall in love with will not be decided by your DNA, or by his/her DNA, or by what you learned in the bosom of your family, or in the school of hard knocks, or in graduate school. Whom you fall in love with will be determined by whom you happened to be standing next to when Cupid's arrow strikes. That individual is likely to be someone rather like yourself, someone from your "set," because those are the kinds of people you most often happen to be standing next to. But there is no guarantee of this, and no good evidence that it matters much as far as your future prospects are concerned.

We don't know when you might be vulnerable to Cupid's arrow, but it may be that *you* know. Ask yourself this: What if some really attractive person were to look deep into my eyes and confess that he/she loved me? Would you feel a thrill or would you wince? If you are in a committed relationship already, wincing is better. If you have built up an edifice of years of companionate affection, then being struck by Cupid's arrow can be like stepping on a land mine—wrack and ruin all around. This never happened to me, I'm glad to say, but I've lived through it with friends and the explosion simile is apt. One friend, I'll call him Humbert, fell in love with a girl younger than his daughter. I pictured an irresistible Lolita, but when at last I met this twenty-year-old paragon, she looked about fifteen and acted about twelve. Eventually, the scales fell from Humbert's eyes, and he escaped the affair with only his marriage, his finances, and his self-confidence in ruins.

> Once upon a time, the world was sweeter than we knew. . . .
> But, somehow, once upon a time never comes again.
> —SONG LYRIC BY LEE ADAMS

But what if your own romantic dream fades, say after the standard four-year period, and you find yourself committed but no longer enchanted? The first thing to do is to stop feeling cheated; we are all in the same boat, and its name is Human Nature. You won your lottery, and that kept you feeling high perhaps for longer than if you had won something more mundane, like a million dollars. The only people whose delirium persists indefinitely are the losers, the ones whose beloved always remained out of reach; would you want to trade places with them?

The next thing to do is to work on the companionate affection that should have been developing while you were preoccupied with romance and Roman candles. Think about your mutual investments in shared experience, perhaps in a child or two, in your intimate knowledge of each other's qualities, good and not so good. If there *are* children involved, then—unless their other parent is psychiatrically out of control or dangerous—I will adopt the hard-line position that you *must* make your relationship work, you owe it to those innocent babies that you brought into the world. You and your partner both have the responsibility of getting those children to life's starting line, and that means, roughly, getting them through high school with grades appropriate to their innate abilities and without the handicaps of a record of delinquency, drug addiction, or a child of their own. In chapter 8, I have reviewed the evidence showing that children reared by single parents are some *seven times* more likely to be abused, drop out of school, have an out-of-wedlock baby, or become delinquent and later criminal, than are children reared with the active participation of both resident biological parents.

Before coming to grips with the question of *how* to make the relationship work, it will be useful to consider why so many relationships do not work at present. I hardly need say that the loyal participants in the Minnesota Twin Registry have also contributed some interesting (and surprising) data that are relevant to this issue.

## The Genetics of Divorce

Love comes along, casting its spell;
Will it sing you a song? Will it say a farewell?
—Who can tell?
>                                   —HOAGY CARMICHAEL

Several years ago, my colleague Matt McGue and I mailed a short questionnaire to about half of the members of our Registry who had a same-sex twin.[15] Completed surveys were returned by 3,316 individuals, aged thirty-four to fifty-three years, of whom about 7.5 percent of the men and 5.9 percent of the women had never married. There were 1,516 pairs in which both twins returned surveys, of whom about half were MZ pairs and about 63 percent were female pairs (women, bless 'em, are always better about returning surveys). The questionnaire asked how many times they had been married, how many times divorced, and whether their parents had ever been divorced. We also asked them the same questions about their current spouse (if the respondent had never been divorced) or about their first or ex-spouse (if the respondent *had* been divorced).

About 20.3 percent of our sample had been divorced at least once, a rate just slightly higher than the 18.4 percent predicted from the 1980 U.S. census data for Minnesotans in the same age range as our subjects. The divorce rate was 22.6 percent for couples that had ever been married, and two and a half times greater for childless unions than for marriages that produced children. The divorce rate for the parents of these twins was lower, about 13 percent, partly because those parental marriages *had* produced offspring. What we were most interested in, however, was whether we could predict the divorce risk for a given marriage from a knowledge of whether the cotwin, the twins' parents, or the spouse's parents had ever been divorced.

We found, first, that divorce in either set of parents increased risk by about 50 percent (i.e., from 22.6 percent to 31.9 percent) and these effects were independent and additive—that is, if either you or your spouse's parents have divorced, your risk is 50 percent higher, but if both sets of parents have been divorced, the risk is 100 percent higher than if both yours and your spouse's parents had stayed married to each other. Second, if you or your spouse happens to have a fraternal or DZ twin, then if that twin is divorced, your risk increases also about 50 percent, independently of what both sets of parents did or did not do. Third, if you happen to have an identical or MZ twin who is divorced, the probability that your marriage will fail jumps up about 132 percent (from 17 percent to 39 percent)![16]

But marriage and divorce are both two-person games. It seems reasonable to assume that, on the average, each spouse contributes about 50 percent of the total risk that the marriage will fail. Yet our data suggest that we can predict about half of that total risk knowing only the relevant genetic factors (estimated from the behavior of the parents and the cotwin) brought to the table by only one of the partners! To make all this clearer, McGue (former math major who understands these things better than I do) has computed the risk for divorce of a hypothetical couple who both happen to be MZ twins born in Minnesota. If neither set of parents ever divorced, and if the MZ cotwins of both husband and wife are still married to their first spouses, then our lucky couple has only about a 5 percent chance of ending up in the divorce courts. If, on the other hand, both sets of parents divorced as well as both cotwins, then, alas, the risk for this marriage rockets up to 77.5 percent!

Does this mean there is gene for divorce? Certainly not. People get divorced for all sorts of reasons. But most of those reasons have to do with the participants' temperament, personality, interests, attitudes—with his or her *psychological traits*—and these, as we have seen, all have strong genetic roots. For example, in a subsequent study of many of these same twins who had also filled out Tellegen's personality inventory, the MPQ, we found that the personality differences measured by this test accounted for about one-third of the heritability of divorce risk.[17] Which personality traits proved most important is an interesting question that I shall return to shortly. Meanwhile, you might want to hazard a guess: Aggression? Social Closeness? Social Potency? Impulsiveness? Harm Avoidance? Traditionalism?

It is important to see that the complex trait we are talking about here is not the all-or-nothing property of *being* divorced but, rather, the graded or quantitative property of *risk* for divorce. People with enough of this trait to have split long since under current circumstances would still have been married a hundred years ago, when divorce was a much higher hurdle to cross. Cultural, religious, and legal factors determine the height of the hurdle, while psychological factors, all of them partly genetic, determine how high you are willing to jump. *Some* of those people are better off—happier—now that divorce is more accessible, than they would have been then. No doubt it is better to make a new start rather than being confined in an intractably miserable relationship.

However, I firmly believe that many people now divorced, "like the base Indian, threw a pearl away richer than all his tribe." They are like people whose homes have become so dirty and cluttered, the lawn unmowed, the basement full of junk, that they just burn it down and move away. How much better instead to roll up their sleeves, clean up and clear out the mess, and then resolve to do better in future. They have a big investment in that home, in that marriage, and it simply makes no sense to abandon it until all potential avenues of salvage have been explored.

## Happiness in Marriage

There have been rooms full of self-help guides and marriage manuals published (a good one is by Albert Ellis, which allows you to look over the shoulder of a very sensible marriage counselor).[18] I will not try to plow that same ground here. Instead, I will limit myself to a few things I have learned during my brief career as a psychotherapist, my longer career as a researcher, and my practically unblemished forty-six-year career as a husband. I hope you will find them interesting and—who knows?—perhaps even useful.

## Personality Traits

In our MPQ study mentioned above, it turned out that people high on Social Potency (extroverted, take-charge people) were at higher risk for divorce than more introverted people. Not surprisingly, people with a strong sense of traditional values are at relatively low risk. It might surprise you (at least, it surprised *us*) to learn that the Traditionalism scale of the MPQ is strongly influenced by genetic factors. One would have thought that children learn their social and religious values from their parents, yet identical twins reared apart by different parents correlate more strongly on this variable than on any other personality trait. Related measures, such as Conservatism, Right Wing Authoritarianism, and Religiousness also owe about half their variation across people to genetic differences between people.[19] Moreover, the strongest similarity between spouses is not IQ or education, not body size or even age, but rather their scores on Traditionalism. And if both husband and wife have high scores, they are less likely than the average couple to end up in the divorce courts.

Risk takers or fearless people have an increased risk for divorce, as do people high on the trait of impulsiveness. Probably the correct interpretation of these last two traits is that impulsive and more daring people are more likely to do things that create friction with their partners, up to and including physical abuse and extramarital affairs. Happy people are at lower risk, and I believe that this trait would have shown a stronger relationship if we had been able to measure our subjects' true happiness set point. Robert Louis Stevenson said that "there is no duty so much underrated as the duty of being happy." Because happiness is contagious, having someone cheerful in the house tends to put everyone in a good mood.

But these personality traits are rather strongly heritable, and our 1996 study showed that it is the heritable component of personality that predicts divorce risk. Does this mean that if you are an extroverted, risk-taking, free thinker your home life has to pay the price? Only if you decide to let your genetic steersman make all your decisions for you. Think about driving in traffic. Those same traits—impulsiveness, fearlessness, a tendency to disregard the rules—could get you into one accident after another. If you let your genetic steersman have his head to that degree, then you should surrender both your driver's license and your marriage license. But the chances are that you can control yourself driving in traffic, and this means that if you really want to and make the effort, you can control yourself in other situations also.

## Jealousy

This green-eyed monster that causes so much marital strife works differently in men than in women. David Buss, a psychologist at the University of Michigan, predicted this on evolutionary grounds.[20] Men need to be sure that the babies they are diapering and saving up to send to Harvard are really theirs, carriers of their own genes. Male sexual jealousy is based on the primal fear that some other rascal might sneak in and plant his seeds in your garden. Women, on the other hand, have no doubts about whether the baby that they carried for nine months is their own. Female jealousy is directed at the possibility that some siren might steal your mate's love and commitment so that his strength and resources will be devoted to her and hers rather than to you and yours.

To test this conjecture, Buss and his colleagues had men and women vividly imagine discovering that their mates (1) had sex with someone else or (2) had fallen in love (thus far Platonically) with someone else. In addition to asking his subjects how they felt about each fantasy, Buss also measured their physiological reactions while they were engaged in these painful reveries. As predicted, Buss found that men found sexual infidelity more disturbing, while women were most upset by the idea of their lover being in love with someone else. As is true of all such tests of psychological sex differences, some women reacted more like the typical male and some men more like the average woman, but on average, the differences were clear.

It has been shown recently that college women are more likely to assume that a love relationship will lead to sex than that a sexual relationship will lead to love. College men tend to think that both directions of causation are about equally likely.[21] These investigators thought they had wriggled out of the evolutionary dilemma, but as Buss and his colleagues point out,[22] the natural selection argument is the most parsimonious explanation of both sex differences. Most men know from personal experience that casual sexual contacts can occur without emotional involvement before or afterward. Most women, however, will acknowledge that the plot that suits them best can be found in the refrain: "First comes love, then comes marriage, then comes baby in a baby carriage."

Now picture the Olsons, who live in the middle of the block with the Smiths on one side and the Joneses on the other. Both Mrs. Smith and Mrs. Jones are ten years younger than Mrs. Olson, and even Mr. Olson, who is not very sensitive, vaguely realizes that this makes them a bit threatening to his wife. Mrs. Jones is a bosomy lady and a bit of a flirt. Because Mr. Olson finds her attractive, he tries to keep his distance in order to avoid giving his wife the wrong impression. Mrs. Smith, on the other hand, a divorcée with two young children, seems shy and helpless, and Mr. Olson feels sorry for her and is always ready to help out when she seems to need someone to shovel her walks or replace a fuse. It never occurs to Mr. Olson that from his wife's point of view, Mrs. Smith is the real threat.

Or consider Craig and Sally, a hippie couple who solicited my help when I was still practicing psychotherapy back in the sixties. They had been living together for about four years and seemed to me to be genuinely in love. But they had a problem. They belonged to a kind of commune whose members held advanced and liberated views about life, the environment, the evils of war, the virtues of recreational drugs, and about love and sex. Both Craig and Sally subscribed to the party line, which meant, among other things, that love between two people should not rule out spontaneous sex with other people. But Craig and Sally were not getting along; Craig often seemed surly and resentful, and Sally couldn't understand why.

After meeting with them once together and once with each alone, I offered my diagnosis: "You kids live in a world that's foreign to me, but I know that if I were Craig, I couldn't help feeling jealous about Sally's making out with other men, and I think it would make me feel hurt and mad and generally miserable. I know you two think that people shouldn't feel this way, but I think people *do* feel this way, especially men, because that's the way we are made. We can't really help it." I had feared they might make fun of my old-fashioned views, but Craig's eyes teared and his voice choked while Sally reacted with maternal solicitude: "I don't have to do those things, baby; I didn't think you cared!" It was one of my few triumphs as a therapist.

## Resentment

When two people live together, year in and year out, there is bound to be occasional friction. She doesn't show proper respect for my opinions; he just leaves a mess for me to clean up; she isn't interested in my plans or my ideas; he doesn't seem concerned about my feelings. Resentment festers, and the feeling grows that reparation is required. She needs to apologize and say she's sorry, he needs to see the error of his ways. Sometimes, indeed, it is a good idea to talk it out, to explain as calmly and reasonably as possible what it was that upset you in order to improve mutual understanding. But, usually, the best idea is to forget it. These things happen, and unless you make it into a big deal today, by tomorrow it won't matter.

Most of us are inclined to the conviction that all such wrongs should be righted, that we shouldn't "let them get away with it." And we let ourselves stay angry and resentful, sometimes even precipitating an open altercation that almost inevitably creates new reasons for resentment. I think I had been married for some thirty years, a highly trained, reasonably well-known professor of psychology, before I finally learned that this is a dumb way to behave. For thirty years, I clung to the counterproductive belief that if I was mad or hurt or disappointed by something my wife said, or did, or didn't do, then it was her responsibility to make it right and my responsibility to stay mad until she did it. Now, if I find myself irritated about something (and, strangely, that happens much less often now), I feel that it is my responsibility to get over it without making any fuss. I know that I am happier as a result, and I believe my wife is, too.

## The Powers of Positive Reinforcement

The great psychologist B. F. Skinner had all his best ideas while on the faculty at my university and, later, during his many years at Harvard, Skinner and his students proceeded to demonstrate how good those ideas were. He showed that the best way to shape the behavior of rats, pigeons, or people is by means of positive reinforcement or reward, rather than through punishment. As explained in chapter 8, if you want to get the white rat to press the lever, you must start by pressing the button that delivers a pellet of food reinforcement when the animal happens to go toward the lever. Then, when he's spending most of his time in that neighborhood, press the button only when he rears up on his hind legs near the lever, then only when, perhaps by accident, he touches the lever, and, finally, when he actually presses it. Works every time.

Skinner loved to tell a story about two bright undergraduates at Harvard who came somewhat shamefacedly to ask his advice. They had found themselves rooming with a "jock" who cared only for sports and girl chasing and shared none of their intellectual or aesthetic values. These boys had taken Skinner's psychology course and decided to try to shape their roommate's interests to be more compatible with their own. Now they wondered if they perhaps had gone too far. Whenever their roommate regaled them with his latest triumph on the football field or on a date, they simply ignored him, seemed not to hear or care. But whenever he asked a question or expressed an opinion about any remotely academic or artistic topic, they looked up from their books with interested expressions and responded with conviviality. By the end of the semester, their plebeian roommate was showing signs of becoming an aesthete like themselves and talking of changing his major. Skinner reassured them that both they and their roommate seemed to have learned something useful.

I am *not* advocating that you should start treating your spouse like a rat in the Skinner box. But I do suggest that you begin noticing how you yourself react whenever your spouse does something nice, expresses interest in what you say—gives you a pellet of positive reinforcement. Those pellets induce a pleasurable feeling, don't they? They enhance your own feelings of well-being, make you less ornery, and easier to live with. That works in both directions, as explained in a law of psychology that was discovered before Skinner came along: the Golden Rule.

# A Family Love Story

My Norwegian-American father was born on a farm in North Dakota, the eldest of nine children, all of whom married in the old-fashioned way, for keeps. Dad's youngest brother, Laurence Lykken, for example, lived with his wife, Hazel, on a farm near Grafton, North Dakota for seventy-two years. And they seem to have been happy years, judging from these two notes that they exchanged (Hazel had been deaf from girlhood, so their extended communications had to be in writing). Here is Laurence on the occasion of their sixtieth anniversary:

> Dearly beloved wife; I don't think I could have gotten a better wife than you. Was so in love with you 60 years ago. Sure was lucky I proposed to you that first night I took you home from the dance at the Benny Johnson farm. I fell in love with you that first date. I always like to stay home with you alone. We have had a wonderful life—very few that would come up to the way we lived together. Know there's not any man who loves his wife more than I do, and have ever since I started to go with you. I think about you and love you more now than in the old days when I fell in love with you. Thank you for everything.

And here is Hazel, writing on their seventieth anniversary:

> Dearest Laurence and the best husband ever. I love you with all my heart and when you're not with me I feel so lost. You have given me everything I have wanted. I have tried to be a good wife for you and one thing I know—no one pals around together and goes places like you and I do together. I could write a book about you, I love you so dearly.

Hazel never wrote her book, at least not with pen and paper. Her book, and Uncle Laurence's, was their seventy-two years together, as lovers, partners, parents, and best friends.

# PART FIVE

❀

# THE THIEVES OF HAPPINESS

> We deem those happy who from the experience of life have
> learned to bear its ills, without being overcome by them.
> —JUVENAL

It seems natural to think that Positive Emotionality and Negative Emotionality must be at opposite ends of the same continuum, like *thin* and *fat* or *good* and *bad*. My colleague Auke Tellegen has shown, however, that Positive and Negative Emotionality are two basic traits of temperament that are separate and distinct. That is, some people are high on both—people whom you would describe as highly emotional—while others are low on both—people you might characterize as phlegmatic. Happiness or well-being is a component of Positive Emotionality along with Social Potency (enjoying leadership roles and visibility), Achievement (the motivation to excel, to accomplish something), and Social Closeness (enjoying close personal relationships). Negative Emotionality, on the other hand, is composed of Stress Reaction (nervousness, worry, anxiety, feeling vulnerable), Alienation (feeling cheated, badly treated, unlucky), and Aggression (feeling irritable, hostile, wanting to punish someone).

The problem is that each of these components of Negative Emotionality can interfere with feelings of well-being; they are potential happiness thieves. The Behavioral Activation System (BAS), the brain mechanism involved in positive thinking and goal-directed activity, can be inhibited by stimulation of the Be-

havioral Inhibition System (BIS), which mediates fearful with-
drawal. That emotional person who has a good talent for
happiness when things go well too often has those contented
feelings stolen away if something triggers those contrary feelings
of anxiety, alienation, or aggression. Fearfulness (which is something different from anxiety, as I will explain later) is another
personality trait that can interfere with happiness.

In 1997, the National Center for Health Statistics (NCHS) reported a study of more than 43,000 American adults who had been
questioned as to whether, and how often, they had experienced
various negative moods during the previous two weeks.[1] The five
moods queried were boredom, restlessness, depression, feeling
"upset because of something someone said about you," and feeling
"very lonely or abandoned." Each item was scored from 0 ("never")
to 4 ("very often") so that the total scores ranged from 0 to 20.
About 8 percent of the total group reported high levels of negative
feelings (scores of 10 to 20) during the previous two weeks. In
contrast to the studies of "satisfaction" or "contentment" previously
reviewed, this study found significant differences between demographic groups in the prevalence of negative emotions. For example, 9.1 percent of women reported high levels, as compared with
only 6.3 percent of men. Twice as many black respondents reported
strong negative emotions as compared to whites: 14 percent versus
7 percent. Of those with less than a high school education, 12.9
percent reported strong negative feelings during the prior two
weeks, compared with 6.4 percent of high school graduates.

How can we reconcile these findings with our other evidence
that women, on the average, are just as "contented" or "satisfied" as
men, that black Americans are just as happy on the whole as whites
are, and that subjective well-being is negligibly correlated with educational attainment? Because susceptibilities to positive and to negative emotions are only weakly related to each other, it is possible
to be high or low on both tendencies. Yet there is no doubt that on
those preceding days when they were feeling blue or lonely or
upset, these respondents were not feeling happy.

In the next few chapters, I will discuss ways in which one
can keep these thieves of happiness at bay. First, however, we
must come to grips with the worst thief of all, depression.

# 12

# HAPPINESS THIEF 1: Depression

When things come to the worst, they generally mend.
—SUSANNA MOODIE

The cure for this ill is not to sit still, or frowst with a book
by the fire;
But to take a large hoe and a shovel also, and dig 'till you
gently perspire.
—RUDYARD KIPLING

Morbid depression, surprisingly, is not the result of too much negative emotion but, rather, the absence of the positive. The truly depressed person feels not only wretched, sad, and joyless, but also *hopeless*. It is no fun to feel stressed out and anxious, or to feel angry and vengeful, or that people aren't treating you right. But at least these negative feelings are compatible with hope. "If only this lump turns out to be benign." "If only my boss would come to realize my value." "If only my worm of a husband would admit how wrong he was and ask forgiveness." But not to be able even to imagine a happening that would bring relief short of death itself, to truly see one's world as an unweeded garden gone to seed, to feel that all one's future holds or could hold is weary, stale, flat, and unprofitable—that is depression.

Serious depression is not only a thief of happiness; it is a life-threatening illness. Most suicides are a consequence of morbid depression. Some sufferers have bouts of depression that alternate with periods of manic elation, a condition known as *bipolar affect-*

211

*ive disorder.* In *primary major depressive disorder,* only the episodes of morbid depression are seen. Susceptibility to both illnesses is strongly determined by genetic factors.* If your identical twin suffers from bouts of depression or manic-depression, there is a 40 percent to 60 percent chance that you too will be affected. Because morbid depression (and mania as well) involves a disturbance in certain neurotransmitters (the molecules that convey nerve impulses from one brain cell to another), and because most sufferers experience these problems only intermittently, the genetic defect is not the illness itself, but rather the susceptibility to the illness. Morbid depression sometimes develops spontaneously, but it is often precipitated by distressing life experiences, including other debilitating psychiatric disorders. Many people afflicted with schizophrenia become seriously depressed, as do people haunted by irresistible obsessions or compulsions. People in the early stages of Alzheimer's disease, still able to appreciate how their mental powers are failing, easily fall victims to despair. My brother, Robert, in this state of Alzheimer's, talked of suicide, so my other brother and I hid Robert's pistol. Later, when Robert's mind and personality died, several years before his body did, I wondered if we had done the right thing.

Fortunately, however, in almost every instance (except, alas, encroaching dementia) effective help is now available. Most depressed people respond well to one or another of the numerous antidepressant medications. The fact that different families of antidepressants are known to differentially effect different neurotransmitters, especially *norepinephrine* and *serotonin,* suggests that serious mood disorders can result from dysregulation of different components of the brain's mood machinery. A skillful (or lucky) diagnostician may be able to select the medication that remediates the problems of a given patient with the fewest side effects.

For patients with bipolar disorder (what used to be called

*See T. Reich, P. Van Eerdewgh, J. Rice, J. Mullaney, J. Endicott & G. Klerman. The familial transmission of primary major depressive disorder. *Journal of Psychiatric Research,* 21 (1987), 613–624.

manic depression), the mineral lithium has proven especially effective in preventing the manic phases, although no one as yet knows how or why it works. Some bipolars become agitated and paranoid in the manic state, and it is decidedly unpleasant for them as well as for others. For most, however, at least the early or hypomanic phase is delightful; they feel really together, full of confidence and energy, creative and optimistic. When one is feeling that good and functioning well, it is tempting to forego the daily pill. But the drift from this inventive and productive state into unrealism and loss of control is insidious. Reckless purchases, bad investments, and disastrous romantic entanglements can result. One member of a pair of fraternal twins in our early studies had bipolar disorder. One day, after I had not heard from him for months, he phoned me full of camaraderie, explaining that he had decided to rent the Minneapolis Auditorium and that, of course, he wanted me on the program. "George, you haven't been taking your lithium have you?" After a long pause he replied, in a different tone, "Am I going off again?" Happily, his grip on reality, while tenuous, was just strong enough for him to agree to make an emergency appointment with his psychiatrist.

It is widely believed that an important fraction of all individual human achievement has been accomplished by people with the bipolar tendency, working tirelessly in the hypomanic phase with great enthusiasm and self-confidence.[2] William Gladstone, mentioned earlier, was almost certainly a bipolar, and his periods of hypomania helped him to be a renowned orator and parliamentarian, a prolific author and scholar, and "something like the Moses of modern liberalism."[3]

When I was a graduate student in the early 1950s, I worked one summer on the psychiatric wards of the Minneapolis General Hospital. The current armamentarium of psychoactive drugs was then not yet available, and those wards were full of very disturbed patients, some kept in restraints. The staff consisted of two interns, doing a two-month rotation and largely ignorant of this branch of medicine, some experienced nurses and strong-armed attendants, who really ran the place, and one part-time psychiatrist who showed up briefly, three days a week, to press the button on the electric shock machine. The film *One Flew Over the Cuckoo's Nest* gave a very accurate picture of the way in which disturbed or troublesome patients, irrespective of diagnosis, were assigned a course of "shock treatments." Laid out, supine, on the treatment table, surrounded by four staff members, each holding firmly an arm or a leg in anticipation of the impending grand-mal seizure, a rubber bulb in his mouth to prevent tongue biting, and electrodes clamped lateral to the temples, the frightened patient waited, wide-eyed, for oblivion. The burst of current seemed to induce instant unconsciousness, followed by the fierce clonic spasms of the seizure. Once again relaxed, the patient was lifted onto a gurney to be taken to the recovery room while the next victim was made ready. The scene these days, happily, is greatly different. Muscle relaxants prevent the spasms that would sometimes break the patient's bones. Sedatives dispel the terror of anticipation. For people with serious mood disorders who do not respond well to the available drug therapies, the once-feared electroconvulsive treatment (ECT) has now become so benign that it is given on an out-patient basis.

If you are reading this book, however, I hope I can safely assume that you are not morbidly depressed, at least not at this moment. Therefore, I should like to discuss the sorts of moderate or mild depressions, the "downs," the "blues," the little periods of mild melancholia, to which most of us are subject from time to time.

The great problem with mild depression (indeed, with any depression) is not just the sad and hopeless feeling it engenders, but rather that depression is autocatalytic; it feeds on itself. There seems to be a law of human nature that we abhor an unexplained emotion. If I were secretly to implant an electrode in the part of your brain that generates these feelings of depression and then covertly to activate this electrode by remote control,[4] it is very likely that you would soon be generating numerous logical reasons to explain why you are feeling as worthless, as hopeless, perhaps as guilty as that brain stimulus has made you feel. If the electrode keeps doing its insidious job, you will soon have more immediate and tangible reasons for feeling as badly as you do. You will have become bad company to your spouse, a burden to your children. You will not have the energy or drive to deal with your ordinary obligations. And you will be more aware of your failings than anyone else because your rational, orderly mind will be monitoring them closely and explaining to you secretly, not only your inadequacies in great detail, but also *why* you are letting everyone down: because you are a useless person, probably a bad person. And therefore you will feel even worse and function even more poorly; this is the vicious cycle of depression. Here is how a wise British psychiatrist puts it:

> Many hundred times have I wearily explained to a patient's relatives that the supposed causes to which he and they attribute his morbid depression have nothing whatever to do with it, and his preoccupation with them is a symptom and not a cause of his illness. They never troubled him before he took ill and he will never give them another thought once he gets well. To attempt to argue him out of them is like attempting to argue a patient out of having tonsillitis.
> —HENRY YELLOWLEES, O.B.E., M.D., F.R.C.P., D.P.M.[5]

The first and hardest job in working with even a moderately depressed patient in psychotherapy is to get her (depression is much more frequent in women than in men) to understand—to *really* understand—that she is suffering from a temporary imbalance of her brain chemistry, that she has an illness rather like the flu (or like Dr. Yellowlees's tonsillitis), and that she should stop doing the things that make it worse and start doing the things that can make it better. In particular, she must stop *justifying* how she feels, stop explaining it to herself. "If your nose was running and your stomach was upset, would you say: 'Well, I had it coming, I'm such a worthless person!'? That would be silly and just make you feel worse. Well, it is silly now and it is making you worse, so you must try to stop doing it."

Happy people are active, always busy doing something, whereas depressed people, having lost interest in everything as well as their self-confidence, tend to sit and mope. We cannot ask a depressed person to do everything she would normally be doing if she felt like herself because she simply will not be up to it. But moping is bad for her, so she has to work out a compromise. She must find something useful to do, something that she *can* do even feeling as she does, even though it doesn't really interest her. For both women and men, this will often be some sort of work around the house—cleaning, fixing, straightening up, mowing the lawn, weeding the garden—something that doesn't involve other people or require great creativity or spirit. Doing something simple but useful is usually better than seeking diversion through entertainment, because when one is depressed, it is hard to get interested in books or movies. On the other hand, if one feels any urge at all to read an Agatha Christie mystery or to watch some favorite TV program, then go for it. What we are trying to do here is to ride this thing out, to let the brain chemistry right itself without our doing anything to make it worse.

One simple but effective treatment for the ordinary blahs or blues is physical exercise. In one remarkable study of depressed students at the University of Kansas, all women, the patients were divided into three groups, one to be untreated, one given training in relaxation, and third enrolled in a ten-week program of jogging and aerobic dancing. When reassessed later, the untreated women were still depressed, the group doing the systematic relaxation were generally better, but the exercise group had improved dramatically.[6] Vigorous exercise can be done on one's own, but its therapeutic effect is enhanced when done with others—tennis with a friend or joining an aerobic dance class—because this both enhances the motivation to continue and helps to repair the sense of isolation that depressed people tend to feel.

Were I to have a down period lasting more than a few days not attributable to illness or some depressing life event (and which I would therefore tend to blame upon my own myriad deficiencies and faults!), here is what I would do to fight back. I would avoid socially or intellectually demanding tasks, but keep active doing simple things. I would take Willie, my bull terrier, for a long walk before breakfast as well as our regular after-din-ner hike. (That would be good for both of us.) I would clean up my offices at home and at the university—several days' worth of mindless but useful activity right there. And I would start taking an herb called Saint-John's-wort which was used in ancient Greece to drive off evil spirits and is used by modern Europeans as a natural specific for depression. The *British Medical Journal*[7] recently reported a meta-analysis of two dozen controlled studies of the antidepressant effects of the herb's mysterious but appar-ently harmless active ingredient, hypericin.[8] The results were ex-cellent and remarkably consistent.

I commented in chapter 2 that great achievements and other joyful experiences resemble earthquakes in that they tend to make smaller waves on one's lake of happiness for some time afterward, as one happens to recall those happy events. The more serious of the bad things that can happen—the death of a loved one, misfortunes, marital breakups, and the like—also produce aftershocks when we contemplate them later. The only loved one I have lost who was a part of my daily life was our first bull terrier, Polly Peachum. Real animal people will understand that it is not so strange, as it must seem to others, to speak of the loss of a dog almost in the same breath as the loss of a child. But I spent more time with Polly during her ten years with us than with any friend; she loved me unreservedly, as dogs will, and when we had to have her "put to sleep," as they say, it was truly like a death in the family. A year later, we got our second BT, Slick Willie, and he filled many of the empty places in our lives. Yet even now, years later, something reminds me of Polly, and I feel a pang. But I can't say that these reminiscences are depress-ing—they are poignant and moving, and they make me feel briefly sad, but not *bad*. After all, we humans enjoy sad and senti-mental stories now and then, I don't know why. Perhaps they remind us of our connection with other living creatures, all of us perishable, all worthy of respect and concern. If I had ever been so unlucky as to lose a child, I believe—I hope—that after the first period of anguish and desolation, I would come to be able to think of him in a similar way, teary-eyed but still thankful for the memory.

I think that emotional wounds are slowest to heal when we keep them too much to ourselves. In traditional societies, sufferings are shared with the extended family, and I think this sharing is both natural and often necessary for recovery. Those of us without a family to rally round must lean on friends or, in some cases, therapists. If the anguish is unabated after several months, the only way may be to talk it out. A modern invention that makes good psychological sense is the support group: meeting with others who have had similar losses and can share one's grief. There are even support groups for people who have lost a pet, like Polly. My family was my support group when she died, but had I been alone in the world, it would have helped to talk with others who could truly understand how one feels. And beware the temptation to believe that continued suffering is somehow obligatory, that we owe it to the departed to continue to mourn, or even that the world will appreciate the awful perfidy of your faithless spouse only if you allow it to ruin your life. Some temperaments can shrug off disasters more easily than others can, of course. If you tend to be a brooder, if your inclination is to incubate a nest full of unhappy memories, then you have a choice: You can let your genetic steersman keep you weeping on that nest, or you can wrench yourself away, take yourself in hand, turn your back on the past, pull up your socks, get on with your life—there seem to be an unlimited number of these equivalent, hortatory clichés, perhaps because they all provide the needed prescription for a common complaint.

And where is it written that we should expect to be happy, vigorous, up-and-doing, all of the time? Even Slick Willie, our incumbent dog, gets the blahs now and then. One of the high points of Willie's day is our afternoon game of yard ball (driveway ball during the long winters). Although Willie never seems to get sick, once every couple of weeks, when I throw the ball for him to fetch it, he walks rather than runs and walks back even slower. Now and then the ions aren't right or something, and his joie de vivre is in short supply. I have days like that, but

I don't feel I've been cheated. One must learn to take the bitter with the better, as some wise person said.

## The Implications of Prozac

How many times do you have to see a two-headed calf before you believe it?

—MARK TWAIN

In the 1970s, researchers at the pharmaceutical house of Eli Lilly announced the discovery of a new drug, fluoxetine hydrochloride, that is a highly selective inhibitor of serotonin uptake, thus having the effect of enhancing the activity of brain pathways that use this molecule as the neurotransmitter. This new compound, trade-named Prozac, was put on the market in the late 1980s and proved to be a highly effective antidepressant for many patients who responded less well to the tricyclic family of drugs such as imipramine (Tofranil) or amitriptyline (Elavil). There was a media scare in 1990 suggesting that patients on Prozac were at risk for suicidal and even homicidal violence, but this seems to have been a consequence of the drug's being used with already disturbed and suicidal patients who had not responded well to other medications. As psychoactive drugs go, Prozac is remarkably free of significant side effects and free also of addictive properties. Some 10 million people around the world have taken or are taking Prozac today. (These last two statements are not as contradictory as they may appear. I have taken the same antihistamine for years to control my hay fever, but I am not addicted to it. I have not developed a tolerance to it, so that I need more and more, nor do I crave it when I run out—I just sneeze a lot.)

What is especially interesting about this drug, and what led psychiatrist Peter Kramer to write his book *Listening to Prozac*,[9] is that its normalizing or euthymic effects often go beyond "merely" ameliorating morbid depression. Kramer's book provides numerous case histories of patients, often successful, productive people, whose innate temperaments seem to become different, healthier, while taking this medication. People troubled with shyness, with self-doubt, or with minor but annoying compulsions felt liberated, as if they had been reborn. Psychologists and researchers in the other life sciences are trained to think in terms of group statistics and to scorn individual cases and other "anecdotal evidence." But, like many physicians, I think there is a lot to be learned, or at least suggested, from case histories. As Mark Twain reminds us, once you have seen a two-headed calf, you don't need a large-scale controlled study to prove that it can happen. It is tempting to suppose that Prozac, at least for some people, actually raises the congenital happiness set point.

In spite of Mark Twain, however, my own guess is rather different. Prozac has not been tried on a sample of those average people who think they are in the upper third of the population in subjective well-being. Such a study would be fascinating: two hundred average adults, half of them getting Prozac for six months while the other one hundred take a placebo pill that looks just like the real thing. Then, for the final six months, fifty of group 1 are switched to the placebo and fifty of group 2 start getting the active drug. No one knows who is getting which compound until the year is up and the computer, which randomly assigned people to groups, gives up its secrets. This makes it a "double-blind" study, meaning that neither the patient nor the scientists collecting the data know who is getting what, so that neither the subjects' self-reports nor the observers' evaluations are contaminated by that knowledge.

If such a study showed that average, well-adjusted people felt even happier than usual when the pills they were taking contained Prozac rather than milk sugar, then we should be forced to the conclusion that we all can aspire to be like that English lady who "can't help being happy." My guess, however, is that, in spite of its apparent specificity of action in the brain, Prozac works its wonders not by raising the happiness set point, but rather by disabling a variety of happiness thieves, including depression, shyness, timidity, and unpleasant compulsions. I doubt that Dr. Kramer's patients have been given what amounts to an improved set of happiness genes. Instead, they have been freed up to begin making the most of the potential they were born with.

# 13

## HAPPINESS THIEVES 2:
## Fear and Shyness

Courage is resistance to fear, mastery of fear—not absence
of fear.
                                                —MARK TWAIN

We should be careful to get out of an experience only the
wisdom that is in it—and stop there; lest we be like the
cat that sits down on a hot stove-lid. She will never sit
down on a hot stove-lid again—and that is well; but also
she will never sit down on a cold one anymore.
                                                —MARK TWAIN

A s is true of all human attributes, people differ innately in
their fearfulness, in their tendency to react to the unknown
or to threat with a pounding heart and sweaty palms and
dread. The Harm Avoidance scale of Tellegen's personality inventory, the MPQ, measures individual differences in fear reactivity.
Scores on Harm Avoidance have a heritability of about 50 percent. Most people enjoy the pleasurable excitement of watching
an occasional scary or horrific movie but would balk at parachut-
ing from an airplane for the fun of it. Sky divers and bungee
jumpers notwithstanding, you cannot be happy if you are truly
frightened. People who engage in risky pastimes enjoy the high
they get from skating on the edge of fear,[1] but that edge for them
is higher than for you and me and requires a greater risk to get
there. It is interesting that many criminals, notably burglars and
muggers, enjoy their work because of that same high.[2] For shy
and fearful people, however, not only risky pastimes but many
tamer pleasures, including ordinary social interactions, may be
too stressful to enjoy.

221

The developmental psychologist Jerome Kagan has reported that about 20 percent of healthy children are easily aroused and distressed by stimulation early in the first year of life and then, at ages two and three, are inclined to avoid unfamiliar stimulation.[3] Most (but not all) of these children tended to remain relatively inhibited and shy at later ages. Those easily distressed infants who remained inhibited in later childhood were likely to have parents who reacted to their children's sensitivity by shielding them from the stimulation that disturbed them. Parents who exposed their fearful children to a wider range of stimulation, on the other hand, more often found their youngsters able to adapt and to lose their early hypersensitivity. Like me, Kagan began his career as a radical environmentalist, but the data, his own and others, eventually carried him "kicking and screaming" into the hereditarian camp. But Kagan rightly points out that "the power of genes is real but limited." Skillful parenting can mitigate the effects of an excessively shy or inhibited temperament. This is not to say that every child can be turned into a free-wheeling extrovert, but when one comes to think it through, thank God for that.

Fear, of course, like our sense of pain, is an adaptive trait. I once examined a child of six who had been born with a congenital insensitivity to pain and then reared by criminally neglectful foster parents. The front third of his tongue, most of his lips, and the end joints (distal phalanges) of each of his fingers were missing; he had chewed them off before anyone bothered to have his sharp baby teeth removed. Interestingly, this child's fearfulness was higher than average. I had wanted to measure his tolerance for electric shock and spent considerable time reassuring him, putting the electrodes on my own fingers. I showed him that I had to turn the dial up to 10 or so before I could feel anything, then up to 30 at least before the shock began to hurt, and finally much higher still before it was as strong as I was willing to stand. When at last he let me put the electrodes on his stubby fingers, however, as soon as he could feel the strange tingle of the current, he bade me stop. I could stick a sterile hypodermic needle in his arm without eliciting a flinch as long as he was looking the other way, talking to the nurse, but not when he could see what I was doing.

Kagan also found that about 15 percent of boys, but only 5 percent of girls, "displayed a combination of low reactivity, very low heart rate, and consistently low fear." A child who is relatively fearless from birth is almost at much at risk as this painless boy was, and equally in need of skillful parenting. Not only is he likely to attempt risky things that could get him injured, but he will also be inclined to resist parental discipline. Where the average child will "do this" or "stop doing that" at least partly out of fear of the consequences, the relatively fearless child may ignore the injunction, argue, or have a tantrum. Unless the parent has the good sense and the energy to win each of these battles, such a child will learn that resistance or counterattack *works*, and his undisciplined behavior will get worse with each such lesson.

These children, moreover, are likely to become more rather than less fearless with experience due to our remarkable human ability to adapt or habituate to repeated stimulation. After Johnny is used to climbing the fence, he is tempted to climb the tree, and then, when he feels at home in the tree, why not climb up on the roof or up that steep cliff? When parents cannot meet the challenge of socializing these adventurous and difficult children, they may grow up as psychopaths.[4] When the outcome is happier, they grow up to be the kinds of people we like to have around when danger threatens or when volunteers are needed for a trip to the moon.

But the child we are concerned with in this chapter is at the opposite extreme of the bell curve of innate fearfulness. Even as toddlers, they are timid, shy, they do not dare to climb or explore or to risk making the big people angry. And as they get older, many of the games and adventures that most children enjoy seem to be too risky for them. Here again, one hopes such children will be blessed with skillful parents who will gently and patiently urge them out of their corners, one desensitizing step at a time.

My three sons were about average in their harm avoidance tendencies, but I did a little desensitizing with them anyway. For example, before they could walk, I used to swing them by their arms, up and back between my legs, swings just big enough to make them wide-eyed but not quite frightened. As might be expected, their tolerance grew for bigger and more vigorous swings until we ran out of room and I ran out of breath. I think fathers are more inclined to do this sort of desensitizing than mothers, but I also think that mothers often are better at it, perhaps because children tend to feel safer with them.

My six-year-old grandson, Zeke, gashed his chin in a fall the other day and had to be taken to the doctor for stitches. His mother reports that he didn't cry a drop. This story really begins thirty-six years ago, when his father, also six, had to be taken to the hospital to sew up a similar gash in his forehead. En route, I told him that American Indians are well known for their bravery, and one of their secrets is *not letting on.* "If you keep a straight face and don't show that you're scared or that it hurts, then you'll be less scared and it really won't hurt as much." The reason for this, which I did not go into at the time, is that emotions are a blend of your internal feelings and the feedback to your brain of your bodily reactions; if you *act* scared, then you are more likely to *feel* scared. Jesse took his stitches like a man, and the doctor commented on how brave he was. On the way home, he said, "Gee, Dad, it really worked!"[5] Jesse, in turn, taught Zeke this same lesson the first time he had to have his chin sewed up, and it was still working on this second trip. There is an interesting corollary to this principle: If inhibiting the expression of negative emotions lessens their impact, then *disinhibiting* the expression of positive emotions—giving exuberant expression to feelings of joy, love, and pleasure of all kinds—should *increase* the enjoyment that attends them. And it does.

When our sons were ten, twelve, and fourteen, I was doing an experiment that involved giving painful electric shocks. Like all sensible experimental psychologists, I recruited my wife to be the first subject. She understood that the shock had to really hurt for the experiment to work and so, while I was adjusting the intensity at the start of the session, she let me increase it to the maximum. (None of the young men who served as subjects later would tolerate more than 75 percent of maximum; my wife is no sissy.) When my boys visited the lab the next weekend, they wanted to try out the shock that their mother had "taken all the way to the top." The two older boys also made it to maximum and the ten-year-old got to 85 percent. These boys were no more fearless or pain-tolerant than those young men (although I think my wife probably was), but they were reassured by the knowledge that their mother had done it before them, and perhaps also a little by the fact that it was their father operating the controls. But the point is that they were a little braver after this experience than before because they had discovered they could take it.

Even with this kind of help while growing up, really timid children do not become bold adventurers. However, they will find more of the world and its possibilities open to them. Left entirely to their own devices, on the other hand, they may lead a rather cloistered existence, like Proust or the sister in Tennessee Williams's *The Glass Menagerie*. One can be happy in the cloisters, of course, but it can be lonely and the options are few.

When I was a young clinical psychologist, a man I'll call Ralph was referred to our university hospital for regressive shock therapy, a radical and dangerous procedure now long since abandoned. Ralph was in his early thirties, and for some ten years he had been afraid to leave his parents' house except for short walks in the dead of night. Ralph had a bad case of agoraphobia, or fear of crowds and open places. I was assigned to do the psychological work-up on Ralph before his course of shock treatments was begun. I got interested in his case and asked to be allowed to try to help him in a less drastic manner. After several conversation sessions to gain his confidence, I began giving Ralph some homework assignments. "This afternoon, Ralph, I want you to walk downstairs, five flights, and go to the front door of the hospital. Then you can come right back." The next week, he had to make the same trip each day but on the elevator with other people. When Ralph had mastered the elevator, I assigned him to one of the regular afternoon patient walks, around the block with one of the attendants in charge.

Within a month or so, Ralph was ready to set out on his own, first short walks, then longer ones, then a walk to the drugstore, then an actual purchase at the drugstore. A bridge runs across the Mississippi River not far from our hospital, and Ralph was very nervous about bridges. It took at least a week of trying before Ralph made it across, but he was so proud! By this time, Ralph had come to realize that he *could* do it, that he was already freer of the limitations of his illness than he had been for years, and that he could go farther still. The last I heard from Ralph, he had an apartment of his own, he had a job, and he also had a girlfriend. It is important to see that my role in this was rather like that of a parent with a shy child. I was interested in Ralph's problems, I gave him gentle pushes in the right directions, and I was as pleased as he was with each success.

If Ralph had turned up thirty years later, in the 1980s, he would have been recognized to be suffering with "panic anxiety," thanks largely to the work of psychiatrist Donald Klein.[6] Ralph would now be treated with drugs like Xanax that forestall panic, but he would still need someone like me to urge him to explore his world in ever-increasing circles in order to convince himself that devastating attacks of overwhelming panic were no longer lurking around the next corner.

## Stage Fright

In addition to snakes and spiders, another innate fear disposition that seems universal in our species is stage fright, finding oneself to be the focus of attention of a multitude of eyes. Few actors or speakers would feel the same apprehension if they could perform standing at the back of the hall with the audience gazing, say, at slides projected on a screen. Among other primates (and in some human cultures), a sustained direct gaze is a threat signal, and the occasions when our ancient ancestors found all eyes focused on them were likely to have been dangerous situations calling for escape or avoidance behavior. One reason we admire "high-talking chiefs" and are inclined to accept their leadership is that they have the unusual ability to function with apparent confidence before an audience of eyes.

I had an attack of acute stage fright years ago, a serious and embarrassing handicap for an academic psychologist. It began just before I went with my family to spend a sabbatical year in London where, shamefacedly, I had to refuse invitations to lecture. Getting a grip on myself, I enrolled in a Dale Carnegie course being held one night a week in a London hotel. These courses are based on that commonsense principle of systematic desensitization, very much like the progressively more demanding tasks I had set for Ralph. By the end of the eight weeks, like my fellow sufferers, I was able not only to stand up comfortably in front of the group and talk, but even to give an impromptu talk on a subject presented at the last minute. My real graduation was being able to accept an invitation to speak before a group assembled by the eminent professor Hans Eysenck at the Maudsley Hospital in London. Years earlier, I had written a critical (and rather sophomoric) review of one of Eysenck's many books. This was rather like walking into the lion's den, although Hans was perfectly friendly and forgiving. Since that time, I have talked before audiences of all sizes and appeared on television (which is much easier because there are fewer visible eyes), and I seem to be cured.

## Coping with Fear and Stress

Social fear, especially, can greatly restrict one's abilities to do the things that need doing and one's opportunities to enjoy life's many possibilities. The point of these reminiscences is to make it clear that, although it is always best to begin the desensitization process in childhood, it is never too late. If shyness and fear stand between you and what you need to feel fulfilled, if these thieves are stealing your happiness, take some action, find some professional help, fight back. Remember, too, that when a shy person has a friend, even another shy person, the two of them together may be braver than either is alone.

The Minneapolis telephone directory lists eight organizations offering training or counseling in transcendental meditation and allied arts, all related to ancient Hindu or Buddhist practices, and all offering balm and surcease from the cares and stresses of mundane existence. Because they all are at least vaguely religious in character, it is difficult to tell whether their widespread popularity is testimony to their therapeutic efficacy or to their appeal to a yearning for contact with the supernatural. But there is another, simpler form of meditation that serves as an effective stress reliever without the otherworldly trappings which some, like me, may find a bit off-putting. Here is how it works:

When you think you will have thirty to sixty minutes free of interruptions, sit down in a comfortable chair, both feet on the floor, hands comfortably in your lap. Close your eyes and tell yourself that, for the next half hour at least, you are not going to move except to breathe and to swallow, as necessary. This turns out to be difficult at first; your nose will itch or you will have an urge to change the position of your hand or to change your posture slightly. But you must not give in to these temptations. You are not required to chant mantras or to focus your mind on anything—except the rule of not moving. After what at first may seem a long while (it will probably be only five minutes or so unless you are unusually nervous and stressed out), the itches and squirmy impulses will recede and your mind will drift. Let it go where it listeth. You are entirely awake, but also entirely relaxed. There is some sort of magic in the motionlessness, as if the inhibition of all movement somehow spreads to include the inhibition of emotional concern. The first time you try it, you might want to set a kitchen timer for thirty to sixty minutes. You are not allowed to open your eyes to check the clock, so you may want the reassurance of knowing that the timer's bell will prevent you from investing your entire afternoon in this curious state. Try it: It is simple, agreeable, and it is good for you.

The tranquilizing drugs that are now so widely prescribed do actually work wonders for most mild social anxiety, but these drugs are also widely abused. An occasional pill may help you elude the social fear that is stealing your well-being, but they won't provide a source of happiness that isn't there already. If it takes more than one tablet of Valium to make you feel comfortable about giving that committee report or meeting your fiancée's parents for the first time, then you should think about a short course of psychotherapy or reading one of Albert Ellis's excellent self-help books.[7] You might also read the case histories of shy, inhibited, oversensitive, or self-depreciating patients in chapters 4, 6, and 7 of Peter Kramer's book *Listening to Prozac*; these people seem to have been rescued from happiness thieves by a combination of that wonder drug, Prozac, and skillful psychotherapy. If you can see yourself in Tess, Lucy, Allison, Jerry, William, or the others, then you might want to have a talk with your HMO psychiatrist.

# What Will People Think? (WWPT?)

My mother-in-law, Gladys, was a good mother and a remarkable woman in many ways. In fact, one of her talents persuaded me, a hard-nosed psychological scientist, that the butterfly of extrasensory perception is real, if only someone could find a way to pin it down. Gladys seemed more embarrassed by than proud of her telepathic gift. She affected disinterest in card games, for example, but the real reason she avoided playing is that it troubled her to know which cards were in the other players' hands. There are many stories about Gladys's premonitions, but the trouble with most such anecdotes is that one doesn't have a count of the times when similar expectations proved false. Here is one example, however, of how Gladys, without trying, made a believer out of me.

Gladys had been appointed to some governor's committee to inspect Minnesota's state mental hospitals. The group was to go by bus on one of their inspections on a Saturday. On the previous Thursday, Gladys confessed to misgivings. "I have the strangest feeling that someone on that bus is going to wet their pants, of all things! I don't know who it will be, but I for one am not going to drink any coffee that morning." Saturday arrived, and the bus pulled out on schedule. About half an hour into the trip, an elderly lady sitting behind her leaned forward and whispered, "Gladys, the most awful thing has happened! I've wet my pants! I think my bladder must have fallen. Can you help me?" Gladys got the driver to stop at the next gas station and helped her aged friend clean up in the women's toilet.

Many otherwise-sober identical twins are convinced that they are somehow telepathically connected to their cotwins' minds. Many of their "proofs" can more easily be explained as examples of similar people reacting in similar ways to similar situations, but I have heard anecdotes from twins that are as hard to explain away as some of Gladys's experiences. The trouble with these apparent telepaths is that they cannot perform on cue, cannot pick lottery numbers or horse race winners. If Gladys had had more control of her gift, she might not have been so troubled by that common bogey, "What will people think?" Like many people of her generation, Gladys worried excessively about what others might think if she did this or failed to do that. Had she been able to intuit "their" reactions in advance, she would have known that the people she cared about would have thought as she did, and that what the others thought was irrelevant.

Happily, although I have sometimes been discomfited by evidence that my wife may have inherited some of her mother's telepathic tendencies, Gladys did not pass this WWPT? trait along to her daughter. A good example of how one ought to deal with such concerns occurred one summer Saturday when the Metropolitan Opera was making its annual visit to Minneapolis. Harriet had tickets for the evening performance of *Faust* with our son Joseph, then age twelve. When it was time to leave, Joe came down the stairs, scrubbed and dressed in his favorite shirt, which his mother got him at a rummage sale for a quarter, some well-worn Levi's, and his high-top tennis shoes. That was a time when people dressed up to go to the opera—long dresses and black tie in the evening and at least tea party outfits for the matinees. Harriet was about to explain all this to Joseph, then bit her tongue and said, "You look nice, Joe. Let's go." Joseph was delighted by *Faust*. Now, of course, everyone dresses as they wish at concerts or the theater. Perhaps Joe started the trend.

# 14

# HAPPINESS THIEVES 3:
# Anger and Resentment

Anyone can become angry—that is easy. But to be angry
with the right person, to the right degree, at the right time,
for the right purpose, and in the right way—this is not
easy.

—ARISTOTLE[1]

Reckon the days in which you have not been angry. I used
to be angry every day; now every other day; then every
third and fourth day; and if you miss it so long as thirty
days, offer a sacrifice of thanksgiving to God.

—EPICTETUS

When angry, count four: when very angry, swear.

—MARK TWAIN

It is a little-appreciated fact that anger is perhaps the most
common antidote for feelings of fear and weakness. If one can
get mad at somebody—at one's spouse, one's children, one's
dog—then one feels stronger, in command, and fear and weakness fade into the background. This incompatibility of fear and
anger works in both directions, of course; if the fear stimulus is
stronger, then anger hides its face. That is why we often tolerate
mistreatment from people we are afraid to antagonize and then
get angry later at people whom we do not fear or, in the safety of
fantasy, at the harmless image of our previous tormentor. The
Freudians call this "displacement" and suggest that we are releas-
ing anger we have bottled up, rather like upchucking a poison
we have been forced to drink. There may be some truth in this,
but I think that it disregards another subtle but important

truth—being angry actually *feels better* than feeling frightened or humiliated.

Most children come to appreciate the instrumental advantages of anger. On the playground, the boy who wins the fight is often the one who gets the maddest rather than the one who is bigger or stronger; genuine rage is intimidating to others. As we already saw in chapter 8, some foolish parents inadvertently teach their youngsters to respond angrily, coercively, to interpersonal frustrations by letting the child win by throwing tantrums. I can remember discovering the advantages of righteous indignation when I was about ten years old. A boy in my class at school had angrily refused some rebuke from the teacher, and his outrage seemed so genuine that she in effect apologized. After turning that scene over in my mind for several days, I tried out my new discovery on my mother, attempting to conceal my trepidation with feigned indignation. Having never once lost a battle of wills with my four older brothers, my mother simply looked at me over her glasses and said, "Go to your room!" I went and that was that.

During the late 1960s, my wife and I joined the local Democratic-Farmer-Labor ward club for the purpose of supporting the fledgling anti–Vietnam war movement. One member of that club plainly had been reared by a mother very different from mine. He dealt with every disagreement with angry aggressiveness, and he simply intimidated the rest of us. One felt that the only effective way to deal with him would be to hit him with a brick. He was a business executive, and it may be that his belligerent style had proved effective in that milieu. His permanently frazzled wife confided to mine that they seldom entertained: "People we invite always seem to be busy that night." One of the serious disadvantages of the choleric approach to life is that no one wants to see you coming.

Most people, if they try, can identify occasions or circumstances in which they self-indulgently permit themselves to cultivate and express irritation. Driving alone in traffic, many of us enjoy muttering criticisms about the skills, character, or parentage of other drivers. I can get reliably irritated reading the letters to the editor or certain columnists in the newspaper, and there is no doubt that I feel stronger, more vigorous and self-confident, when I am irritated than I do when I am feeling worried or apprehensive or discouraged.

Adolf Hitler is said to have ranted about the unfairness of the Versailles Treaty and other rage-inducing topics in order to wrench himself out of an occasional funk. Moreover, Hitler's talent for choleric rages (undoubtedly potentiated by his addiction to amphetamines)[2] so intimidated his generals that he very nearly brought them and all of Germany with him to his final Armageddon. Unlike Hitler, I am known for my sweet disposition. Yet I can remember at least a couple of times when my children were small when I guiltily realized that I was being sharp and irritable with them, not as a responsible parent, but because it made me feel better than I had felt before they gave me the excuse to get angry. Many people can be seen to hoard grievances and develop a kind of chronic irritability as they get older because, when one is irritated, the juices start flowing and one feels stronger, more puissant. A good fictional example of a sociopathic character whose entire adjustment to life was based on this principle is Leroy Fleck, the contract killer in Tony Hillerman's novel *Talking God*.[3]

But while feeling angry may be better than feeling scared or weak, it is not nearly so gratifying as just feeling happy. Although righteous indignation can serve a useful function now and then, you and especially your family will be better off if you can manage to keep anger in its place. This is harder for men than for women, partly because of the cultural notion, stronger in some cultures than in others, that anger is manly. Bouchard's data on MZ twins reared apart suggest that aggression, the behavioral manifestation of anger, is more strongly influenced by genetic factors in men than in women. Men score significantly higher on the MPQ Aggression scale than women do.

Two of the items in that list of self-ratings filled out by our MTR twins read like this:

*Irritability:* The tendency to be frequently irritated by people, events, interruptions, by the things people say or do—a "short temper"; what you feel regardless of whether you show your feelings.

*Rage:* Whether you get angry frequently or seldom, when you *do* lose your temper, how mad do you get? Give yourself a "4" if people avoid you when you are angry, a "5" if you get physically violent.

For the 198 pairs of middle-aged twins we tested twice, three years apart, the adjusted MZ correlations were .55 and .89 for Irritability and Rage, respectively, compared with adjusted DZ correlations of .06 and .03.[4] What this suggests is, first, that the stable components of irritability and, especially, of rage-readiness are strongly influenced by genetic factors, and, second, that these genetic effects, like those of the happiness set point, are "emergenic" and do not tend to run in families. *But*, and this is very important, if you were endowed by nature with an especially choleric disposition, this does *not* mean that you must give way to it. These four hundred twin individuals varied substantially in their self-ratings on the Rage item over the three years (the retest correlation was only about .40), which means that it is possible to master this tendency if you try. If you choose to let your genetic steersman run your life, then, if you have inherited the choleric tendency, you can expect to be involved in periodic explosions for which you (and/or your loved ones) will have to take the consequences. But it is your life, and you would be wise to take control of it yourself.

A substantial fraction of all homicides results from altercations in which the perpetrator (call him Perp) feels that his honor has been impugned by the victim (call him Vic). What if Perp, now languishing in jail, had waited until the next day to decide how to respond to the offense? What if he had asked himself then how important Vic's comments, opinions, or actions really were to him and how high a price was he willing to pay in order to see Vic suitably punished?

If bulls or stallions have been castrated as youngsters, they are much less aggressive and dangerous as adults. If we inject those adult steers and geldings with testosterone, the hormone complex secreted by the male testes, they may begin to show aggressiveness, especially during the mating season. Does this mean that testosterone, the "male hormone," is responsible for male violence and aggression? Well, not exactly. It appears that male aggressiveness is largely learned, and that testosterone serves as a kind of facilitator or releaser of those learned tendencies. If a troop of male monkeys who have established a dominance hierarchy among themselves are subsequently castrated, the hierarchy is retained. If the number-two monkey is then injected with testosterone, he becomes more aggressive indeed but only toward poor Number Three and other monkeys lower in the hierarchy. He is still submissive to Number One, as he had learned to be before the operation. In the wild, one cannot predict which males will become dominant to which other males from their testosterone levels. But after the dominance hierarchy has been established, the top males will be found to have higher blood levels of testosterone than the subordinates lower down. Male hormones are important in aggression, but not causal in any simple way. Biology is always more complicated than one expects.

Once, when a member of the Minnesota Corrections Department was sitting in on my graduate seminar, he brought to class with him two inmates (plus two husky armed guards). One of his exhibits was a classic, fearless psychopath, the type of individual that Cleckley characterized as "Not deeply vicious, but carries disaster with him lightly in each hand." The other inmate was what I call a sociopath, someone who began as a little boy with a difficult temperament (although not so difficult as a psychopath's) and who grew up unsocialized largely because of parental malfeasance. These two had much in common in their criminal histories, but one difference was striking. The sociopath was always getting into fights, while the fearless psychopath walked away from violence. In the discussion, it became clear that the psychopath's relative fearlessness made him able to react in a more rational way—he was unafraid of "what will people think," the bugaboo that has been killing young men the world over since the Stone Age. "People can get hurt out in the yard.

Why should I get myself messed up over something some
_____ says?" On the other hand, other inmates seemed to sense
that it could be dangerous to back this man into a corner where
he couldn't walk away.

Since we can't help getting angry, what we must work on is
what we do when anger flares. The instinct is the same one that
causes lions or hyenas to snap at one another when feasting com-
petitively on a fresh kill. It is adaptive for them as it once was for
our ancestors because the most fearsome snappers tended to get
the most meat. But it is no longer adaptive in most situations,
and now most flares of anger are occasions when the "genes'
prehistoric song" must be resisted.

My big, gentle Norwegian father set a good example. I remember one time after dinner when he went to the closet for his
hat before walking to the store for his after-dinner cigar.
"Where's my hat, Frances?" "Oh, Henry, I gave that grimy old
hat to the Goodwill. Wear that nice new one I got you." "Damn!"
my father said. Then, after putting on the new hat that he'd never
liked, he muttered, "Double damn!" and then he walked out.
When he got back fifteen minutes later, the brief storm was permanently over. My father almost always did the right thing.

## Resentment

I am sure that my colleagues in the shrink business have done
much good for many patients over the years, but some of them
have done much harm as well, both directly in dealing with patients and indirectly in pontificating for the public. Most educated people have been persuaded to believe in an erroneous and
naïve radical environmentalism and, in particular, to attribute all
of their personal faults and problems to the way they have been
treated, especially in childhood. When I was a graduate student
undergoing a psychoanalysis for training purposes, I got to re-
flecting on whose fault it was that I had never gotten very far
with my intention to read my father's *Encyclopaedia Britannica*
from Aalto to Zwingli; I thought it was probably my father's
fault. My wise professor-analyst suggested kindly that perhaps I

just wasn't that interested. (My son Matthew read my copy of the *World Book Encyclopedia* from cover to cover when he was about ten, but Matthew was naturally more studious than I was, and the *World Book* is not as intimidating as the *Britannica*.)

Although altogether too many children have been sexually abused by family members, the recent epidemic of "recovered memories" of such abuse has been largely iatrogenic or doctor-caused. Several years ago, while waiting to give a talk at the annual meeting of the American Psychological Association, held in San Francisco that year, I wandered into an adjoining crowded meeting room to hear the speaker concluding: "So, if your patient cannot remember any sexual abuse, it is your duty as a therapist to help her—or him—remember!" I could hardly believe my ears. It is rather like a physician advising colleagues: "If your patient has not yet been infected by [some ineradicable virus], then it is your duty to infect him now."

When one imagines that one's failings or other problems are someone else's fault, when one adopts the resentful shroud of victimhood, then one's chances of resolving one's problems and getting on with one's life are abrogated. Most of us are the way we are because our genetic steersman pushed us in that direction. Even when there is some truth in the blaming, what is the point of continuing to obsess and gripe about it? Five of my ten grandchildren have African-American ancestry. In the course of their lives, they are certain to meet with occasional bigoted slights as a result. But they are also, in the present climate of opinion, certain to be from time to time advantaged because of their heritage. Happily, their parents will make it clear to them that their futures are in their own hands, and from the present vantage point, they look like happy futures.

# PART SIX

⁕

# HAPPY SENIORS

Do not go gentle into that good night.
Old age should burn and rave at close of day;
Rage, rage against the dying of the light.
                                        —DYLAN THOMAS

The problem with Dylan Thomas was that he began raging while he was still a boy, and it killed him before he reached his seniority. Had he waited, he would have discovered that there are compensations that accrue with elder status. You don't have to go to poetry readings or rock concerts, for one thing (unless for some reason you really want to). Thomas made the common mistake of assuming that the fellow creature whom he observes on some other square of the chessboard of life must feel as he thinks he would feel, should they suddenly change places. He neglected to take account of our extraordinary human adaptability. Those happy young men in the linoleum business would have cringed to see themselves, while still seniors in high school, where they would be ten years later. When I was a boy of fifty, I would have cringed to see myself now, white-haired, "all but one of my fires out."

But although it is much harder now to touch my toes before I step into the shower, I felt good when I got up this morning. I'm looking forward to my day, and to the next one, and the next. And most of my contemporaries seem to be in similar fettle. Part

239

of what misleads the young into attributing gloom and despair to the old is that many of us seniors have lined faces which, in repose, *look* angry or sad. Harriet and I go to the Guthrie Theatre on the Wednesday matinees, when most of the audience is on the far side of three score and ten. When I study them before or between acts, as they sit there in repose, I see few happy-looking faces. But when they are enthusiastically applauding, later on, their faces are alight with real joy. We saw a revival of Kaufman and Hart's *You Can't Take It with You* the other day, and hundreds of white (mostly female) heads laughed all the way through.

These last two chapters examine happiness among the aged.

# 15

# HAPPY IN RETIREMENT

The years between 50 and 70 are the hardest. You are
always being asked to do things, and yet you are not
decrepit enough to turn them down.
—T. S. ELIOT

Just remember, once you're over the hill, you begin to pick
up speed.
—CHARLES SCHULZ

Americans who, like me, are old enough to retire, can look
forward to living another twenty years or so, and the question is: Shall this penultimate chapter in the book of one's
life be happy or sad, gratifying or grim? I was the youngest of
five boys, nine years younger than the fourth, the youngest in
my class from third grade onward, even the youngest in my company at Great Lakes Naval Training Station, because I enlisted on
my seventeenth birthday in 1945. Therefore, it seems odd now
to find myself the eldest member of my psychology department
faculty, a colleague of former students who have become distinguished researchers in their own right, with worldwide reputa-
tions in the field to which I helped introduce them years ago.
Oddly enough, I rather enjoy this elder status and am looking
forward to becoming professor emeritus in another year. I shall
keep my office in Elliott Hall and continue doing what I'm doing
now, minus only the few obligatory tiresome duties that are part
of any salaried position. I used to rather dread the thought of

retirement. But now that it is ready for me, I find that I am ready for it.

For one thing, I have found some excellent role models. My father, who was an inventor, continued happily working at his drafting table until the day he died at age seventy-seven. Or consider Paul Meehl, who was chair of the psychology department when I was a graduate student. Paul is a former president of the American Psychological Association, a member of the National Academy of Sciences, and the recipient of nearly every honor and award available to psychologists. One might have thought that retirement for him would becalm his lake of happiness and leave him bored and melancholy. Instead, he has been happily working on unfinished projects, publishing books and papers, awakening nearly every morning secure in the knowledge that the day is his to do with as he likes. Or consider my friend Rufus Lumry, professor emeritus of chemistry, who knows things about protein molecules that no one else knows yet and who is busily writing it all down. Rufus turns up on campus about noon most days, in time for lunch at the Campus Club, and leaves his cluttered office in the chemistry building often after midnight, having spent the hours in between, confiding what he knows to a generation of physical chemists yet unborn. Both Paul and Rufus insist that their retirement years have been among the happiest in their respective lives.

My eldest brother, Henry, is a retired business executive now in his eighties, who lives with his wife in a retirement community in Florida. Henry was always an organizer and he is still at it, shepherding his gray-haired friends and neighbors into various activities that Henry enjoys, and which I expect they do, too. Henry is fond of gadgets, and the personal computer is, of course, a kind of universal gadget. Henry is currently working with what must be at least his third computer, and he greatly enjoys putting it through its paces. A computer is like a talented and complaisant friend who can always be counted on to do whatever you want to do, as long as you ask nicely (that is to say, correctly). Henry, like me, was always a bad speller (spelling ability has strong genetic roots), and having a computer spell-checker makes writing much less irksome for both of us.

Many people devote their lives to jobs that cannot be carried on as easily into retirement as mine can. Academics have the advantage in that most of us can continue to do in retirement many of the things that produced the ripples in our lakes of subjective well-being throughout our careers. The father of a young colleague of mine was a professional firefighter who was required to retire at sixty-five, and he resented it greatly. Fire-fighters live half their lives at the firehouse, they eat half their meals and sleep half their nights there, and they develop a strong sense of camaraderie with their colleagues. Then there are the periodic adventures, full of risk and excitement. Police officers and people in the military face similar problems when the time comes at last to take off the uniform for good. My friend's dad spun his wheels for a time, feeling uprooted. But then he discovered that he had outlived many of the men in his neighborhood and that their wives often needed someone handy with tools, as he is, to make minor repairs around their houses—jobs their husbands used to take care of. He finds it interesting and gratifying to have become the neighborhood foster-husband.

Our research group has collected data showing that it is not only former college professors (and Thoroughbred stallions) that enjoy being put out to pasture. You will recall that our middle-aged Registry twins, thirty to fifty years old when we first recruited them, answered, on average, 76 percent of the questions on the Well Being scale in the happy direction. The seventeen-year-old twins in our Twin/Family Study, with their lives mostly ahead of them, produced virtually identical results. But how about us seniors? What do the elderly report when asked those questions listed in chapter 2? Are their lives interesting? Do they find ways to liven up their days, to have fun? Can they report that "Most mornings, the day ahead looks bright to me"? My colleague Matt McGue, inspired by our good luck in locating and recruiting twins identified from Minnesota birth records, identified in the same way twins born sixty or more years earlier and tracked down most of the survivors. Some four hundred of his seniors, aged sixty-five to ninety-one, filled out the Multidimensional Personality Questionnaire used with our other samples, and Matt has kindly permitted me to examine the results. On the MPQ Well Being scale, these elderly twins, whose average age was 70, answered not 76 percent but 84 percent of the items in the happy direction!

It has to be remembered that the people, young and old, who participate in our researches are not currently incapacitated by illness, either physical or psychiatric. No hospital or nursing home patients filled out our questionnaires. But McGue managed to recruit about the same proportion of his surviving elder twins as we had achieved earlier with the middle-aged group. Therefore, it seems a safe prediction that, when their Social Security checks begin coming in, most of our Registry twins will find their feeling of personal well-being trending upward, rather than the reverse. At my time of life I find this an encouraging prospect.

## What Have Seniors Got to Be So Happy About?

It is likely that those few of our early ancestors who survived long enough to acquire wrinkles and gray hair were even happier than are the Social Security recipients of today. Older people once were respected by the young—they still are, I'm told, in Latin countries—and were thought to have accumulated useful wisdom so that their long stories were worth listening to, even if now and then they were repeated. Their children and grandchildren did not go to live vast distances away—neither the "empty nest" nor the nursing home had as yet been invented. Those early elders saw their peers expire first-hand, and perhaps they felt lucky to have been spared themselves. Now one reads in the newspaper the obituaries of school chums not seen for decades, not to mention the demise of celebrities (Mickey Mantle, Jimmy Stewart) who seem always to have been a part of one's life, and such news comes as an unexpected, shocking intimation of mortality.

Many of my generation once consoled themselves in their

bleaker moments with dreams of future glory, dreams that then seemed faintly plausible but which are only silly, now that the future isn't what it used to be. I have to face up to the fact that I am never going to learn to speak French or be elected to the National Academy of Sciences (the most exclusive club to which psychologists aspire). Physical and mental debilities begin to proliferate. Voices are too soft, and print is too small. I meet friends and colleagues in the halls or on the street, and their names rise to the surface of my mind, like air bubbles in molasses, but not until it is too late. Some nights, in bed, just bending one's leg brings on a painful cramp, which never used to happen. (It turns out that one capsule of quinine, the drug usually prescribed for malaria, will hold those cramps at bay for the rest of the night—one of the mysteries of pharmacology.) Why is it then that most of us retain a cheerful outlook?

At least part of the reason why most seniors turn out to have a strong sense of subjective well-being is that many of the doleful or querulous members of their birth cohort have died off! We know that being happy is good for you. Happy people get sick less often and recover from illness or accident faster than unhappy people do. If unhappy people are more vulnerable, they are more likely to be the first to lay down their burdens and expire, leaving the happier survivors to carry on. Figure 15.1 shows that, at least in Minnesota, about 50 percent of the males in my (1928) birth cohort had left the field of play by 1997, and about 40 percent of the women.[1] (The shape of these curves confirms Charles M. Schulz's comment, cited above, that when one is over the hill, one picks up speed.)

If I had been clever enough to begin collecting happiness data from my contemporaries forty years ago, then we could test the hypothesis that, on average, the ones who failed to make it to my age now were less happy people than the ones who have survived. The best I can do instead is to report on the fiftieth reunion of my 1945 high school graduating class. They were a surprisingly jolly collection of codgers, even before the wine began to flow, and I was especially impressed to note that some

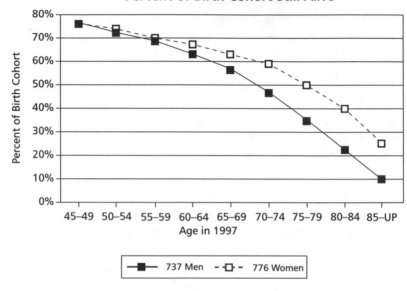

FIGURE 15.1

The proportion of each age group of Minnesotans who, in 1997, were still alive. Note the relative longevity of women as compared with men.

of the "girls" were still as flirtatious as I remembered from a half century earlier.

Although quite irrelevant to this discussion, I cannot resist recounting how that evening ended. Not having known these people, my wife was reluctant to attend this reunion, so I went with my boyhood friend Roger Sahr, whose wife had similar views. Driving back about midnight, I unconsciously made a turn I hadn't made in at least forty years and stopped in front of the house where my parents had lived at that time. "Roger," I said, "do you see what I've done?" "Yes," he replied. "You've gone home." How could anyone *not* be interested in studying the mysteries of the mind?

Although no one has done the necessary longitudinal study, I believe that the genetic talent for happiness does contribute to longevity. However, I also think that there are aspects of the retirement years that make more waves and fewer troughs on one's lake of happiness than when one was trammeled with the uncertainties of youth or the obligations of middle age.

## It's Not My Problem Anymore

One reason many older people feel an extra measure of contentment has to do with the devolution of responsibility to the next generation. My younger colleagues now run the research project that I began and which has grown to require an annual budget of a million dollars. They are far better managers than I ever was, and I attend the research meetings now like a guest at a concert. I can tune in on the melodies and tune out the discords that are no longer my problem to orchestrate. For more than thirty years, I have been custodian of my family's two cabins at a northern lake. While I have usually enjoyed that role, I now enjoy the prospect of my sons taking over those responsibilities. While one continues to take satisfaction from doing useful work, after retirement one can select such undertakings more for their intrinsic appeal than out of any sense of obligation.

Forty years ago, by accident, I got interested in polygraphic interrogation. By publishing the results of two experiments, I became the proprietor of a significant fraction of the world's scientific literature on the so-called "lie detector," that uniquely American invention that wise old Senator Sam Irvin called "Twentieth Century witchcraft." I also became one of the only persons with scientific credentials to whom victims of erroneous lie detector tests could turn for help. My 1981 book, *A Tremor in the Blood: Uses and Abuses of the Lie Detector*," was the only scientific monograph on the polygraph test—that bloodless third degree to which millions of Americans were being required to submit in order to get or keep their jobs, or in the often vain hope of convincing the police that they were innocent of some criminal charge. Over a period of some twenty years, I testified as an expert witness in courts and courts-martial all over the United States and Canada. Many of these cases, together with other more recent developments—such as the marriage of the mystique of the computer to the myth of the lie detector, a union that has spawned a litter of mischievous mythlets—are reviewed in the second edition of *Tremor*.*

The first lie detector was developed and promoted by (alas) a Harvard Ph.D. named William Moulton Marston, whose imaginative talents led him later to create, under the pen name of William Mouton, the comic strip character *Wonder Woman*. Readers may recall that this lady possessed a magic lasso that, once wrapped around some villain, forced him to utter only the truth. But the idea of a lie detector test goes far back into human history. That splendid title for my book came from Daniel Defoe, the author of *Robinson Crusoe*. In a pamphlet published in 1730, *An Effectual Scheme for the Immediate Prevention of Street Robberies and Suppressing All Other Disorders of the Night*, Defoe explained: "Guilt carries Fear always about with it; there is a Tremor in the Blood of a Thief, that, if attended to, would effectually discover him." What Defoe—as well as the FBI, the CIA, the Secret Service, and the U.S. military—failed to realize is that there is frequently a tremor in the blood of the innocent accused as well. Darwinian natural selection, which caused us to evolve our powers of speech and also our ability to speak falsely— because these talents both proved to be adaptive—did not cause us to evolve some involuntary physiological response, like Pinnochio's lengthening nose, which we show when, and only when, we're lying.

I have enjoyed doing battle with the polygraph proponents. Moreover, when my research was in the doldrums, it has been comforting to have this *pro bono* sideline with which to justify my professional existence. But I am ready now to let someone else step into the breach. Happily, my former student and now colleague Bill Iacono has now become the leading scientific expert on polygraphy and I can refer all calls from lie detector victims or their lawyers directly to him. There are many benefits to an academic career and one is the gratification of knowing

*D.T. Lykken, *A Tremor in the Blood: Uses and Abuses of the Lie Detector*, 2d ed. (New York: Plenum, 1998.)

that the family business has passed into the capable hands of an intellectual scion. Another is to know that it's not my problem anymore.

There are a couple of problems at my university that once would have troubled me. I think I know what needs to be done to solve them. One concerns our dumb "punishment first, trial later!" method of dealing with allegations of wrongdoing against members of the faculty.[2] The other is the university's Human Subjects Committees that were designed to prevent physicians from secretly experimenting on their patients but now, because of the lack accountability, threaten to prohibit much harmless but important psychological research.[3] In fact, if I were a younger man, I might even act on the realization that a university is a microcosm replete with the baleful phenomena of bureaucracy. Bureaucracy is a problem that society needs to master before it masters us. It should be easy to research this problem within a university where remedies could be suggested and tried out before application to the larger world outside. But I am an older man, and so I am content just to compose an indignant response to the appropriate administrator, and leave the problem for others to solve.

Can there be grandparents, no matter how loving and devoted, who have not found comfort in the knowledge that the problems of their grandchildren are not theirs to solve? I know a couple whose retirement dreams had to be abandoned when their daughter, having split with her husband, moved with her two children back into the grandparental nest. They seem as happy as ever, being as adaptable we all are. But I suspect that, when they reach seventy, they may answer only 76 percent of the Well Being questions in the happy direction, rather than 84 percent like the rest of us retirees.

Five of my grandchildren have African-American heritage, and, if I were their father, I would worry about the tendency of our public schools to place "diversity" and "multiculturalism" at the top of their agenda. Their objective is, or should be, to minimize ethnic stereotyping and to inculcate a common set of skills and values. But teaching minority children about a culture and encouraging them to believe that their ways of learning and feeling are innately different than those of their white schoolmates seem a strange way of achieving those goals. Happily, my son Jesse and my daughter-in-law Veneta know that "multiculturalism" is an oxymoron, and that a real sense of community depends upon sharing a common culture. When required to indicate the race of their children, they specify "human." They are happy to have their son Zeke recognized as gifted, but they are unwilling for Zeke to be made into an African-American poster boy. Zeke's grandparents are glad to have his nurturance in such capable hands.

## Are Things Getting Better or Worse?

Nothing is more responsible for the good old days than a
bad memory.
—ROBERT BENCHLEY

The optimist proclaims that we live in the best of all
possible worlds; and the pessimist fears this is true.
—JAMES BRANCH CABELL

My wife and I have had a running argument for as long as I can remember as to whether the secular trend is up (my view) or down (hers). I have what she thinks to be a foolish faith in technology, the belief that human inventiveness will gradually solve most of our problems, many of which, of course, were created by technology in the first place. She is especially concerned with the future of our wildlife and the environment generally and, it must be admitted, that picture looks rather bleak. If it were not for Harriet and her talented pro bono lawyer, Brian O'Neill, I think that the last remnants of our native timber wolf, *Canis lupus*, ancestor of all the doggie pets on which Americans spend billions annually, would have been exterminated from the lower forty-eight states by the brave hunters and trappers whose greatest joy in life is to kill things. It is interesting that Harriet, the pessimist, gets a higher score on the happiness scale than I do. One's expectations about the great world outside are not necessarily determined by one's confidence about self and family.

As the optimist in the family, I take great satisfaction from the fact that, at our north woods cabin on the Gunflint Trail, we take our drinking water directly from the lake. There are not many places left where that is possible. I asked a biochemist colleague once whether we should be testing that lake water on a regular basis. "You are," he replied, "and you're using one of the most sensitive tests we know of, the bioassay!" (that is, human consumption).

One major concern that still engages both our interests is the fate and future of the millions of American children now living with abusive or overburdened or incompetent parents, often single parents. I say "living with" rather than "reared by" because incompetent parents do not accomplish the main responsibility of true parents: namely, the socialization of their children. They fail to imbue their children with the kind of conscience that prevents antisocial rule breaking, or with the senses of empathy and altruism and personal responsibility that we expect of our fellow passengers in this crowded lifeboat. Not having learned the lessons themselves, such parents fail to teach their children the satisfactions of becoming responsible, productive citizens. Nearly 50 percent of American children today, either because of early divorce or out-of-wedlock birth, are being reared without the active participation of their biological fathers. In my book *The Antisocial Personalities*,[4] I show that this guarantees that these youngsters will be approximately *seven times* more likely to be abused, to become delinquent, to drop out of school, to become themselves teenage parents of out-of-wedlock children, or to end up in prison. In short, millions of America's children are now being denied their supposed birthright of life, liberty, and the pursuit of happiness.

As usual, Harriet's expectations are more pessimistic than my own. She fears that our own well-socialized grandchildren will grow up to be rather like zoo keepers, having to feed and take care of (and often to cage) a large dependent and/or feral fraction of their generation whose biological parents, in an ideal world, would never have been permitted to breed.

I, on the other hand, have been promoting the notion of parental licensure,[5] and I have been impressed by the interested reception given this apparently radical idea by psychologists, journalists, and thoughtful citizens. An old expression has it that "Your rights end where my nose begins!" The people I have talked to find it easy to see that the reproductive rights of feckless, would-be parents end where the life and future of an innocent infant begins. Barbara Carlson, a candidate for mayor of Minneapolis in 1997, announced that she favors parental licensure, and Tony Jaros, a state legislator from Duluth, plans to introduce a licensure bill drafted along lines I have suggested. I think that requiring of biological parents the same minimal credentials we require now of adoptive parents is an idea whose time will eventually come.

# 16

# THE FINAL CHAPTER

Why is it that we rejoice at a birth and grieve at a funeral?
It is because we are not the person involved.

—MARK TWAIN

I think the dying pray at the last not "please" but "thank
you," as a guest thanks his host at the door.

—ANNIE DILLARD

It is impossible that anything so natural, so necessary, and
so universal as death, should ever have been designed by
providence as an evil to mankind.

—JONATHAN SWIFT

I discovered death on the evening of December 26, 1936. My
mother's older sister, Ann, a tiny, shy, unmarried woman,
lived with us, and Auntie Ann had given me for Christmas a
model airplane kit that I felt sure had cost more than she could
afford. Thinking about that, sentimentally, in bed, it suddenly
occurred to me that Auntie Ann would die one day, and that my
father and mother would, too, and even my brothers! They
would all be gone and I would be alone! I can still recall the
sense of utter desolation that this dawning realization caused. I
cried myself to sleep, and the next morning, I awoke feeling that
my life had changed, that I was "alone and parted from all joy
and gladness." I remember being with my friends in the neighborhood that day or the next, thinking how they would feel if
they knew what I knew. I have wondered since whether this is a
common experience, whether other people can recall a time in
their lives when the inevitability of death changes suddenly and
traumatically from an abstract concept to a gut-wrenching reality.

Even during the several days that this sense of desolation lasted, it was not my own demise that troubled me. What was giving me so much pain was the anticipation of how I would feel after a loved one had died, and perhaps my inability to imagine feeling anything after my own death ruled that out of consideration. Now, sixty years later, the awareness of my own mortality still harbors no great anxiety or regret. "To die; to sleep" seems a peaceful prospect and, because I am not a religious man, I do not have Hamlet's fear about "what dreams may come, when we have shuffled off this mortal coil."

But I do fear the kind of nightmare that frequently precedes death in American hospitals and nursing homes. Poor young Ben, my niece's husband, whose galloping cancer not only caused searing pain but also obstructed his breathing so that, during his last hours, he repeatedly experienced the terrifying sensation of being strangled. My aged mother, who lost with her memory her sense of familiarity so that, for two years before the end, she awoke every morning in a place she didn't recognize among people who all were total strangers to her. My brother, Robert, whose personality expired from Alzheimer's disease about four years before his bodily shell followed suit. It can be ugly, painful, frightening, and humiliating, and it is our fault, yours and mine, because we have not had the will or the courage to figure out a way to prevent such things from happening.

Some brave and considerate physicians used to be willing to take the necessary steps when the time came. Sigmund Freud smoked too many cigars for too many years and ultimately developed a disfiguring, painful, and terminal cancer of the jaw. The great man lingered on, still working, for several years more, but finally told his physician, Max Schur, "My dear Schur, you remember our first talk. You promised me then that you would help me when I could no longer carry on. It is only torture now, and it has no longer any sense." Dr. Schur thereupon honored his pledge by giving his patient an injection of morphine sufficient to provide him a permanent peace[1].

One afternoon forty years ago, my father drove the cleaning lady home and then, returning in his absentminded way, he drove through a stop sign and was hit, broadside, by a fast-moving car. Thrown from the car, Dad struck his head on the curbing and was taken, unconscious, to the hospital. The chief of neurosurgery was a friend of mine and kindly agreed to take over the case. Around midnight, I was summoned to the hospital. My friend, gowned and with his gloved hands clasped in front of him, came out of the surgery and told me kindly, "The skull fracture is much worse than I had realized at first. We might be able to save him, but there will be a lot of brain damage." I recognized this to be a question. My father's life had always been a life of the mind; he could not bear to know that his mind was now half gone and, if he did not know it, then the man who awoke would no longer be my father. His sudden loss would be grievously hard on my mother, but to find her strong, kindly husband turned into a helpless and tormented half-man would be harder still. "Let him go, then," I told my friend, and he nodded and went back into the operating room. Ten minutes later: "Your dad's gone, Dave. I'm sorry. He never felt a thing."

Now, however, it appears that only Dr. Kevorkian has the necessary courage, and he is pilloried for having it. I could look forward to the Final Chapter of my life with a much greater feeling of security if every hospital had a wing called the thanatorium with small suites where people who were ready to die could spend their last hours. We have the technology to banish pain and fear by adequate medication. With family members in attendance, the patients, if they were conscious, would be able to say their last good-byes in peace before being kindly put to sleep. But we shall have to learn to think more rationally about these matters if any progress is to be made. One test may turn out to be whether government and the medical profession can ever come to grips with the fact that the narcotic, heroin, is an ideal geriatric analgesic. Heroin soothes pain at least as well as morphine does and produces less gastric upset in old people. Moreover, it makes the patient feel good. But heroin is not listed in the American pharmacopoeia because it is illegal and strongly addictive—and we don't want to let people become drug addicts just because they are dying!

But I have signed my living will and my durable power of attorney and joined the local chapter of the Hemlock Society. Thus prepared, I expect to enjoy my retirement. I hope to see my grandchildren enter into young adulthood but if not, I hope at least that my own final chapter will be as brief as the one you have just read.

# NOTES

## INTRODUCTION

1. D. G. Myers and E. Diener, "Who Is Happy?," *Psychological Science 6* (1995): 10–19.
2. D. T. Lykken and A. Tellegen, "Happiness Is a Stochastic Phenomenon," *Psychological Science 7* (1996): 186–89.
3. D. G. Myers, *The Pursuit of Happiness* (New York: Avon Books, 1992).

## CHAPTER 1

1. William (or "Tiger, tiger") Blake, 1757–1827.
2. A. Campbell, P. Converse, and W. Rodgers, *The Quality of American Life* (New York: Sage, 1976).
3. F. M. Andrews and S. B. Withey, *Social Indicators of Well-Being* (New York: Plenum, 1976).
4. R. Inglehart, *Culture Shift in Advanced Industrial Society* (Princeton, NJ: Princeton University Press, 1990), 32.
5. For twin correlations, the formula is $(B - W)/(B + W)$, where B is the mean square between pairs ($B = (N*Var(S))/2(N-1)$) and W is the mean square within pairs ($W = (\Sigma(D^2))/2N$); where Var(S) is the variance of S, N is the number of pairs, D is the within-pair difference, and S is the within-pair sum.
6. It is more accurate to say that fraternal twins share about 50 percent of their polymorphic genes on average. Most of our genes are shared by nearly all humans because they constitute the instructions for making a human being rather than an ape or a butterfly. But perhaps one-fourth of our genes are polymorphic; from one person to another in the human population there may be two to twenty or more slightly different genes, different alleles that can occupy the locus of a given polymorphic gene. Fraternal twins, like ordinary siblings, share about half of these polymorphic genes on average.
7. Norman Cousins, *The Anatomy of an Illness as Perceived by the Patient* (New York: Norton, 1979). Cousin's disease was ankylosing spondylitis, a painful and usually progressive arthritislike degeneration of the joints of the lower spine that then works upward. Cousin's therapy during the acute phase of the illness included funny films and books, plus massive injections of vitamin C to help jump-start his adrenals.
8. To understand how we can be sure there was such an Eve, consider the set of all mothers now alive. Since some mothers have more than

258 Notes

one daughter and others have none, the set of all grandmothers, living or dead, who had daughters with children, must be smaller than the number of those daughters. By similar reasoning, the number of great-grandmothers, whose daughters had daughters with children, must be smaller still. You had sixty-four great-great-great-great-great-grand-mothers but you got your mitochondria from only one of them (the one whose great-granddaughter was the great-grandmother of your maternal grandmother). If we go back farther, we shall meet the woman who was the source of both yours and my mitochondria and, farther still, we shall meet Eve, the source of all the human mitochondria in the 6 billion of us now alive.

9. See R. Dawkins, *The Selfish Gene* (New York: Oxford University Press, 1976).

10. Some evolutionary psychologists, turning a blind eye to evidence like that summarized in chapter 2, assume that genetic variation affecting most important traits has largely disappeared in our species as a consequence of natural selection. While much of human psychology is influenced by innate genetic tendencies, instincts, "mental organs," and the like, these savants believe (against all evidence) that human traits show negligible heritability or, if they are heritable, that they are not important traits. This compromise between the tabula rasa of the radical environmentalist and the facts of behavioral genetics gives these evolutionary psychologists an area of scientific study while shielding them from the uncomfortable debate about biological equality. Charles Darwin's freethinking grandfather, Erasmus, once observed that "Unitarianism is a featherbed for falling Christians." One might similarly say that this halfway haven of evolutionary psychology provides a featherbed for falling radical environmentalists.

11. D. G. Myers and E. Diener, "Who Is Happy?," *Psychological Science* 6 (1995): 10–19.

12. Bill Iacono is McKnight Distinguished Professor of Psychology at the University of Minnesota, a past president of the Society for Psychophysiological Research, and, I am proud to say, a former student of mine.

13. D. T. Lykken, "Research with Twins: The Concept of Emergenesis," Presidential Address, Twenty-first Annual Meeting of the Society for Psychophysiological Research, Washington, DC, 1981; *Psychophysiology* 19 (1982): 361–73.

14. E. Suh, E. Diener, and F. Fujita, "Events and Subjective Well-Being: Only Recent Events Matter," *Journal of Personality and Social Psychology* 70 (1996): 1091–1102.

15. *The New Yorker,* July 28, 1997, 76.

16. See Bowlby, *Attachment and loss: Vol. 1. Attachment* (New York: Basic Books, 1969).

17. For example: Albert Ellis, *How to Stubbornly Refuse to Make Yourself Miserable About Anything—Yes, Anything!* (Secaucus, NJ: Stuart, 1988).
18. See, for example, the chapters by Orians and Heerwagon and by Kaplan in *The Adapted Mind: Evolutionary Psychology and the General of Culture*, J. H. Barkow, L. Cosmides, and J. Tooby, eds. (New York: Oxford University Press, 1992).
19. D. T. Lykken, "The Genetics of Genius," in *Genius and the Mind: Studies of Creativity and Temperament in the Historical Record*, A. Steptoe, ed. (New York: Oxford University Press, 1998).
20. Robert Louis Stevenson.

## CHAPTER 2

1. These items are from the 198-item form of the MPQ, used by permission of the University of Minnesota Press and Dr. Tellegen.
2. In January 1997, the German magazine *Stern* ran a cover story on our research ("Ist Glück erblich?"). In researching their story, they discovered a pair of identical twins, young women in their twenties, who had been separated at birth and reared apart, having met for the first time very recently. A German version of our Well Being scale was given separately to both women. Their scores were identical, both 37, exactly at the mean for our Minnesota twins.
3. The twin similarity is measured by the intraclass correlation which is equal to (BPV-WPV)/(BPV + WPV), where BPV is the between-pair variance and WPV is the within-pair variance.
4. D. D. Johnson in *Smithsonian*, October 1980. To protect the confidentiality of the MISTRA records, the only details about this twin pair repeated here are those already in the public record.
5. T. J. Bouchard, Jr., D. T. Lykken, M. McGue, N. Segal, and A. Tellegen, "The Sources of Human Psychological differences: The Minnesota Study of Twins Reared Apart," *Science* 250 (1990): 223–28.
6. The evidence for this claim (that children reared together in the same *bad* home, by the same incompetent or abusive parents, is reviewed and discussed in D. T. Lykken, *The Antisocial Personalities* (Mahwah, NJ: Erlbaum, 1995).
7. The other important studies of twins reared apart include: N. Juel-Nielsen, "Individual and Environment: A Psychiatric-Psychological Investigation of MZ Twins Reared Apart," *Acta Psychiatric Scandinavia Suppl.* 183 (Copenhagen: Munksgaard, 1965); J. Newman, H. Freeman, and K. Holzinger, *Twins: A Study of Heredity and Environment* (Chicago: University of Chicago Press, 1932); N. L. Pedersen, R. Plomin, J. Nesselroade, and G. McClearn, "A Quantitative Genetic Analysis of Cognitive Abilities During the Second Half of the Life

Span," *Psychological Science* 3 (1992): 346–53; J. Shields, *Monozygotic Twins Brought Up Apart and Brought Up Together* (London: Oxford University Press, 1962).

8. See, e.g., Bouchard *et al.* (1990).

9. D. T. Lykken, T. F. Bouchard, Jr., M. McGue, and A. Tellegen, "Heritability of Interests: A Twin Study," *Journal of Applied Psychology* 78 (1993): 649–61.

10. D. T. Lykken, "Research with Twins: The Concept of Emergenesis," *Psychophysiology* 19 (1982): 361–73. See also C. C. Li, "A Genetical Model for Emergenesis," *American Journal of Human Genetics* 41 (1987): 517–23, and D. T. Lykken, M. McGue, A. Tellegen, and T. J. Bouchard, Jr., "Emergenesis: Genetic Traits That Do No Run in Families," *American Psychologist* 47 (1992): 1565–77.

11. The Kentucky Derby, the Preakness Stakes at the Pimlico Race Course in Baltimore, and the Belmont Stakes comprise the three great annual events—the "crowning" events—of American Thoroughbred flat racing.

12. Oliver Sacks, *An Anthropologist on Mars* (New York: Knopf, 1995), 223.

13. Sacks, *op. cit.*, 191.

14. Sacks *op. cit.*, (p189).

15. Sacks *op. cit.*, 224.

16. Sacks *op. cit.*, 222.

17. Sacks *op. cit.*, 194.

18. Sacks *op. cit.*, 199.

19. Sacks *op. cit.*, 210.

20. Sacks *op. cit.*, 226.

21. Grandin, T. and Scariano, M. *Emergence: Labeled autistic.* (Novato, CA: Avena Press, 1986).

22. D. T. Lykken, "The Genetics of Genius," in *Genius and the Mind: Studies of Creativity and Temperament in the Historical Record,* A. Steptoe, ed. (Oxford: Oxford University Press, 1998).

23. T. J. Bouchard, Jr., and M. McGue. Familial studies of intelligence: A review. *Science* 212 (1981): 1055–1059.

24. M. McGue, T. J. Bouchard, Jr., W. G. Iacono, and D. T. Lykken. "Behavioral Genetics of Cognitive Ability: A Life-Span Perspective," in *Nature, Nurture, and Psychology,* R. Plomin and G. McClearn, eds. (Washington, DC: American Psychological Association, 1993).

25. Plomin *et al.*, 1977; Scarr and McCartney, 1983

26. M. McGue *et al.*, *op.cit.*

27. This man, an acquaintance of my colleague T. J. Bouchard, Jr., was kind enough to provide our research group with an outline of his autobiography.

28. Children still living at home resemble each other and also their parents more than they will when grown and on their own. The seventeen-

year-old DZ twins in our Minnesota Twin/Family Study correlate about .32 on Well Being and the midparent vs. midtwin correlation is about .20. However, these similarities are due to their current living arrangements and not to their genes.

## CHAPTER 3

1. W. Dunham, *Journey Through Genius* (New York: John Wiley & Sons, 1990).
2. J. M. Keynes, "Newton the Man," in *The World of Mathematics,* vol. I, J. R. Newman, ed. (New York: Simon & Schuster, 1956).
3. A. Campbell, *The Sense of Well-being in America* (New York: McGraw-Hill, 1981), 115.
4. R. A. Niemi, J. Mueller, and T. S. Smith, *Trends in Public Opinion: A Compendium of Survey Data* (New York: Greenwood Press, 1989), 242.
5. J. R. Flynn, IQ Gains Over Time, in *Encyclopedia of Human Intelligence,* R. J. Sternberg, ed. (New York: Macmillan, 1994), 617–623.

## CHAPTER 4

1. L. L. Heston and R. Heston, *The Medical Casebook of Adolf Hitler* (London: William Kimber, Ltd., 1979).
2. Associated Press, September 27, 1993.
3. D. T. Lykken, *The Antisocial Personalities* (Mahwah, NJ: Lawrence Erlbaum Associates, 1995.)
4. D. T. Lykken, "Factory of Crime," *Psychological Inquiry* 8 (1997) 261–270.
5. See, for example, H. Begleiter and B. Kissin, eds., *The Genetics of Alcoholism* (New York: Oxford University Press, 1995).
6. J. C. Westman, *Licensing Parents: Can we Prevent Child Abuse and Neglect?* (New York: Plenum Press, 1994).
7. D. T. Lykken, "Incompetent Parenting: Its Causes and Cures," *Child Psychiatry and Human Development* 27 (1997): 129–37.

## CHAPTER 5

1. D. G. Myers, *The Pursuit of Happiness* (New York: Avon Books, 1994), 128–29. The Studs Terkel quote is from his 1972 book, *Working People Talk About What They Do All Day and How They Feel About What They Do* (New York: Pantheon Books).
2. D. Davis-Van Atta, *et al.,* eds., *Educating American Scientists: The Role of the Research Colleges* (Oberlin: Oberlin College Press, 1985). (Of Ivy League graduates, 7.8 percent got Ph.D.s, compared with 4.3 percent Big Ten graduates.)

3. The Terman studies were published in eleven volumes over a span of seventy-one years as the original group was followed up. The first volume was L. M. Terman, *Genetic Studies of Genius, Vol. 1. Mental and Physical Traits of a Thousand Gifted Children* (1925). The data cited here are from L. M. Terman and M. H. Oden, *The Gifted Child at Mid-Life* (1959). The most recent volume, which summarizes the entire study and then examines the "Termites" in old age, is C. K. Holahan and R. R. Sears, *The Gifted Group in Later Maturity* (1996). All volumes were published by the Stanford University Press.
4. The counterproductivity of focus on rewards is documented by A. Kohn, *Punished by Rewards* (New York: Houghton Mifflin, 1993).
5. See Milhaly Csikszentmihalyi, *Flow: The Psychology of Optimal Experience* (New York: HarperCollins, 1990). (If pronouncing this fine psychologist's surname tends to interrupt your own flow, try saying "chick-SENT-me-hi.)
6. L. J. Peter and R. Hull, *The Peter Principle* (New York: W. Morrow, 1969).
7. M. Csikszentmihalyi, *Finding Flow* (New York: Basic Books, 1997). (See note 5 above for pronunciation.)
8. Quoted in J. R. Chiles, "We Got Us Some Sky Today, Boy!," *Smithsonian,* July 1997.
9. M. Csikszentmihalyi, 1990, 32.

## CHAPTER 6

1. All of us share about three-fourths of our genes; these are the ones that made us into humans rather than butterflies or elephants. But about one-fourth of our gene loci—the pages in our personal genetic blueprints—can be occupied by one of two to twenty or more slightly different or polymorphic genes. These are the ones that produce individual differences between people.
2. A. R. Hochschild, *The Time Bind: When Work Becomes Home* (New York: Metropolitan Books, 1997).

## CHAPTER 7

1. Grantly Dick-Read, *Childbirth without Fear* (1953).
2. M. D. Storfer, *Intelligence and Giftedness* (San Francisco: Jossey Bass, 1990), 324.

## CHAPTER 8

1. Psychiatrist Thomas Szasz, best known for his claim that the only thing wrong with the sufferer from schizophrenia is that other people treat him as if he were crazy.

2. F. J. Sulloway, *Born to Rebel: Birth Order, Family Dynamics, and Creative Lives* (New York: Pantheon Books, 1996).
3. Reprinted with permission from the *Diagnostic and Statistical Manual of Mental Disorders, Fourth Edition*. Copyright 1994 American Psychiatric Association, Washington, DC.
4. Judith R. Harris, "Where Is the Child's Environment? A Group Socialization Theory of Development," *Psychological Review* 102 (1995): 458–89.
5. Terrie Moffitt, "Adolescence-Limited and Life-Course-Persistent Antisocial Behavior: A Development Taxonomy," *Psychological Review* 100 (1993): 674–701.
6. D. T. Lykken, "Incompetent Parenting: Its Causes and Cures," *Child Psychiatry and Human Development* 27 (1997): 129–37.
7. Much of the ensuing discussion of psychopathy is taken from my 1995 book, *The Antisocial Personalities* (Mahwah, NJ: Lawrence Erlbaum Associates).
8. G. Frank, *The Boston Strangler* (New York: New American Library, 1966).
9. Casseno, "He's in Prison for Good, but Not Before a Murder," *Minneapolis Star Tribune*, June 13, 1993, 1.
10. S. Shakur (a.k.a. Monster Kody Scott), *Monster: The Autobiography of an L.A. Gang Member* (New York: Atlantic Monthly Press, 1993).
11. M. Horowitz, "In Search of Monster," *The Atlantic Monthly*, December 1993, 32.
12. R. Lindsey, *The Falcon and the Snowman* (New York: Simon & Schuster, 1979).
13. R. Lindsey, *The Flight of the Falcon* (New York: Simon & Schuster, 1983).
14. For more on Ted Bundy, see Ann Rule's *The Stranger Beside Me* (New York: Norton, 1980) or S. Michaud and H. Aynesworth, *Ted Bundy: Conversations with a Killer*. New York: New American Library, 1989.
15. See Ann Rule's biography of Diane Downs, *Small Sacrifices*. (New York: New American Library, 1988).
16. For more on Neville Heath, see G. Playfair and D. Sington, *The Offenders*. (New York: Simon and Schuster, 1957).
17. See Robert Caro's biography, *The Years of Lyndon Johnson: The Path to Power*. (New York: Knopf, 1982).
18. See William Manchester's biography, *The Last Lion: Winston Spencer Churchill*. (Boston: Little, Brown, 1983).
19. See Edward Rice's *Captain Sir Richard Francis Burton*. (New York: Charles Scribner's Sons, 1990).
20. See Tom Wolfe's *The Right Stuff*. (New York: Farrar, Straus, Giroux, 1979) or Chuck Yeager's *Yeager, an Autobiography*. (New York, Bantam Books, 1985).

21. V. B. Carter, *Winston Churchill: An Intimate Portrait* (New York: Konecky and Konecky, 1965).
22. Leon Dash, *Rosa Lee: A Generational Tale of Poverty and Survival in Urban America* (New York: Basic Books, 1996).
23. D. T. Lykken, "Incompetent Parenting: Its Causes and Cures," *Child Psychiatry and Human Development* 27 (1997): 129–37.
24. Child psychiatry professor Jack Westman has made a detailed and careful estimate of the costs of incompetent parenting in his provocative book, *Licensing Parents: Can We Prevent Child Abuse and Neglect?* (New York: Insight Books, 1994), 95.
25. Louis Sullivan, "Families in Crisis," address by the then-Secretary of Health and Human Services, delivered before the Council on Families in America of the Institute for American Values, January 6, 1992.
26. M. S. Forgatch, G. R. Patterson, and J. A. Ray, "Divorce and Boys' Adjustment Problems: Two Paths with a Single Model," in *Stress, Coping, and Resiliency in Children and the Family,* E. M. Hetherington, D. Reiss, and R. Plomin, eds. (Hillsdale, NJ: Lawrence Erlbaum Associates, 1994), 96–110.
27. H. N. Snyder and M. Sickmund, *Juvenile Offenses and Victims: A National Report* (Washington, DC: Office of Juvenile Justice and Delinquency Prevention, 1995), 31.
28. *Minneapolis Star-Tribune,* March 21, 1993, 15A.
29. Irving Kristol, *New York Times,* November 3, 1994, 3.
30. M. Ingrassia and J. McCormick, "Why Leave Children with Bad Parents?" *Newsweek,* April 25, 1994, 64.
31. *Chicago Tribune,* January 2, 1994, 1, 6–7.
32. J. K. Wiig, *Delinquents under 10 in Hennepin County* (Minneapolis, MN: Hennepin County Attorney's Office, 1995).
33. Snyder and Sickmund, 1995, 169.

## CHAPTER 10

1. The ponderal index is the cube root of weight in pounds divided by the height in inches. If we measure fattiness the way a physiologist would, e.g., by the specific gravity or weight as a function of volume, then admittedly women average fatter than men. But, in a chapter about sex differences, it makes sense for a male author to be diplomatic.
2. A. Feingold, "Gender Differences in Body Images are Increasing," *General Psychologist* 32 (1996): 90–98.
3. R. Inglehart, *Culture Shift in Advanced Industrial Society* (Princeton: Princeton University Press, 1990).
4. D. Myers, *The Pursuit of Happiness* (New York: William Morrow, 1992), 80–84.

## CHAPTER 11

1. S. L. Mellen, *The Evolution of Love* (San Francisco: Freeman, 1983).
2. The bonobo is the "pygmy chimp" of Zaire, thought to be most like us of any of the apes.
3. E. Berscheid and E. H. Walster, *Interpersonal Attraction* (Reading, MA: Addison-Wesley, 1978), 177.
4. For example, S. M. Drigotas and S. E. Rusbult, "Should I Stay or Should I Go? A Dependence Model of Breakups," *Journal of Personality and Social Psychology* 62 (1992): 62–87; C. Hendrick, *Close Relationships* (New York: Springer-Verlag, 1985).
5. E. Berscheid and B. Campbell, "The Changing Longevity of Heterosexual Close Relationships." In *The Justice Motive in Social Behavior,* M. J. Lerner and S. C. Lerner, eds. (New York: Plenum Press, 1981), 227.
6. C. Hendrick and S. Hendrick, "A Theory and Method of Love," *Journal of Personality and Social Psychology* 50 (1986): 392–402.
7. C. Hazen and P. Shaver, "Romantic Love Conceptualized as an Attachment Process," *Journal of Personality and Social Psychology* 52 (1987): 511–24.
8. H. Fisher, "Monogamy, Adultery, and Divorce in Cross-Species Perspective, in *Man and Beast,* M. H. Robinson and L. Tiber, eds., (Washington: Smithsonian Institution Press, 1991), 95–126; H. Fisher, *The Evolution and Future of Marriage, Sex, and Love* (New York: Norton, 1992).
9. M. R. Liebowitz, *The Chemistry of Love* (Boston: Little, Brown, 1983).
10. J. Money, "The future of Sex and Gender," *Journal of Clinical Child Psychology* 9 (1980): 132–33; see also Tennov, note 11 below.
11. D. Tennov. *Love and Limerence* (New York: Stein and Day, 1979).
12. D. T. Lykken and A. Tellegen, "Is Human Mating Adventitious or the Result of Lawful Choice? A Twin Study of Mate Selection," *Journal of Personality and Social Psychology* 65 (1993): 56–68. It should be noted that the sample sizes listed here are nearly 50 percent larger than those reported in the cited paper due to the collection of additional cases since that paper went to press.
13. J. L. Gould, *Ethnology* (New York: Norton, 1983), 266.
14. K. Lorenz, *King Solomon's Ring* (New York: Crowell, 1952).
15. M. McGue and D. T. Lykken, "Genetic Influence on Risk for Divorce," *Psychological Science* 3 (1992): 368–73.
16. Taking the divorce status of a twin's parents and of the cotwin together, we found that we could account for 52.5 ± 5.4 percent of the variation across people in risk for divorce. Turkheimer *et al.,* in a paper presented at the 1992 Behavior Genetics Association conference, reported lower estimates, but the divorce rate in their sample was only

6 percent, which suggests that the highest levels of divorce risk (high enough to exceed the higher threshold in the population from which they sampled) may often result from special environmental circumstances.

17. V. Jockin, M. McGue, and D. T. Lykken, "Personality and Divorce: A Genetic Analysis," *Journal of Personality and Social Psychology* 71 (1996): 288–99.

18. Albert Ellis, *Rational-Emotive Couples Therapy* (New York: Pergamon Press, 1989).

19. See N. G. Waller, B. A. Kojetin, T. J. Bouchard Jr., D. T. Lykken, and A. Tellegen, "Genetic and Environmental Influences on Religious Interests, Attitudes, and Values: A Study of Twins Reared Apart and Together," *Psychological Science* 1(2) (1990): 1–5.

20. See D. M. Buss, "Sex Differences in Human Mate Preferences: Evolutionary Hypotheses Tested in 37 Cultures." *Behavioral and Brain Sciences, 12,* (1989): 1–49; D. M. Buss, *The evolution of Desire: Strategies of Human Mating.* (New York: Basic Books, 1994); D. M. Buss, R. J. Larson, D. Westen, and J. Semmelroth, "Sex Differences in Jealousy: Evolution, Physiology, and Psychology," *Psychological Science, 3* (1992): 251–255.

21. D. A. DeSteno and P. Salovey, "Evolutionary Origins of Sex Differences in Jealousy? Questioning the 'Fitness' of the Model." *Psychological Science, 7* (1996): 367–372; C. R. Harris and N. Christenfeld Gender, Jealousy, and Reason. *Psychological Science, 7* (1996): 364–366.

22. D. M. Buss, R. J. Larson, & D. Westen, "Sex Differences in Jealousy: Not Gone, Not Forgotten, and Not Explained by Alternative Hypotheses." *Psychological Science, 71 (1996): 373–375.*

## PART V

1. B. S. Jonas and R. W. Wilson, *Negative Mood and Urban Versus Rural Residence. Advance Data from Vital and Health Statistics,* no. 281 (Hyattsville, MD: National Center for Health Statistics, 1997).

## CHAPTER 12

1. See T. Reich, P. Van Eerdewgh, J. Rice, J. Mullaney, J. Endicott and G. Klerman, "The Familial Transmission of Primary Major Depressive Disorder," *Journal of Psychiatric Research* 21 (1987): 613–24.

2. See. For example, D. J. Hershman and J. Lieb, *The Key to Genius.* (Buffalor, NY: Prometheus Books, 1988), and K. R. Jamison, *Touched with Fire.* (New York: Free Press, 1993).

3. Adam Gopnik, "The First Liberal," *The New Yorker,* February 10, 1997, 78.
4. Perhaps, to make this experiment work, we should have to implant the electrode in the part of your brain that inhibits feelings of well-being.
5. This passage is from a fine little book by one of the great clinical psychiatrists, Henry Yellowlees, *To Define True Madness* (Harmondsworth, Middlesex: Penguin Books Ltd., 1953).
6. L. McCann and D. S. Holmes, "Influence of Aerobic Exercise on Depression," *Journal of Personality and Social Psychology* 46 (1984): 1142–47.
7. K. Linde, G. Ramirez, C. D. Mulrow, A. Pauls, W. Weidenhammer, and D. Melchart, "St John's Wort for Depression—An Overview and Meta-analysis of Randomised Clinical Trials," *British Medical Journal* 313 (1996).
8. Some authorities recommend avoidance of alcoholic beverages, aged cheese, red meat and yeast bread while taking Saint-John's wort; see N. D. Brown and J. Donald, "St. John's Wort Overview," *Phytotherapy Review and Commentary* (Seattle, WA: Bastyr University's Department of Continuing Education, 1995). If this herb can counter depression even in the face of these depressing precautions, it must be a wonder drug indeed!
9. P. Kramer, *Listening to Prozac* (New York: Viking Press, 1993).

## CHAPTER 13

1. See M. J. Apter, *The Dangerous Edge* (New York: The Free Press, 1992).
2. See J. Katz, *Seductions of Crime: Moral and Sensual Attractions in Doing Evil* (New York: Basic Books, 1988).
3. J. Kagen, *Galen's Prophecy* (New York: Basic Books, 1994).
4. I discuss psychopaths and their interesting kin in *The Antisocial Personalities* (Mahwah, NJ: Lawrence Erlbaum Associates, 1995).
5. Jesse came over recently to show us his latest tattoo, which had involved ninety painful minutes with a hot needle; his lessons in pain tolerance are still working, not always for the best.
6. See for, example, D. F. Klein and J. G. Rabkin, eds., *Anxiety: New Research and Changing Concepts* (New York: Raven Press, 1981).
7. For example: Albert Ellis, *The Practice of Rational-Emotive Therapy (RET)* (New York: Springer, 1987); Albert Ellis, *How to Stubbornly Refuse to Make Yourself Miserable About Anything—Yes, Anything!* (Secaucus, NJ: L. Stuart, 1988); Albert Ellis, *The Essential Albert Ellis: Seminal Writings on Psychotherapy* (New York: Springer, 1990).

## CHAPTER 14

1. According to Daniel Goleman, from whose excellent book, *Emotional Intelligence,* I borrowed this epigraph, it was taken from Aristotle's *The Nicomachean Ethics*
2. Hitler's amphetamine addiction is documented in Leonard and Renate Heston's fascinating *The Medical Casebook of Adolf Hitler* (London: William Kimber, 1979).
3. T. Hillerman, *Talking God* (New York: Harper & Row, 1989).
4. "Adjusted" means the average cross-twin, cross-time correlation divided by the mean retest correlation, i.e., the same adjustment that gave an MZ value of .85 and a DZ correlation of .41 for Abstract Intelligence.

## CHAPTER 15

1. The Minnesota State Board of Health kindly provided me with the live-birth statistics back to 1910, as well as the 1997 population estimates by age/gender group. Because not all current residents were born in Minnesota, and some of each birth cohort later moved out of state, these curves are only approximations.
2. Our Alice in Wonderland method of handling allegations of misconduct against members of the faculty goes like this: First, some administrator adjudicates the matter and, should the professor be found guilty, punishment is specified. Only then, after the hanging, is the accused provided with an evidentiary hearing before a jury of his/her peers, and then only if s/he appeals the prior verdict, under the tenure code, to the faculty senate's Judicial Committee. By this time, of course, the university administration is committed to its prior position and the procedure is adversarial and expensive for all concerned. Oddly, when the allegations are of scholarly or scientific misconduct (e.g., plagiarism, faking data, and the like), we provide the hearing before rather than after sentence is pronounced. Until recently, I have felt a frustrated obligation to try to persuade the powers to extend this fair and sensible system of due process to all allegations of misconduct. Now, somehow, I am content to wait and see if reason will prevail.
3. Every American university now maintains Human Subjects Committees (called, for obscure reasons, Institutional Review Boards or IRBs) that must give prior approval before any faculty research involving human subjects can proceed. This practice began in response to abuses in which medical researchers put experimental subjects at risk without first obtaining their free and informed consent. I remember as a graduate student witnessing a brain surgery in which, for reasons unrelated

to the patient's epilepsy, an electrode was inserted three times deep into an unaffected brain region, each insertion doubtless destroying many brain cells and their interconnections. A neurologist and the neurosurgeon were doing a bit of informal experimenting, as physicians had done since Galen's time, usually with no lasting harm to their unsuspecting patients. But the practice plainly was wrong, and the IRBs have put an end to most of it. They are also threatening to put an end to much harmless and useful psychological research as well. Indeed, much of the work reviewed in my *Antisocial Personalities* could not have been done under the mindless, pettifogging scrutiny of an IRB, at least not the one that I was dealing with recently.

I wanted to ask inmates at our local maximum security prison to fill out the same personality inventory, the MPQ, that we have administered to thousands of twins of all ages. I was particularly interested in testing my prediction that these inmates, once they have had six months or so to adjust to prison routine, are probably as happy as they were before their last arrest, just about as happy indeed as are most law-abiding citizens outside the prison walls. The warden and the state corrections people had approved the plan and the prison psychologist had volunteered to collaborate. It was agreed that neither the individual scores nor who had or had not been willing to participate would become part of any inmate's record. As the only incentive to participation, I would provide each volunteer with a computer-generated report of how his scores compared with those of men in general, the same sort of feedback that we have always used with twins and other research subjects. It was a simple, innocent, inexpensive little project that seemed to me worth doing.

But my Human Subjects Committee was scandalized! Prisoners are vulnerable and must be handled gently if at all. I will mention only one of the loony "stipulations" demanded by the IRB before this project would be allowed to proceed. I was informed by this committee of faculty colleagues, professors of English, architecture, law, etc., and chaired by a professor of occupational therapy, that it would put these men "at risk" to inform them of their scores "outside the context of individual counseling." That is, the only way I could provide my inmate volunteers with the promised incentive feedback would be to hire a licensed "counselor" to meet with each felon privately to explain his scores, to answer any questions, and to ensure that learning he scored higher on Aggression than 76 percent of men in general did not cause him lasting psychological injury. The consequence of this fatuity, of course, was that the project was stillborn.

We have known for some time that long prison sentences do not act as a deterrent. (I must exclude from that "we," of course, those legislators who enacted bills requiring long sentences for drug dealers, the only effect of which upon the citizenry has been the forced early release of dangerous criminals to make room for the dealers who are at once replaced on the street.) Most of us have also known that prisons do not function as "reformatories." Reasonable people would have been interested to learn that imprisonment beyond six months in a well-run institution does not actually punish the offender either, and that the only function imprisonment does serve is to keep dangerous criminals off the street.

Even those professors on the IRB would have found this interesting were it presented to them in a different context. They are all intelligent, highly educated, well-intentioned people—yet, given the responsibility, and the authority, to regulate a function they know nothing about, in a bureaucratic system where they are accountable (to higher bureaucrats) for their errors of omission, but not accountable at all to the persons regulated for their errors of commission, they predictably behave in a mindless, arbitrary, bureaucratic way. If I were a younger man and realized what an encumbrance and real threat this was to my chosen profession and to me personally, I would feel obliged to take up arms on this issue as well. I would organize other victimized researchers and demand audience with higher authority, pointing out some of the easy and obvious ways to remediate the situation: e.g., we should require every IRB to be composed of faculty half of whom actually do research with human subjects, and it would be particularly helpful if each proposal had to be discussed *ab initio* in the presence of the interested investigator.

4. D. T. Lykken, *The Antisocial Personalities* (Mahwah, N.J.: Lawrence Erlbaum Associates, 1995).
5. D. T. Lykken, "Want to Have a Baby? Not Until You Get Your License!," *Law and Politics,* December 1995; "Psychopathy, Sociopathy, and Crime," *Society* 34 (1996): 29–38; "Incompetent Parenting: Its Causes and Cures," *Child Psychiatry and Human Development* 27 (1997): 129–37; "Factory of Crime," *Psychological Inquiry* 8 (1997): 261–70; "The Causes and Costs of Crime and a Controversial Cure," *Journal of Personality* (1998); "The case for parental licensure," *Psychopathy: Antisocial, Criminal, and Violent Behaviors* (New York: Guilford Press, 1998). See also J. Westman, *Licensing Parents* (New York: Insight Books, 1994); and D. Blankenhorn, *Fatherless America* (New York: Basic Books, 1995).

## CHAPTER 16

1. The story of Freud's death is told in an article by Alan Stone in the *Harvard Mental Health Leter* for January 1997, pp. 4, 5.

# INDEX

# ABOUT THE AUTHOR

David Lykken is professor emeritus of psychology at the University of Minnesota, a clinical psychologist, a past president of the Society for Psychophysiological Research (SPR), and a behavior geneticist. He is the author of *A Tremor in the Blood: Uses and Abuses of the Lie Detector* (1981; 1998), and *The Antisocial Personalities* (1995) as well as numerous scientific papers, including "The American Crime Factory" (*Psychological Inquiry,* 1997), and "The Causes and Costs of Crime and a Controversial Cure" (*Journal of Personality,* 1998). His honors include the American Psychological Association's award for Distinguished Contribution to Psychology in the Public Interest (1990) and the Society for Psychophysiological Research's award for Distinguished Contributions to Psychophysiology (1998).